Christianity and Party Politics

Christianity and Party Politics aims to discuss and evaluate the contemporary relationship between party politics and religion. This book focuses on the important role of the Church in both electoral politics and public policy formulation in the twenty-first century, and argues that, contrary to the established secularisation argument generally applied in Europe, religion continues to be a powerful influence, particularly within British politics.

Steven begins by examining the basics of electoral and party behaviour, how religious affiliation has traditionally influenced the way people choose to vote, and how recent surveys have suggested it continues to do so. Moving on to discuss how this affects the behaviour of party politicians, the role of the Christian Church as an interest group is analysed; to what extent is this major societal institution continuing to influence public policy decisions?

Broadening the debate out to the international context, the work evaluates how the relationship between party politics and religion has been affected by global factors. This discussion is developed through analysing the influences on the way in which Christian groups choose to lobby and influence public policy. Steven suggests that increasing European integration is forcing Christian groups to become more proactive in their approach, to combat the decline in the more 'automatic' domestic influence they previously enjoyed. In relation to this, the influence of American politics is analysed, debating whether tactics from the more pluralist US system are being adopted by Church leaders elsewhere.

Providing a valuable and long overdue contribution to the field, this work will provide readers with a detailed knowledge of how the worlds of politics and religion interact.

Martin H. M. Steven lectures in Politics at the University of Glasgow. He researches within the field of comparative political behaviour, with particular emphasis on parties and elections in Britain, and has published in journals such as *Representation, POLITICS* and *Religion, State and Society*.

Routledge Studies in Religion and Politics
Edited by Jeffrey Haynes
London Metropolitan University, UK

This series aims to publish high quality works on the topic of the resurgence of political forms of religion in both national and international contexts. This trend has been especially noticeable in the post-cold war era (that is, since the late 1980s). It has affected all the 'world religions' (including Buddhism, Christianity, Hinduism, Islam and Judaism) in various parts of the world (such as the Americas, Europe, the Middle East and North Africa, South and Southeast Asia, and sub-Saharan Africa).

The series welcomes books that use a variety of approaches to the subject, drawing on scholarship from political science, international relations, security studies and contemporary history.

Books in the series explore these religions, regions and topics both within and beyond the conventional domain of 'Church–State' relations to include the impact of religion on politics, conflict and development, including the late Samuel Huntington's controversial – yet influential – thesis about 'clashing civilisations'.

In sum, the overall purpose of the book series is to provide a comprehensive survey of what is currently happening in relation to the interaction of religion and politics, both domestically and internationally, in relation to a variety of issues.

Politics and the Religious Imagination
Edited by John Dyck, Paul Rowe and Jens Zimmermann

Christianity and Party Politics
Keeping the faith
Martin H. M. Steven

Christianity and Party Politics

Keeping the faith

Martin H. M. Steven

Routledge
Taylor & Francis Group

LONDON AND NEW YORK

First published 2011
by Routledge
2 Park Square, Milton Park, Abingdon, Oxon OX14 4RN

Simultaneously published in the USA and Canada
by Routledge
270 Madison Avenue, New York, NY 10016

Routledge is an imprint of the Taylor & Francis Group, an informa business

© 2011 Martin H. M. Steven

The right of Martin H. M. Steven to be identified as author of this
work has been asserted by him in accordance with the Copyright,
Designs and Patent Act 1988.

Typeset in Times New Roman by
Florence Production Ltd, Stoodleigh, Devon

Printed and bound in Great Britain by
CPI Antony Rowe, Chippenham, Wiltshire

British Library Cataloguing in Publication Data
A catalogue record for this book is available from the British Library

Library of Congress Cataloging in Publication Data
Steven, Martin H. M.
   Christianity and party politics: keeping the faith/Martin H.M. Steven.
      p. cm. – (Routledge studies in religion and politics)
   Includes bibliographical references (p.) and index.
   Christianity and politics – Great Britain.   2. Political parties –
   Great Britain.   3. Great Britain – Politics and government.
   I. Title.
   BR744.S74 2010
   324.241 – dc22   2010026800

ISBN: 978–0–415–55660–6 (hbk)
ISBN: 978–0–203–83416–9 (ebk)

Contents

Illustrations

Figures

Tables

Preface

Scholars have ignored the role of religion in British politics – this is primarily an institutionalist failing, with an over-emphasis on the decline of traditional church attendance, the absence of a confessional party and, linked to this, any significant social conflict related exclusively to religion. However, a more rational perspective reveals the true political influence of the British churches – voting behaviour and turn-out continue to be affected by Christian values, parties continue to sustain Christian subgroups, a state Church continues to sit and vote in Parliament in London, and conscience-based issues pose 'irrational' challenges for policymakers working within a unique constitutional framework.

The overarching focus of this book is the relationship between Christianity and the quality of representative democracy in Britain. The author argues that the continental European tradition of secularism has less resonance in Britain – no constitutional attempt has been made to protect the State or its citizens from the Church, and there has been no need for a confessional party to develop. The British case can be cautiously compared with the United States where Christianity is regarded as being complementary to modern democracy, rather than in conflict with it.

Martin H. M. Steven
Department of Politics
University of Glasgow

Acknowledgements

I would like to thank Jeff Haynes, series editor of *Studies in Religion and Politics*, Nicola Parkin, senior editorial assistant at Routledge, Barry O'Toole, my head of department at Glasgow, as well as my colleagues on the fifth and sixth floors of the Adam Smith Building. Tom Lundberg was a particular help throughout the project, while Fraser Duncan (GCU) and Craig Smith (St Andrews) gave me some excellent preliminary ideas at the start. I would also like to thank François Forêt (Brussels), Xabier Itçaina (Bordeaux), Lucian Leustean (Aston) and John Madeley (LSE) for all their contact via the ECPR standing group on Religion and Politics. I also warmly acknowledge the support of David Denver (Lancaster) for offering me some of his extensive expertise with the statistical passages of this book. Thanks also to the Hansard Society for allowing me to use their London offices as a Visiting Fellow when I was conducting some of my fieldwork – this helped immeasurably, and I was made very welcome.

Material from Chapter 7 first appeared in article form. I acknowledge the help of Wiley Blackwell in permitting me to reproduce 'Secessionist politics and religious Conservatism: the Scottish National Party and faith-based interests', originally published in *POLITICS*, 28 (3): 188–96. I also acknowledge the help of Taylor & Francis in permitting me to reproduce 'Religious lobbies in the European Union: from dominant church to faith-based organisation?', *Religion, State and Society*, 37 (2): 183–93 (also in L. Leustean and J. Madeley (eds), *Religion, Politics and Law in the European Union* (London: Routledge), 175–85). Finally, I am grateful to Lynda Barley for allowing me to reproduce Figure 8, 'Believe in God and usual Sunday church attendance' from *Churchgoing Today* (London: Church of England, 2006).

This book is dedicated to my parents, Harold and Allison, for all their help and support with my academic career.

Martin H. M. Steven
Adam Smith Building
June 2010

Abbreviations

ACTS	Action of Churches Together in Scotland
APPHG	All Party Parliamentary Humanist Group
BBC	British Broadcasting Corporation
BES	British Election Study
BSAS	British Social Attitudes Survey
CBI	Confederation of British Industry
CCF	Conservative Christian Fellowship
CD	Christian Democracy
CDA	Christian Democratic Appeal
CDU	Christian Democratic Union
CSM	Christian Socialist Movement
EIS	Educational Institute of Scotland
ETD	Equal Treatment Directive
EU	European Union
FBO	Faith-based organisation
HFE	Human Fertilisation and Embryology
IVF	In vitro fertilisation
LDCF	Liberal Democrat Christian Forum
MEP	Member of the European Parliament
MP	Member of Parliament
MSP	Member of the Scottish Parliament
NGO	Non-governmental organisation
PC	Plaid Cymru
RCT	Rational choice theory
SCHA	Scottish Churches Housing Action
SIFC	Scottish Inter-Faith Council
SNP	Scottish National Party
UK	United Kingdom
US	United States

1 Introduction

The neglected dimension of British politics

In the late summer of 2008, the then British Chancellor of the Exchequer, Alistair Darling, gave an interview to *The Times* newspaper in which he forecast that the 'worst recession in 60 years' was heading towards the United Kingdom (UK). In the early spring of 2010, Mr Darling gave another interview, this time to Sky News, in which he described how the 'forces of hell' had been released upon him from the then Prime Minister Gordon Brown's office as a consequence of his remarks (Sky News, 24 February 2010). There then followed a series of bullying accusations directed towards Mr Brown that were investigated by the head of the British civil service, Sir Gus O'Donnell – or 'GOD' as he is affectionately known around Whitehall, the heart of British government – who concluded that the accusations had no foundation. In and around the Palace of Westminster, or 'The West Minster' as it was historically known, such disagreements are commonplace – after all, modern British parties are 'broad churches' where a range of personalities and policies frequently collide.

The use of religiously charged metaphors is not unusual in British party politics – indeed, the opening paragraph of this book can itself act as a convenient metaphor for its main focus: the relationship between Christianity and party politics in the UK. While – prima facie – the daily business of British politicians is more preoccupied with the secular and not the sacred, scrape beneath the surface and the importance of religion, and particularly, Christianity, is never all that far away. Indeed, that simple truth constitutes the main contention of this monograph – the absence of conflict or division in relation to religion on mainland Britain should not be equated with an absence of significance, an error that many electoral and party scholars focusing on Britain have increasingly made.

Political scientists have, on the whole, chosen to ignore the role of religion in British politics – this is primarily an 'institutionalist' failing, with an over-emphasis on the decline of church attendance in the UK, the absence of a confessional party, and linked to this, any significant social conflict related to religion.[1] However, a more rational perspective reveals the true political influence of the British churches – voting behaviour continues to be significantly affected by Christian values, parties continue to sustain Christian groups, a state

Church continues to sit and vote in Parliament in London, and more and more conscience-based issues increasingly pose 'irrational' challenges for policymakers. Further, while this book does not include comment on either the 'economics of religion' literature (i.e. the rationalist argument that church attendance is positively affected by an open, American-style religious market – see Stark and Iannaccone 1994), or the 'free-rider'/prisoner's dilemma game theory of the collective action paradigm (i.e. the inherently irrational nature of organisational behaviour – see Olson 1965), it applies a public choice framework, defining churches as interest groups who rationally wish to protect their collective interests within the context outlined above.

Indeed, the United Kingdom hosts a distinctive interface between politics and religion, unique among advanced industrial democracies in Western Europe and North America – yet has been badly neglected by political scientists working in the field. The relationship is both multifaceted and fluid as a consequence of Britain's unwritten constitution and the nature of its party organisational framework. In Western Europe, the political sphere is frequently summarised as being 'secularised' – a straightforward relationship between one party, the Christian Democrats (CD), and one religion, Christianity, which is gradually weakening (Van Kersbergen 1994: 42–5; Norris and Inglehart 2004: 209–10). Meanwhile, in the United States, interaction between political and religious actors is dominated by evangelical Christian interest groups exerting influence in Washington as a result of developing mutually beneficial links with the Republican Party (see Wilcox 2006).

The UK context is rather different. The now former Prime Minister Gordon Brown – mentioned at the start of the chapter – personifies a peculiarly British tradition of being privately motivated by faith without necessarily publicly talking about it, or more to the point, making it part of his formal partisan identity.[2] Cultural, rather than spiritual, heritage becomes much more of a factor when it comes to British politicians approaching the topic of religion – they may be motivated by their faith to do good works and take part in public service – but they do not talk all that much about it. This can obviously be compared with both the United States (US), where politicians cannot be elected to high office without setting out in detail their religious value system and also many other Western European Union (EU) member states where parties adhere to a confessional label. However, that does not mean that the 'religious factor' is not relevant or important to British politics, simply that the relationship is less two-dimensional.

First, the mechanics of Britain's unwritten constitution have created a unique set of Church–State relations.[3] The Church of England maintains bishops in the upper house of Parliament, the House of Lords – known as the Lords Spiritual – while prior to devolution in 1999, the General Assembly of the Church of Scotland was commonly described as being the closest institution to a parliament outside of Westminster (Kellas 1989: 178). The churches have played a vital role in highly politicised issues such as the abolition of slavery in the nineteenth century as well as more modern twentieth and twenty-first century campaigns urging society to tackle Third World debt and child poverty.

Second, the nature of the British party ideologies has created a much more open relationship between religious interests and parties, compared with other EU member states and the United States. There is no Christian Democratic tradition – the right-of-centre party, the Conservatives, is independent of any religious affiliation, and there are Christian groupings in all three major parties. The Conservative Christian Fellowship (CCF) promotes family values, the Christian Socialist Movement (CSM) advocates social justice while the Liberal Democrat Christian Forum (LDCF) endorses moderation, tolerance and progressive ideas. So, in many ways, church identity transcends partisan affiliation in Britain, and not vice versa – as the Republicans do in the US, or the Christian Democrats do across Europe.

In the wider context of the EU, the nature of the relationship between political and religious actors creates a much more rigid structure, and one that is experiencing a discernible trend of secularisation – the State or dominant Church will frequently keep out of political debates, primarily because it is actually unnecessary to do so owing to Christian Democratic party organisations, yet CD support is generally in decline.[4] They continue to function as major political actors in the Netherlands, Belgium and Germany, for example, but place much less emphasis on 'Christian' issues, while in France, Spain and Italy, they have been superseded in importance by 'people's' parties or equivalent blocs (Van Hecke and Gerard 2004; Duncan 2006). It should also be noted that, outside the UK, the Northern European tradition of sustaining Protestant state churches has also somewhat dissipated – in Sweden, for example, the Lutheran Church was disestablished in 2000, and this is also being actively considered in Norway after the Government set up a commission to look into the issue in 2006. Meanwhile, the church tax procedure in Germany has been substantially altered over the decades, and it is now optional. Similarly, in the US, a strictly regulated relationship exists between Church and State, which in turn can be linked directly to the now established relationship that exists between Republicans and the Christian Right.[5]

None of this is to argue that religion matters more to British politics than in the rest of Europe or America, or that it is more influential, but simply that it does not fit neatly into a narrow classification, and specifically, the 'secular Europe' sociological argument (Habermas and Derrida 2003). The 'new orthodoxy' of the 1960s saw scholars view religion as being either irrelevant or contrary to democratic politics in Western Europe (Berger 1967; Martin 1978). Meanwhile, in the US, the role of religion in politics is high profile but also highly controversial with fundamentalist Christians forming interest groups to lobby government over emotive single issues such as abortion or same sex marriage. The British case, then – among other things – illustrates the meaningful conceptual difference between 'freedom from religion' and 'religious freedoms' (see Table 1.1 for a typology among advanced industrial democracies).

Table 1.1 Church–State relations versus Christian parties

Nation	Church–State relations	Party organisation
France	'Dominant' Church kept separate from State	Democratic Movement[†]
Italy	'Dominant' Church kept separate from State	Union of Christian and Centre Democrats[†]
Spain	'Dominant' Church kept separate from State	Popular Party[†]
Germany	Churches receive financial subsidies[*]	Christian Democrats
Netherlands	Churches receive financial subsidies	Christian Democrats
Nordic[**] countries	Churches receive financial subsidies	Christian Democrats
UK	'National' Churches – Church representatives sit in legislature	No confessional party
US	'Separation' – multiple religious interest groups	No confessional party

[*]　Organised regionally
[**]　Since 2000, this no longer includes Sweden
[†]　Christian Democrat either partly or entirely in origin. In Italy, UDC is part of the 'People of Freedom' coalition, together with far right, liberal and populist organisations. Meanwhile, during the Spanish democratic transition, Christian Democrat parties emerged only in the Basque and Catalan regional party systems, although at the national level, Christian Democrats were integrated in the PP.

This book provides a first attempt to reverse the neglect of the religious dimension of British party politics on the false assumption that the 'new orthodoxy' had led to other variables becoming more important. In the UK, churches have an independent role to play in politics – they neither represent a single issue or interest, nor do they represent a party. Linked to this, the parties do not seek to monopolise Christianity as a label or policy platform. There is also no equivalent of politicians such as Joschka Fischer (German Greens) or Sophie in't Veld (Dutch Liberals) in the UK – politicians who are 'politically' atheist and serve in parties that are also publicly/formally secular. The British sociologist, Steve Bruce, argues that secularisation in the UK is irreversible (2002: 73) – however, there is no consistent statistical evidence that supports it becoming any less important to British politics. Policymakers continue to respect the role of religion in politics because they recognise that a substantial proportion of British voters continue to relate their religious views to their political views. It may be difficult to quantify precisely *how* influential all of that is, but what is not in doubt is the fact that it *is* influential.

Prior to the emergence of the 'third way', and Tony Blair's modernisation of the democratic left, many debates in British politics effectively centred around the disjuncture between Thatcherism and Socialism, and the role of redistributive taxation in relation to individual wealth. In 2010 – and the end of the New Labour project – the key issues in British politics are politicians' expenses and illegal wars. The Conservative-Liberal Democrat coalition government's new challenge is not the question of how to redistribute societal assets but their vision of how the role of the State as a whole relates to individuals. Kidd (2009) argues that the whole notion of 'personal responsibility' is one that modern British politicians are attempting to capture electorally. For so long as that continues, religion will matter to British politics[6] – both to its parties and to its parliaments.

A separate but related dimension to this is the relationship between Christianity and the quality of representative democracy in Britain. The key contention of this aspect of the research is that the UK can be placed much closer to the US than to the rest of Western Europe, in terms of the role religion plays in the public sphere. The continental European tradition of secularism[7] has substantially less resonance in Britain – no constitutional attempt has been mounted to protect the British State or its citizens from the Church, and there has been no need for a confessional party to develop either. It is possible to refer to common 'Anglo-American' values in this respect where Christianity is regarded as complementary to modern democracy, rather than being in conflict with it – and this book will explore this idea in more depth throughout each chapter.

The UK is – ostensibly – a secularised country with falling levels of active church attendance, yet institutional religion continues to play an important and prominent part in democratic life. Eisenstadt's 'multiple modernities' thesis (2000) can be applied to Britain where centuries-old Christian traditions mix with postmodern secularism. But why is this? *Christianity and Party Politics* supports the argument that the answer lies with British public opinion and voting behaviour – despite the fact that the extant literature in the field has increasingly neglected this aspect on the false assumption that the 'new orthodoxy' had led to other variables becoming more important. Not only is that not necessarily true, but the decline in importance of religion within this context is also misrepresented.

The context: British elections and parties

The UK's longstanding two party system, sustained by a majoritarian 'First-Past-the-Post' electoral system, has deep roots in the sort of social cleavages that help to define other European countries, along with a lengthy tradition of forming single party governments. Operating in the context of the 'Westminster model', parties hold power consecutively on their own, generally without coalitions, rarely serving more than two parliamentary terms under the same leader.[8] Labour and the Conservatives can be likened to the Republicans and Democrats in the US, or other parties in anglophone countries that do not have proportional representation electoral systems. The party that wins the most seats (more than the other parties combined) also wins sole power in the House of Commons, and proceeds to push through its legislative programme with very little opposition.

In this respect, the power of the party is highly significant in British politics as, ultimately, there is no written constitution or separation of powers to prevent the governing administration doing what it likes. It is also the party to which elected politicians owe their first loyalty – in America, candidates choose their party, working their way up through state-level legislatures. In other parts of Western Europe, parties are obviously powerful (for example, the Netherlands has an especially strong list system) but there also exists much more decentralisation (with the exception of France, which has an elitist approach to training politicians, in any case). However, in the UK, a career in politics first and foremost means a career in a party, and the self-interest of parties and overall quality of democracy are not necessarily always synonymous.

The Conservative Party is the oldest political party in the world, capable of tracing its origins back to the civil wars, with a parliamentary membership sometimes described as being the 'most sophisticated electorate in the world' due to its MPs' ability to vote for the leader that is most expedient at that particular moment. It also wears John Stuart Mill's description of it as 'by the law of their existence the stupidest party' as something of a badge of honour (*Considerations on Representative Democracy*, 1861) – the 'stupidity' in question referring to a distrust of any fanciful ideological baggage, as opposed to a lack of capacity for intelligence. After thirteen years in opposition – and a succession of four different leaders – the party regained power in the May 2010 General Election, as part of a coalition with the Liberal Democrats,[9] with David Cameron becoming Prime Minister. Mr Cameron's ability to blend traditional Tory values with twenty-first century presentational qualities is seen as his main asset, although the victory in 2010 was far from convincing. The three pillars/factions of the party centre around first, the merits of the free market economy; second, 'one nation' Conservatives who believe in the importance of civil society and social cohesion; third, traditionalist Tories who believe in the Union, the Royal Family and the established churches. The second strand was overtaken by the first when Margaret Thatcher became leader – not really a 'conservative' at all, Mrs Thatcher promoted free market values and deregulation in a radical and unprecedented way. Meanwhile the third strand lurks, providing the party with a socially conservative base that does not exist in any of the other main parties.

The Labour Party grew out of the British trade union movement, with which it maintains close links, albeit slightly less close following the leadership of Tony Blair. Blair, along with erstwhile allies Gordon Brown and Peter Mandelson, created 'New Labour', after the General Election defeat of 1992, and the sudden death of their leader, John Smith, in 1994. Repealing 'Clause Four' – the section of the party constitution that committed it to a redistribution of wealth in society – was both crucial and problematic, and continues to provide the party with ideological divisions. From a 'Blairite' perspective, it was about moving the party forward and towards the centre while still retaining its social democratic credentials first established by the likes of Hugh Gaitskell and Tony Crosland; for others, it was the abandonment of the entire *raison d'être* of the British Labour movement. After all, when Mrs Thatcher was asked what she considered to be her greatest legacy, she replied 'New Labour'.

The Liberal Democrats are an important party in the UK, but have always been badly affected by the majoritarian electoral system, which offers a huge advantage to the aforementioned two larger parties. Formed after a merger between the Liberal Party and the Social Democrats (SDP) in 1988, the party has struggled to make a meaningful breakthrough in terms of parliamentary seats, although has a much better record in devolved and local government, holding power as part of a Scottish Executive coalition in Edinburgh, for example, between 1999 and 2007. Leaving aside the constraints of the electoral system, the party has also battled with being able to project a unified image to British voters. The current leader, Nick Clegg, is perceived to be on the right of the party, while many of his colleagues are more recognisably on the left. The 'Orange Book' Liberals – keen on the free market and economic liberalism are often at odds with the old SDP members who used to be in the Labour Party. When asked about this, party leaders will often reply 'I am a Liberal because I am a liberal' but this does not really help clarity, as the term 'liberal' is utterly meaningless without context.

There is also a regionalist or sub-state dimension to the United Kingdom party system. Outside of England, the nations of Scotland and Wales sustain active nationalist parties, the Scottish National Party (SNP) and Plaid Cymru (PC). They both support Scotland and Wales becoming independent nation states within the European Union, although traditionally, Plaid placed more emphasis on simply winning greater powers for Cardiff within the UK. The SNP had a successful election in 1974 (October) winning eleven Scottish seats but has hovered around a total of five or six since then, concentrated particularly in more rural areas such as Aberdeenshire and Perthshire. However, since 2007, it has formed a minority government in Edinburgh's devolved parliament. Meanwhile, Northern Ireland has an entirely distinctive party system owing to the social and religious divisions in the province – as has already been mentioned, this is an entirely different dimension from the study of religion and politics, and will not be covered in this book.

An additional aspect to all of this that will obviously be discussed at length at different stages of the study is the absence of a Christian Democratic party in the UK. The reasons for this will be covered in Chapters 2 and 3, as will a wider question – the decline of the party. Much scholarly literature has been devoted to the topic in recent years (for example, Dalton and Wattenberg 2000; Webb *et al.* 2002) and the British context is no different from equivalent comparable Western states. Indeed, the way the British Labour Party transformed itself in the 1990s from being a mass socialist movement into a modern 'catch-all' party is often held up as being the archetypal example of the way parties have to effectively sell themselves in an increasingly challenging and rational issue-based marketplace (see Fielding 2002). Further-more, the way that both the Conservatives and Liberal Democrats have chosen, in recent years, young photogenic leaders, with apparently very little interest in which tradition of the party they actually come from, or what their core beliefs are, speaks volumes. The decline of the party is a major theme in this book, and the final section of this chapter focuses on a related topic.

The scholarly field: politics and religion

Before we come on to that theme, however, we need to be clear about the other dimension to this study: if it is British party politics that provides the research with its main setting, it is the social scientific study of religion that pro-vides it primarily with its methodological backdrop. The study of politics and religion[10] is both nebulous and eclectic. It is generally considered to be a scholarly field in the United States, but more of a theme or sub-field in Britain. In the US, scholars can actually make a scientific career out of focus-ing solely on politics and religion – more often than not, these will be political scientists who see a very close relationship between studying elections and voters in America, and studying religion and politics. So influential is the Christian lobby in the contemporary US that the two seamlessly blend, with an American voter's faith an increasingly strong predictor of partisan identification (Flanigan and Zingale 2006: 114–15). In Western Europe, especially France, the subject is dominated by sociologists of religion. An academic conference on politics and religion can range in focus from an International Relations analysis of the 9/11 terrorists attacks to a philosophical discussion of Weber's 'Protestant ethic' theory. So where does this book fit in with this rather 'Catholic' theme?

First, the present author's field is parties and elections – more broadly, comparative political behaviour – and the title of the monograph indicates that the focus will emphasise this dimension. With that in mind, the rich seam of European literature on social cleavages, initiated by Seymour Martin Lipset and Stein Rokkan (1967), provides the initial basis of much of the analysis. Lipset and Rokkan used a political sociology framework to analyse the roots of party systems in Western Europe, arguing that the sort of historical social variables that existed prior to the start of the twentieth century continued to mould the organisation of political parties in the middle of the twentieth century. The first source of division had been between centre and periphery, via the Reformation; the second between Church and State, with the latter adopting roles that had previously been the former's; the third between land and industry, with the onset of the industrial revolution; and the fourth, between owner and worker, with the development of socialism (1967: 15).

Clearly, the religious cleavage is the one upon which this book will focus the most, as it attempts to explain its importance. Ultimately, the key task of this book is to illustrate the relevance of religion (and in particular,

Christianity) to the British party system at the start of the twenty-first century, so it is vital that it acknowledges the historical and comparative context in the process. Christianity, as well as being a belief system, is also a religious denomination, sustaining an organisational structure, property and other fixed assets. The way all of that interacts with political organisations such as parties lies at the heart of this book.[11]

Linked to this, the absence of Christian Democracy in Britain – while well-known – has not been discussed in any great depth, and this is a key dimension that the aims of this book would seek to rectify. The emergence of Christian Democratic parties in Europe after the Second World War was primarily a reaction to the secularist direction of the left at the time. Since then, CD parties have gone on to dominate political systems across Western Europe (both North and South), and in many they continue to do so. Britain, however, was exceptional in this regard – but that itself raises a question: what are the social origins of the British party system? Did Christianity play any role in it historically, and if so, how does this relate to the more contemporary picture? Linked to this, to what extent does religion act as a variable with regard to voting behaviour?

It is also perhaps worth stating what this book is not going to do. This book is not going to spend time focusing on, for example, the constitutional framework of Church and State. Such issues might well be discussed in relation to political behaviour but not in a stand-alone way. This book is, of course, interested in issues such as bishops in Parliament, the challenges of an unwritten constitution and EU human rights, but only because they are relevant to British party politics. This book is also not especially concerned with overtly sociological matters – that is, how many people attend church, race and ethnicity questions, immigration and so on. Again, clearly, there is a link between some of this and voting behaviour/party politics but only the dimensions that are relevant will be addressed. Further, this book has no great interest – formally – in international relations, wars or diplomacy. The topic of politics and religion has unquestionably received a 'shot in the arm' from the rise of Islamic fundamentalism in the last ten or twenty years, but there will be no attempt to analyse the role of Britain in the Middle East or Afghanistan, for example. Last, this book is not going to provide a detailed historical account of how Christianity – in the past – may have provided an important basis for party politics in the UK; while this aspect will be covered in passing when relevant, ultimately the focus of this book is contemporaneous.

The appeal of religion to social science has been a story of many twists and turns – at times, the latter has been almost entirely convinced that the importance of the former had become of almost no consequence. Peter Berger, the pre-eminent American sociologist of religion, was perhaps the first to write about the secularisation of Western societies (1967), and was followed by his British colleague, David Martin, who penned his 'general theory of secularization' in 1978. This 'new orthodoxy', while understandable, had an unfortunate tendency to cross that very delicate line between offering an academic explanation for certain examples of behaviour and actually going on to predict what will happen as a consequence. The perceived wisdom at the time was that religion was on its way out, an inevitable casualty of modernisation and economic development. Western European countries such as the UK, France and Germany were blazing a trail that the rest of the globe would eventually follow – or so it was argued.

However, the 1980s saw the rise of the Religious Right in the US, and the 1990s saw the collapse of atheistic communism in Eastern Europe, along with the development of Islamic fundamentalism. Another sociologist based in the US, José Casanova, was credited with challenging the notion that the societal influence of religion was in terminal and irreversible decline, when he wrote *Public Religions in the Modern World* (1994). Focusing on a variety of case studies (Spain, Poland, Brazil and the US), Casanova pointed to various examples of religion continuing to play a major role in the public sphere of modern societies across the globe.

Nevertheless, there remain sociologists, foremost among them Steve Bruce of the University of Aberdeen, who are committed to the theory that church attendances are in free fall, and that therefore 'God is Dead' (2002). Bruce's key approach is to focus in detail on aggregate church attendances that, he argues, provide irrefutable evidence that religion is in decline. Others, however, including Berger, are less evangelical in their scholarly atheism, with Shmuel Eisenstadt's work on 'multiple modernities' perhaps the leading theory, suggesting that the secularised Europe does not offer a deterministic path other modern or modernising societies are destined to follow. Indeed, Eisenstadt even argues that religious values have often been at the core of European modernisation, as opposed to on the periphery or merely accommodated by it (see Spohn 2001: 500).

Indeed, the scholarly literature cannot simply be reduced down to a dichotomous divide between those who argue that religion is in decline and those who disagree. There are also scholars who actively discuss the role of religion as a social actor independent of such concerns – for example, the relationship between religion and economic growth. Becker (1996) argues that church attendance can be considered a serious variable when looking at human capital and other household production functions in modern, developed societies. It has already been mentioned at the start of this chapter that the study will adhere to a rational choice methodology. Also, therefore, of interest is the way American political economists study religion as an actor that can be analysed like any other when trying to work out the cost benefits for a democratic society – in other words, the 'religious economy'. Adam Smith was the first economist of religion proper; while a professor at Glasgow, he noted that non-conformist ministers worked harder in Scottish parishes as a result of being independent and not having to rely on state funding – that made them more competitive and also more successful (*The Wealth of Nations* 1776; see Micklethwait and Wooldridge 2009: 21, 64).

This model has been particularly fully embraced by American scholars where the lack of an established Church has meant that all denominations have had to battle for members in a highly competitive spiritual marketplace. Meanwhile, state churches in Northern European nations such as Sweden, Norway and the UK, it must be said, have watched as their attendances have gone into something of a decline. Perhaps the most prominent modern economist of religion is Laurence Iannoconne of Chapman University, California – he has followed in the footsteps of Rodney Stark, of Baylor University, Texas, a strong advocate of the use of rational choice theory in the study of religion. This thesis has particular resonance in the United States where the unregulated society means that the 'start-up' costs of building a new church – or even a new branch of Christianity – are relatively low. The influential Pew Forum on Religion and Public Life recently reported that 44 per cent of Americans have switched denominational affiliation from the one that they were nominally born into (2008: 22). The idea that we can look at churches as if they are interest groups is a controversial one outside of America – and not necessarily one that is always entirely correct, or fits neatly into a straightforward analysis either. In Western Europe, the religious landscape is much less fluid, with the religious beliefs of Europeans more deeply interconnected with the rest of their identity.

The present author is a political scientist, and has no expertise in assessing the relationship between religious adherence and economic growth – the research question of this study is to analyse the influence of religion on politics, not politics on religion. Nevertheless, the wider rational choice analysis can be closely linked to the methodological framework applied here, with its emphasis on both voter and party behaviour, and has much to commend it. Regardless of the theological niceties of what churches believe in, and whether or not they are always a force for good, it is entirely valid for social and political scientists to investigate their societal impact. Indeed, some of the great thinkers of the past – Weber, Marx, Durkheim, as well as Smith – have all turned their minds to the topic. Whether one agrees with Steve Bruce that 'God is dead' (2002) or with John Micklethwait and Adrian Wooldridge, who argue that 'God is back' (2009), points of dispute and discussion are always in plentiful supply.

The issue: Christianity and representative democracy

The earlier section on the field of politics and religion attempted to provide an overview of how social science – and, frequently, American social science – has analysed religion and its influence on society. However, it did not mention the way one of the most influential concepts in contemporary social science – social capital – has also focused on religion in some considerable detail. Indeed, according to Robert Putnam of Harvard University, social capital's most prominent scholar, religion, and particularly Christianity, has had an unparalleled role in developing democratic engagement levels in advanced Western societies such as the US (2000: 65), and this brings us on to what can be considered this book's biggest challenge.

Central to this study stands one overarching theme: is Christianity good for British representative democracy? Clearly, it is not the job of an empirical political scientist to make sweeping normative statements about whether religion is positive for the overall *quality* of democracy. Nevertheless, if the issue exists, and empirical public policy scholars such as Putnam do feel that it is legitimate to discuss it in this way, it would be remiss of this author to ignore the question completely. In fact, it is the natural research question to discuss – is Christianity perceived to be a positive variable for twenty-first century party politics in the UK, especially given the sort of challenges it currently faces? Are party memberships boosted disproportionally by Christians? Is voter turn-out helped by conscientious Christians? Do churches contribute to public debates? It is not the job of this author to decide whether or not it is good that churches or individual Christians do make an impact in this area, but it is the job of a political scientist to assess neutrally whether or not there is some sort of correlation.[12]

Putnam first became interested in religion when he started to worry that the traditionally high levels of democratic engagement in the US were falling: voting, party identification and charitable activities all appeared to be suffering from a crisis of membership; Americans were increasingly 'bowling alone', according to his chosen metaphor (2000). For such a 'nation of joiners', as Tocqueville (1835) called America, to be experiencing such a downturn in its associational fortunes was a matter of grave concern for Putnam, as he regarded it as being of huge importance to wider issues related to trust in government, the quality of public policymaking and even economic growth. Democracy has become the default political system, with around 123/189 United Nations member states regarded formally to be democratic – but in established advanced industrial democracies such as the US and UK, the appetite of citizens for democracy seemed jaded. Partisan identification has been in steady decline for several decades (Dalton and Wattenberg 2000; Webb *et al.* 2002) while electoral turn-out has been falling since the 1990s (Blais 2007). Linked to this, levels of trust are low, and respect for politicians has been badly eroded (Dalton 1999: 63; Hall 2002: 50–1). A number of solutions are possible within the context of British politics: introducing term limits for elected politicians to revive the concept of politics being about public service rather than careerism; greater constitutional reform, including the introduction of a fully elected upper chamber, as well as devolving more power away from London and closer to people in Scotland, Wales and Northern Ireland; and, most directly, electoral reform – which would do away with the existence of 'safe seats' where there seems little point in people voting at all.

As Gerry Stoker argues,

> popular confidence in political process appears to be very low in many countries, while support for the idea of a system of democratic governance is globally high. People appear to like the idea of democracy, but not like the politics that goes along with it.
>
> (Stoker 2006: 32)

According to Stoker, fewer than one in 600 people in the UK can now be considered political activists (2006: 11).

So where is religion – and specifically, Christianity – in all of this? According to Putnam, the answer to the problem in America, at least, could lie with Christianity (Campbell and Putnam 2010). Churches provide very high levels of social capital – a Christian is much more likely to vote, much more likely to identify with a party, much more likely to be involved in charitable works, and much more likely to participate and be a 'good citizen' in general, although there is an ongoing debate about whether or not such correlations are restricted to the US (for example, see Norris and Inglehart 2004: 194–5). Clearly, however, the pressing question is: can any of this be applied to the UK? Putnam is a visiting professor at the University of Manchester's Institute of Social Change, and believes that parallels can be drawn between Britain and America owing to language, culture and history. One of the key aims of this book is to look at this question and decide whether or not he is right.

Outline of methods and chapters

This book is divided into eight chapters, including this introductory one, along with a concluding section. Indeed, the main six chapters can be grouped into three parts or sections: the first focuses directly on the specific electoral context and the way the parties continue to respond to Christian-based voting behaviour; the second on the way the churches act as interest groups, boosted by special political privileges that tie them to the British state establishment; and third, the way the twin policy areas of 'ethics' and 'equalities' pose challenges for party politicians programmed to avoid controversy.

Throughout this book runs a public choice theoretical framework. Public choice is effectively the political equivalent of rational choice theory, which has its origins in economic theory. In essence, it argues that people are rational actors who will always base their decisions on self-interest (see Downs 1957). This clear and accurate theory – while not perfect – is most effective at explaining why religion continues to be of importance to electoral and party politics in the UK. It can be contrasted with a theoretical framework more traditionally associated with British politics, that of institutionalism, which, at its core, states that we cannot ignore the structures and restrictions of institutions when analysing the development of political events and the behaviour of political actors (see March and Olsen 1984). History, context and organisational factors all play a part in the way political systems function, which cannot be simplistically boiled down to a collection of individuals all pursuing their own interests.

While this is unquestionably true, it does not provide a satisfactory explanation for why Christianity clearly still matters to British politics. Historical context or ideological frameworks count for nothing if modern office-seeking politicians estimate there to be any electoral risks involved. At the heart of this book, then, is a very simple thesis – the Christian Church continues to have power in Britain because it continues to affect public opinion, which in turn affects public policy. The days of British people packing into their local parish church on a Sunday morning due to social pressures may have long gone but that does not mean the political influence of religion has gone too. Indeed, the over-arching theme of this book mentioned in the last section has a public choice core – Robert Putnam's analysis of the relationship between Christianity and democratic engagement in America is rooted in Olson's paradigm regarding the inherently illogical nature of collective action (2000: 288). Each chapter will discuss the merits of public choice theory in more detail, but it is helpful to highlight its use at the start.

With regard to the research methods utilised, the study combines qualitative and quantitative research. Chapter 2 contains most of the latter, with a statistical emphasis on voting behaviour, and an analysis of British Election Study and British Social Attitudes Survey data. In addition to this, a significant number of interviews – face-to-face, telephone and focus group – with British Members of Parliament, Peers and other interested parties have been conducted, and these appear throughout the text, with their names listed in the index with times where appropriate. No archival work has been conducted – the premise of trawling through documents in any of the party archives in London, Oxford and Manchester was ultimately considered to be pointless. It is highly unlikely that the influence of Christianity upon policy documents – or some sort of equivalent – exists or is made available for public consumption.

It was also considered to be similarly futile to conduct a large-scale survey questionnaire of elected politicians – a smaller-scale one conducted by the present author as part of his doctoral research produced often uninformative results, and Chapter 3 goes into more detail about this. Asking politicians about their religiosity, and whether or not it affects their politics, inevitably leads to rather banal and politically correct answers. The question of whether or not elected representatives are more or less religious than the voting population at large is certainly an important one, but the methodological difficulties linked to answering it proved insurmountable for this particular project. Media sources, however, are used – both internet and broadcast – in an attempt to give the study as much impact as possible.

Part 1 of this book – The electoral context – focuses specifically on voting behaviour and party organisation. Chapter 2 analyses how important religion

– and specifically Christianity – is as a variable in terms of deciding the way people in Britain vote. The chapter brings together survey data from different sources – primarily the British Election Study (BES) and the British Social Attitudes Survey (BSAS) – to provide an up-to-date and in-depth analysis. There is currently no one source for researchers interested in the topic to go to, and this chapter seeks to address that, comprehensively charting the relationship between partisan identification and denomination, church attendance, as well the role of the latter in wider political participation – for example, electoral turn-out. The persistence of the denominational cleavage has been augmented by a new type of Christian voter who is much more likely to turn out at elections and be politically active. The aggregate number of Christians in Britain may be falling but the total remains high enough to be regarded as significant, while the growth of unconventional or conservative evangelical churches has produced an added dimension to this important area of electoral behaviour.

In Chapter 3, we turn our attention to the parties themselves. With no Christian Democratic party, the Conservatives, Labour and the Liberal Democrats all possess Christian factions/subgroups, but how do they go about trying to capture the 'religious vote' both at election time, and during parliamentary terms? A detailed analysis suggests that it is easier to be openly Christian in the Conservative Party than in either Labour or the Liberal Democrats, both of whom have elements of the secular European leftist tradition. Indeed, linked to this, while the Conservatives under the leadership of David Cameron have modernised their image, there remains a predilection for the family values and a distrust of the equalities agenda. However, it would be wrong to overstate this – the Labour Party, for example, has traditionally close ties with the Catholic community in Britain, and there is no evidence that the Conservatives actively target Christians in a strategic way. The key point is that all the parties are conscious of the importance of the Christian vote in Britain, and respond accordingly.

Part 2 – The Christian lobby – centres around the two state churches of Britain: the Church of England and the Church of Scotland, analysing them as they act as interest groups in the party system. Chapter 4 concentrates on the role of bishops in Parliament. As a result of public choice constraints, the Church of England continues to have a legislative presence in Parliament in the form of twenty-six senior bishops voting in the House of Lords. Perhaps conscious of their privileged position, high-ranking Anglican leaders are frequently prepared to engage with modern politics on its own terms, speaking out on issues such as the global economic downturn, the 'war on terror' and creeping secularism in an inclusive and progressive way, effectively acting as the 'conscience of the nation' in the process. Further, parliamentary bills have been blocked by the votes of bishops, resulting in policy proposals being altered. The presence of the Church in Parliament is one of the best examples of the way politicians are reluctant to 'pick a fight' with the churches, due to the spread of Christian identification across different sections of the British electorate.

Chapter 5, meanwhile, looks at the Church of Scotland. Christianity in Britain is not homogeneously Anglican – the Presbyterian Church performs a similar function in Scotland. While it is free from all political interference, with Church leaders frequently voicing their concern over issues such as nuclear weapons, the treatment of asylum seekers and poverty, it remains – like the Church of England – in a privileged position for similar reasons related to public opinion. The Church is closely associated with wider issues of democratic engagement, devolution and political participation, which can be compared with the role of Anglican bishops in the House of Lords – for example, campaigning for a Parliament in Edinburgh to exist as the sovereign right of the people of Scotland. Interestingly, it does this for instrumentalist reasons, arguing that it would help with social policy delivery – Scotland's 'love affair' with the Labour Party is epitomised by the emphasis its national Church places on social justice issues.

Part 3 – The religious issues – is concerned with the two areas of public policy that are most related to Christian interest: ethics and equalities. Chapter 6 tackles the politics of conscience-based or life issues – for example, abortion, stem cell research and euthanasia. Recent debates at Westminster over how society should regulate these types of challenges make this part of the book especially topical and important. The role of the unwritten British Constitution is central here – the long-standing absence of a British supreme court means that such affairs become politicised, not necessarily in an overtly partisan way, but in the sense that it falls to the parties to debate and legislate in relation to them. Despite the prevalence of free votes being granted to party politicians, we can still see political – and rational – considerations being brought into play. For example, the Labour Government attempted to whip its MPs when they were voting on the Human Fertilisation and Embryology Bill in 2008. The chapter will also look at the way Church of England bishops helped to block euthanasia legislation from going through Parliament. Again, rational choice theory provides us with an explanation – parties desperately try to limit the irrational challenges such issues cause them by controlling them politically.

Chapter 7, meanwhile, is concerned with the equalities agenda. Unlike the last chapter, the partisan dimension to this is much more overt, and as a result, the influence of the Christian lobby is demonstrably much weaker. The Conservative Party's distaste for equalities – the party may have embraced/accepted civil partnerships but it has not embraced the broader agenda – is nonetheless kept in check by the wider consensus that modern, progressive Britain should not discriminate on the grounds of gender or sexuality. The 'hollowing out' of the traditional nation state in the form of European legislation – especially the harmonisation of fundamental citizen rights in policy areas such as education and employment – has led to churches that have traditionally enjoyed an automatic form of domestic political influence beginning to resemble one interest group among many in the context of the wider EU. While the Amsterdam Treaty protects the right of the individual citizen to freedom of religious expression, the EU is an inherently secular body with no mention of Christianity in any of its treaties or directives. In particular, the repeal of 'Section 28', the legislation introduced by the Conservative Government in the 1980s to prevent the acknowledgment of different life-style choices, provides the chapter with its main case study, and shows how desperate the churches are, this time, to try to hold back what they regard as the secular tide.

Chapter 8 concludes that the religious cleavage still matters in British politics – despite sociological theories that argue the reverse. The relationship is multidimensional, and, as a consequence, potentially positive in relation to 'quality of democracy' issues. Churches are able to make an independent contribution to political debates – there is a close and longstanding involvement of the national churches in a range of quite radical and progressive political issues, which ultimately seeks to unite rather than divide. They do not represent a single issue interest, nor do they represent a single party. Religious faith remains strong, religious institutions remain visible, and newer forms of Christian worship and adherence are constantly evolving. The fact that this influence is perhaps less visible in Britain, compared with the US or other EU member states with a Christian Democratic tradition should not mean that political scientists simply ignore it as a variable or a factor.

Part 1

The electoral context

2 Religion and voting behaviour in Britain

From denominational 'cleavage' to the 'alpha vote'

It was Peter Pulzer (1967: 98) who memorably said: 'class is the basis of British party politics; all else is embellishment and detail'. If Pulzer's statement were still true, this would be a very short book. Indeed, far from being an isolated view, Pulzer's statement rather effectively embodies the established scholarly position on the importance of religion to the British political system. Fortunately, there are two issues with his argument one can take – and with the entire premise, for that matter: first, that class is the main social cleavage upon which electoral politics in Britain is centred; second, that the other relevant cleavages (centre–periphery, urban–rural and religious) are not politically significant.

With regard to Pulzer's first question, the prominence of class politics in the UK is not in dispute but it is nevertheless a matter of interpretation to what extent it actually provides the 'basis' of the entire system. The Conservative Party has its origins as a recognisable political movement around the time of Robert Peel's repeal of the Corn Laws, protectionist tariffs that limited foreign grain imports, in 1846 – those opposed to this left and formed the basis of the modern party (see Webb 2000: 42). Many of the priorities of the Whigs' eventual modern-day successors – the Liberal Democrats – are as much concerned with social and progressive liberalism (for example, equal opportunities, the environment and electoral reform) as they are about economic policy. Meanwhile, the nationalist parties – the Scottish National Party (SNP) and Plaid Cymru (PC) – place self-determination for their respective Scotland and Wales at the top of their manifesto pledges, and dislike the suggestion that they ought also to confess whether or not they are 'right wing' or 'left wing'. Only the British Labour Party can truly be described as a 'party of class', with its origins in the Trade Union Movement – and even those origins are now something of a distant memory. The repeal of Clause Four of its constitution, which committed the party to the redistribution of societal wealth, and the arrival of 'New Labour' and the Tony Blair era, means that Labour is now better defined as a 'catch-all' party with a voter appeal that reaches beyond a British 'working-class' mass membership.

Second, the extent to which the other social cleavages are simply 'embellishment and detail' is also a matter for a far more serious scholarly discussion than has so far taken place. Major political issues that have come to dominate British party politics in recent decades include the Troubles in Northern Ireland, European integration and, more recently, the war on terror. Others include identity cards, stem cell research and global warming. Clearly, not all these issues are uniformly *partisan* but the argument that British party politics is simply about class now seems somewhat outdated – if it were ever true in the first place. As the introductory chapter made clear, the central aim of this book is to argue that, by continuously neglecting the religious dimension in British politics, scholars have ignored a highly important aspect of the system – both in relation to how voters and parties behave, but also in terms of how churches and religious organisations themselves seek to participate in politics and influence public policymaking.

This second chapter focuses entirely on one aspect – albeit the central and foundational aspect: the way in which an individual's religious behaviour influences his or her political behaviour, or, put another way, the impact that religious or non-religious values exert upon voter preferences at elections. The chapter analyses this relatively simple dynamic in a relatively simple way – but from different perspectives. First, 'belonging' (religious preference/ religious affiliation or denomination) and 'behaving' (voting for political parties); second, 'believing' (religious practice/religious faith) and 'behaving' (voting for political parties).[1] Also relevant here is the relationship between 'believing' and turn-out at elections – there is a link, albeit a sometimes un-even one, between religiosity and political participation in the United States and other advanced industrial democracies (Norris and Inglehart 2004: 194), and it would be interesting to test this within the context of the UK. Much of the interest in this last dimension has its roots in the Harvard–Manchester joint programme on the role of religion in society, and the social capital literature (Putnam 2000) – Chapter 1 discussed this by way of introduction.

As Denver has pointed out (2007: 56), where British scholars have looked at religion, traditionally, it is the 'belonging' variable in the UK that has preoccupied them much more than the 'believing' variable. This can be contrasted with other Western EU member states, where it is primarily the latter that has sustained partisan splits – in Europe, the post-war development of Christian Democracy was, and still is, a potent institutional symbol of the power of spiritual belief, regardless of denomination, given the existence of both Catholics and Protestants in Christian Democratic movements, in the secular world of elected party politics. Chapter 3 looks at this relationship in more detail. That is not to neglect the importance of the Protestant–Catholic dimension within Christian Democracy, and the way it has incrementally developed across Europe, but simply to highlight at this early stage the distinctive British case.[2]

It might also be noted at the start of the chapter that religion probably constitutes a more complex issue to analyse than the other main social cleavage of class within the context of British politics. Assessing whether or not working-class people still vote Labour, for example, is, on balance, methodologically easier than assessing whether somebody's religious beliefs – whatever they are – impact upon how they vote in an election. Different voters may well have different perceptions of which class they are, but long-established definitions of different socio-economic criteria at least provide a consistent basis for analysis. Religion, on the other hand, has either been ignored as a variable in many British Election Studies (BES) and British Social Attitudes Surveys (BSAS), or merged with other variables – for example, 'ethnicity' (in the case of the former) or 'moral values' (in the case of the latter).

In particular, the British Election Study has been highly inconsistent in terms of its inclusion of questions on religion. In 1970, Bochel and Denver complained about the lax way that religion was being elicited in the surveys: '"What is your religion?" may indicate his "religious preference", but it is hardly a reliable indicator of his status in the denomination' (1970: 207). The most recent BES publications betray a real dearth of information. In *Labour's Last Chance* (Heath *et al.* 1994), *The Rise of New Labour* (Heath *et al.* 2001), *Political Choice in Britain* (Clarke *et al.* 2004) and *Performance Politics and the British Voter* (Clarke *et al.* 2010), a quick look at the indices is sufficient to realise that the religious beliefs of British voters are not going to be mentioned at all. Indeed, even the edited volume, *Critical Elections: British Parties and Voters in Long-Term Perspective* (Evans and Norris 1999), only looks at it briefly in relation to Scotland.

Furthermore, part of the trouble here is defining 'religious' – does it mean 'attends church' or does it mean 'personal faith'? Does attending church more than once a week count as being more significant? 'Believing' is a much more difficult concept to pin down than 'belonging' where one can simply look at official identification statistics from censuses, for example, although even this can pose problems. In the last government census (2001), 71.8 per cent of people stated that they were Christian, which did appear high. The churches themselves release their own official data, although it can sometimes appear unclear as a result of the different definitions of 'member'/attendee (every Sunday, for Communion, every month, and so on). It is also a commonly held belief that respondents themselves claim to have a religious affiliation that is often extremely tenuous. The tendency to over-predict too is also very risky – respondents answer the way they think they should/would like to, in relation to church attendance, and not in a way that necessarily reflects reality. This has been much discussed within the American context where official church membership figures are extremely, almost suspiciously, high. 'Believing', in particular, however, requires researchers to ask the right sort of questions in their surveys, so that time series data can be produced, and this has not necessarily been the case in the British context. Unravelling the precise role of religion in British party politics is a challenge, but one to which we now turn.

Models of voting behaviour

Before we examine these nuances of religious voting behaviour in Britain, we first need to be aware of the different models that have been developed to help us understand how voters behave. Political scientists have grouped three main theories of voting as a result of the behavioural revolution gradually advancing from its origins in the United States – the socialisation model, the party identification model and the rational choice model. In essence, such studies focus on one central question: 'Is voting an act of affirmation or of choice?' (Harrop and Miller 1987: 130).

First, the socialisation, sociological or social determinism model: this approach (for, as Harrop and Miller have pointed out, it is really more of an approach than a model) effectively bypasses the individual voter entirely, choosing instead to focus on the historic links between social groups and parties. Lipset and Rokkan's seminal 1967 work, *Party Systems and Voter Alignments* is the classic text in the field. They explain why certain parties emerged in different European states, and therefore why voters in those countries have a specific range of electoral choices open to them. Despite being over forty years old, the level of scholarly detail in the opening chapter of that edited volume continues to have resonance. In particular, the authors' 'frozen cleavages' thesis remains an insightful commentary on the way that post-war partisan divisions across Western Europe continue to be influenced by much older social cleavages, including religion (see Harrop and Miller 1987; Miller and Niemi 2002: 170; Webb 2002). Although the sociological model more generally is very much of its era, and criticisable on the grounds that it speculates rather than explains, it nevertheless has its merits in its emphasis on the 'why' rather than the 'how' – a methodological attribute many a twenty-first century quantitative specialist would benefit from acknowledging.

Second, the party identification model: this model, also known as the Michigan model owing to its development in the 1960s by political scientists at the University of Michigan (Campbell *et al.* 1960), is not dissimilar to the socialisation approach but takes into account much more directly individual behaviour – for example, the voter's specific class or religion leads them to 'identify' with an individual party. They might not feel all that strongly for 'their' party – or even turn out to vote for it at every election – but they feel that it is on their side, for better or worse. Ultimately, the party identification model traditionally matters in the UK, in relation to religion – there is a well-established link between denomination and party choice that we will discuss in the next section.

Last, the rational choice or median voter model: this was pioneered by the American economist, Anthony Downs (1957). Standing in direct contrast to the Michigan model, the Downsian model emphasises the importance of individual voter choice on party preference. The individual, it is argued, weighs up the choice of party before him or her, before casting their vote for whichever party appears to be capable of delivering the largest cost benefit to them after the election. This simple argument has found particular popularity in the American electoral context, where parties are traditionally weaker than their European counterparts, and have less of a history of mass/cleavage based voting. More contemporary theories such as 'valence' voting and 'retrospective' voting can also be grouped here – the former sees voters casting their ballot in favour of the party they perceive to be the best performer overall, while the latter sees them punishing governments for failing to deliver on previous policy proposals. 'Issue' voting is also part of this general family.

It is the final model that this book embraces most closely – as this chapter will go on to discuss, the old social cleavages that used to exist in Britain, with Catholics voting Labour and Protestants voting Conservative, are clearly of their time, and cannot hope to last much longer. The fact that they do is worthy of note, and confirms the lack of wisdom in ignoring Christianity as a significant actor in British elections, but beyond that, it is of limited importance. Indeed, such cleavages are actually more connected with social class – and the immigrant origins of many British Catholics – than with confessional beliefs, and this will also be elaborated upon in future sections. However, of much more value is the theory of newer, more rational patterns of voting, where Britons decide on the various parties' capacity to govern on the basis of a range of issues, many of which are moral. Here, the role of Christianity as a social force is much more pertinent and current, especially given the concurrent, wider decline in partisan identification levels in the UK more generally – the ability for voters to express their political preferences in a more American style and opt for the candidate that they trust the most, or the party that protects their specific interests more, is substantial.

Linked to this, one of the key themes of this study is the argument that party political leaders in Britain continue to be motivated by rational self-interest when it comes to listening to religious 'lobbies' attempting to influence public policy. If there continues to exist a 'religious vote' (and it should be once again pointed out that the Michigan model still has much to commend it within this context), and a new range of religious-related issues coming to the fore in addition (the environment; stem cell research; trust in politics; euthanasia), then politicians have an obligation to pay attention to religious issues, especially when there is evidence that church attenders are much more likely to vote and generally be engaged with civic and democratic issues.

In short, voting behaviour holds the key to explaining the resilience of religion in the British public sphere. Why does an advanced industrial EU member state such as the UK continue to sustain state churches at the start of the twenty-first century when – prima facie – this is distinctly 'anti-democratic'? Why do the British parties, as Chapter 3 will explain, continue to have highly active and visible Christian factions within their memberships at a time of apparent widespread secularisation, running the risk that such organisations might not be viewed favourably, electorally? The answer to both lies, in short, with public opinion – the British voter continues to use religion as a motivating factor when casting his or her vote. This, in turn, leads both to a continued presence of Christianity in parliamentary representation and to party organisations accommodating Christian values.

The global context: religion and voting in advanced industrial democracies

What does the relationship between religious values and political preferences look like in comparable states in Western Europe and North America? What should we expect when looking at this dimension in the UK? At the heart of such questions lies a debate that can be linked back to Peter Pulzer's opening statement about the importance of class – as Harrop and Miller put it (1987: 177), '[m]uch psephological blood has been spilt on the question of whether religion or class is the most important influence on voting in contemporary democracies'. In particular, Western political parties inevitably focus on socio-economic factors as priorities in their programmes for government as it is in that area of public policy that they can potentially exert most control – it is much more challenging for parties to try to legislate in predominantly 'irrational' areas of society that involve moral or conscience-based issues. Indeed, the problems faced by parties based on nationalist or secessionist principles in advanced industrial democracies rather epitomises this; for example, the Scottish National Party is very keen to point out that it is not an ethnic movement and that its policies are motivated solely by the territory of Scotland becoming a more successful economic growth area – but its limited electoral success suggests that articulating a modern, twenty-first century version of European nationalism is far from straightforward. Meanwhile, religious issues continue to ask challenging questions of parties, in relation to the sort of values they seek to represent and the type of societies they seek to create.

Correlations between religion and voting behaviour have traditionally been strong in the United States (see Smidt *et al.* 2009). As Guth *et al.* state, 'denominations were the ... institutional connection to national politics. Ethnic ties, lifestyle concerns, and the philosophical worldviews generated social and political ideologies that bound the denominations to one political party or another' (2007: 56). Throughout the twentieth century, white Anglo-Saxon Protestants were the backbone of the Republican Party, while Catholics and Jews provided the core for the Democrats (Guth *et al.* 2007: 56–7). As religiosity has weakened (Bruce 2002: 207), however, so too have these alliances and the relationship between religion and politics has altered in character. The differences are now to be found between the religious and the irreligious, as opposed to between the different denominations. Christian right mobilisation was credited with helping the Republicans win the 1994 Congressional elections (Guth *et al.* 2002: 161) while in 2000, the data analysis of Guth *et al.* showed that the most visible correlation was still between the religious right and George W. Bush's Republican Party.

Certainly, aside from voting behaviour patterns, we know that there is a very real and positive relationship between religiosity and political participation in the US. It is for this reason that Harvard political scientist, Robert Putnam, has argued that churches have a pre-eminent role to play in democratic engagement and social capital (2000; Campbell and Putnam 2010). In short, this is owing to the fact that in America, religion is not viewed as being a threat to democracy, or in conflict with democracy, as it has been at various junctures in Western Europe – rather, it is actually *synonymous* with democracy. If someone goes to their local church, they are also more likely to vote, identify with a party, be involved in charitable work and generally engaged with wider American society.

A glance at modern election results reveals that religion also appears to continue to play a high-profile role in West European politics – Italy, France, Germany, Belgium and the Netherlands all have recent experience of being governed by Christian Democrats.[3] Chapter 3 will go into more detail about the modern Christian Democratic parties in Europe but this section will look at Christian Democratic voters. In the historically mixed Northern European countries such as Germany and the Netherlands, the religious cleavage was actually grounded initially in denominational conflict as it involved secular liberals, other Protestant elites and also socialists organising against Catholics on questions of Church–State separation, including state religious education – and subsequently facilitating the emergence of confessional parties. However, anti-secularist motivations were the only key factor in Christian Democrats emerging in the Protestant Nordic countries while in the Southern European Catholic countries, it was also the confessional–secularist dichotomy that characterised Christian actors operating in a political context. That dimension has gradually become the overarching theme of Christian Democracy within the European Union, if it is even possible to talk of such a thing, given how fragmented a philosophy it has become. Indeed, portraying themselves as the party of European integration sometimes appears to be the preferred or easier option for Christian Democrats in relation to defining a core belief.

The twentieth-century manifestation of the European religious social cleavage, then, had become personified by Christians mobilising to form their own parties in order to promote their own social values. As Lipset and Rokkan put it:

> The Church . . . had for centuries claimed the right to represent man's 'spiritual estate' and to control the education of children in the right faith. In the Lutheran countries, steps were taken as early as in the seventeenth century to enforce elementary education in the vernacular for all children. The established national churches simply became agents of the state and had no reason to oppose such measures . . . The parties of religious defence generated through this process grew into broad mass movements

after the introduction of manhood suffrage and were able to claim the loyalties of remarkably high proportions of the churchgoers in the working class.

(Lipset and Rokkan 1967: 15)

In particular, the period immediately after the Second World War was a very successful one for CD parties – in Italy, West Germany, Belgium, Austria and other countries, they became either the dominant or second largest competing at elections.

While significant links remain across Western Europe between religion and voting, the decline in church attendance has inevitably led to a drop in the strength of some dimensions of the correlation – voting patterns are now much less uniform. Catholic Bavaria is still dominated by the CSU and practising Catholics still vote for right-wing parties by a proportion of three or four to one. However, Mitterrand's Socialists made some of their largest gains in the 1980s in the Catholic east and west of France, while Italy's Christian Democrats were convincingly beaten by the Northern League in Lombardy and the White Veneto in 1992. The DC subsequently fell apart and today there exist only Christian Democrat splinter parties.

As Dalton argues (2002: 134), the emergence of a 'new politics' has meant post-materialist issues such as environmental protection and women's liberation have replaced the old 'cleavages' of denominational religion and class, in terms of factors that condition voting behaviour. Nevertheless, Norris and Inglehart (2004: 211) argue that there continues to be a strong global correlation between religiosity and parties of the right; that is, the more religious people are, the more likely they are to be conservative, and therefore, we must be careful not to make sweeping judgements about the decline of Christian Democracy as a political movement that emphasises the importance of religious values. It is that sort of subtle shift of emphasis between religious belonging and religious believing that this book broadly endorses. Ignoring religion altogether as a social variable because the extremes of sectarian conflict have ended or the niceties of denominational affiliation have blurred is to neglect the new ways that religion operates within Western European political systems.

For example, Dalton (2002) shows that the UK lies at the bottom of world rankings in terms of the influence of religion in advanced industrial Western politics: first, in relation to religious denomination, Britain is literally at the bottom (with a Cramer's V of 0.10). Second, in relation to church attendance, Britain is joint bottom with Japan (0.08), and just below Australia (0.09). However, as Dalton points out, the actual spread between the top and the bottom in both cases is not huge – if we ignore Italy from the first category, the cluster of countries' scores is between 0.11 and 0.18 (average 0.15). In terms of the attendance, meanwhile, the average is 0.17. Also, the low British score is the result of the party system, not of religious voting itself. The US also lies towards the bottom of these scores, and nobody would question the importance of Christianity to American politics. As Dalton puts it (2002: 196), 'Despite the paucity of explicitly religious issues and the lack of religious themes in most campaigns, religious attachments still influence party choice'.

Societal context: church attendance in Britain

According to Harrop and Miller (1987: 179), '[w]hen thinking about religious groups in politics do *not* think of the altar or the pulpit: think of the pew'. They go on to state: '[a] secular society is not necessarily a permissive society' (1987: 182). Clearly, we need to be careful not to conflate churches as organisations with individual believers, nor crudely lump together all Christians as one homogeneous group within British society. The cultural differences between an Anglo-Catholic worshipping in London and a Free Presbyterian observing the Sabbath in the Scottish Highlands is quite considerable, and the political implications of those differences are also not without their significance.

While not the main focus for this chapter, there is clearly a need for a stand-alone section on British church attendance and affiliation figures. It has been well documented that church membership has been in steady decline for some time in the UK, but it is helpful to analyse this in detail. Clearly, the actual number of people who identify themselves as 'Christian' is of central import-ance to any analysis of the role of religion in British politics. Even if one wishes to take a more institutional approach and focus solely on churches as interest groups, the actual membership/size of any interest group remains crucial to understanding the aggregate level of influence and power.

When looking at these religiosity figures, we essentially have three sources of data: first, the official government census that is conducted every ten years; second, the churches' own statistics; and third, social science survey data, the most extensive of which is compiled by the Cathie Marsh Centre for Census and Survey Research, based at the University of Manchester, under the auspices of the 'British Religion in Numbers' (BRIN) project.

The decline in British church attendance since the 1960s is widely acknowledged – however, as Figure 2.1 shows, there is still a large number of people who do go to church (this table shows formal Church of England figures and has been reproduced exactly from Barley 2006). So in 2004, just under one million British voters attended church 'normally' or 'routinely', with more than 1.7 million attending each month – a figure that has not changed since 2000, according to Lynda Barley, Head of Research and Statistics for the Church of England (Gledhill, 8 May 2008).

Linked to this, while there has been a decline in the number of Britons who believe in God over the same period, a substantial number still do so. Indeed, the 2004 figure shows a slight increase from 2000. Clearly, defining 'belief in God' is problematic – for example, the 2008 British Social Attitudes Survey created six categories of belief, including relatively ambiguous answers such as 'I don't believe in a personal God but I do believe in a higher power of some

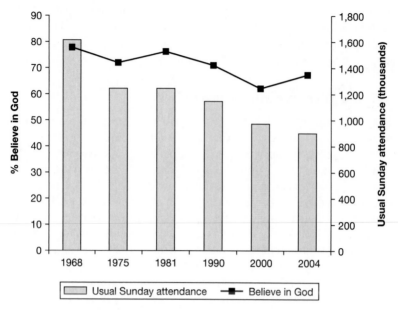

Figure 2.1 Believe in God and usual Sunday church attendance*
* See Barley (2006) *Churchgoing Today* (London: Church of England).
Source: Archbishops' Council, 2006: Gallup ORB/ICM.

kind' (Park *et al.* 2010: 68). But once again, we can be clear that substantial numbers of Britons possess some sort of Christian value system – no matter how vaguely defined.

Last, the number of people who identify with one denomination remains high. In the last government census (2001), 37.3 million people in England and Wales described themselves as 'Christian'. In the UK as a whole, 71.8 per cent of people stated that they were Christian (Office for National Statistics 2004). In Scotland, people were asked their specific denomination, with 2.1 million answering 'Church of Scotland', and a total of 3.3 million as 'Christian' (Office of the Chief Statistician 2005). There is an estimated Muslim population of around 3 per cent. The 2001 census was the first time that the question 'what is your religion?' had been asked in Great Britain (excluding Northern Ireland). While this makes comparisons over time difficult, the 2001 data nevertheless show the continuing strength of church identity, if not necessarily of regular Sunday morning church attendance.

Such bald figures clearly require deeper analysis – there is obviously a difference between people identifying with a church or a religion culturally, and them actually going to worship regularly and actively believing in God. Nevertheless, such high numbers cannot be simply written off so readily by scholars as 'in decline' or politically irrelevant. Indeed, equally basic figures from the World Values Survey, coordinated by Ronald Inglehart (University of Michigan), shows a small increase in church attendance in Britain from the first wave (early 1980s – 13 per cent) through the second wave (1989–93 – 14 per cent) until the third wave (1999–2004 – 15 per cent). Voas and Ling (2010: 67) show that, from 1983 to 2008, the number of people describing themselves as Christian dropped from 66 per cent to 50 per cent, but again, it could be argued this is not as cataclysmic a collapse as some sociologists would argue.

Nevertheless, we do also need to look in more detail at attendance figures as they are probably much more meaningful from a political science perspective, and the specific remit of this book. Christianity's largest denomination in the UK – the Church of England – releases its own figures each year; in 2007, there was an average weekly church attendance of 1.2 million. Such a dramatic difference between the numbers who identify with a church (mentioned on pages 29 and 30), and those who actually attend the church, are quite startling, and the root of the argument that religion is becoming less and less important to British people's lives. The Church itself argues that its figures show a stabilising trend from 2000 onwards. Figures for the Roman Catholic Church (16 per cent of the population) (Office of the Chief Statistician 2005: 7) and Church of Scotland (42 per cent of Scottish population) are broadly similar. Interestingly, as we will see in Chapter 3, this type of large-scale decline in active membership is replicated in the membership figures for British political parties, and poses a challenge for wider social capital and quality of democracy issues.

However, the picture is neither entirely uniform nor bleak for the churches. The influential and much cited 2007 Tearfund report, *Churchgoing in the UK*, found that 53 per cent of Britons identified themselves as Christian, with 59 per cent in total self-identifying as being religious (39 per cent claim to have 'no religion'). Moreover, 15 per cent attend church regularly (7.6 million voters), while 25 per cent attend church at least once a year – and 27 per cent of regular churchgoers now claim to be evangelical. The rise of evangelical churchgoing is something that the churches themselves often point to as evidence that it is wrong to talk in sweeping terms of falling religiosity across Britain. Newer and unconventional forms of worship are springing up, with some churches having to extend their buildings or fund new ones in order to meet demand. In particular, the phenomenon of the Alpha Course must be mentioned here – this is a programme that introduces participants to the basics of the Christian faith. While that sounds relatively unoriginal, the methods used are modern, and it essentially taps into the lack of basic knowledge that many Britons have about Christianity in general. Crucially, the course has an evangelical slant – while it is ostensibly an educational resource, it also acts as a way of bringing people into the church. It has its origins in Holy Trinity Parish Church, Brompton, London, under the leadership of the Revd Nicky Gumbel, and over two million Britons are estimated to have now completed the course (Alpha Course 2010).

Meanwhile, the UK Evangelical Alliance claims to represent around 1.2 million members (Evangelical Alliance, 2003), frequently speaking out on political issues in a distinctive way. While up-to-date data on the way this type of personal faith impacts specifically upon voting behaviour is somewhat 'patchy', we can still identify certain underlying patterns, and these will be discussed in the next two sections. As Grace Davie puts it:

> I have considerable misgivings about projections which examine past and current attendance or membership and use them to predict the future . . . For example, it is becoming ever more evident that most of the modern world, including the United States, is 'as furiously religious as ever' (Peter Berger's phrase); it is very unlikely that Britain remains immune from these trends . . . Cinema going and attendance at football matches are now growing after decades of decline. A similar upturn could easily happen in the churches – indeed it already has in some dioceses. Truro, Chichester and London offer good examples of rising attendance.
>
> (Davie 2005)

This is important to the above three questions discussed in relation to political behaviour. The argument used by scholars that, because the number of people attending church in Britain is in decline, any correlations are not especially significant anyway, is far too simplistic. This also applies to analyses that try to extrapolate religiosity trends from existing data – for example, *Christian Research*, an independent organisation that produces regular reports, forecasts that the number of active Muslims will be more than the number of active Christians by 2050. This type of prediction is ultimately pointless and does not take into account all factors – the Church of England, in particular, disputed the figures quoted for monthly attendance (*The Times*, 8 May 2008).

So, in summary, identification with the Christian Church in Britain remains strong, but active Christian faith has been in steady decline. But how does all of that affect party politics?

Belonging

First, we need to be clear that the longstanding British religious vote still matters, even if its wider importance is perhaps more limited – there continues to be a correlation between denomination and party preferences. If we examine British Election Study data over a fifty-year period, the differences in the denominational vote in Britain are even stronger in 2010 than they were in 1959. As we can see from Figure 2.2, Church of England voters are significantly more likely to vote Conservative than the other Christian denominations. While Anglican support for the Conservatives rises and falls in line with the wider electorate, it generally remains around 10 per cent higher over the period in question. Catholic voters, meanwhile, are consistently the

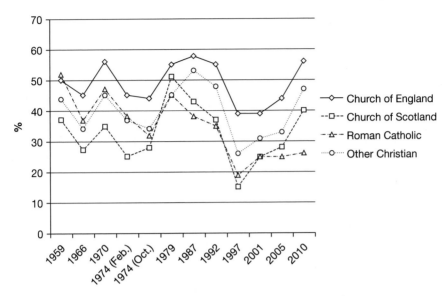

Figure 2.2 Christian vote in British General Elections, 1959–2005 – Conservative Party (%)

Note: No data available for either the 1964 or 1983 General Elections; 2010 data are taken from BES pre-election survey (analysis by author).

Source: Denver 2003, 2007; Seawright 2000.

weakest in their support for the Conservatives, matched more recently by a very substantial decline in popularity among Church of Scotland members – reflecting the long-term decrease in the wider popularity of Conservatives in Scotland. Figure 2.2 charts very clearly this steady and constant decline in Scottish Conservative voters – reflected in the voting behaviour of Scottish Church members.

Meanwhile, Figure 2.3 illustrates the way that – conversely – Catholics are somewhat more likely to vote Labour, as are Church of Scotland members. Again, as with the Conservative vote, while the Church members follow similar patterns to wider electoral trends, we see that Catholics are consistently more likely to stay loyal to Labour than Anglicans, for example.

Interestingly, the century-old link between Methodism and Liberalism appears to be alive and well – non-conformists/other Christians are still much more likely to vote Liberal Democrat than other denominations, despite the smaller numbers involved (Figure 2.4). This alignment has become less distinct since the 1980s, however.

While it is possible to look at the data from the opposite perspective, that is, the percentage of each party vote identifying with a specific religion, Figures 2.2, 2.3 and 2.4 illustrate the most significant correlations for our purposes. It is likely that the different parties have a range of religions within

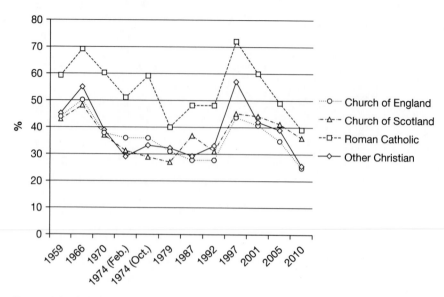

Figure 2.3 Christian vote in British General Elections, 1959–2005 – Labour Party (%)

Note: No data available for either the 1964 or 1983 General Elections; 2010 data are taken from BES pre-election survey (analysis by author).

Source: Denver 2003, 2007; Seawright 2000.

them, broadly reflecting the population of the UK, whereas the very real differences that exist with regard to the way Christians and non-Christians cast their vote is much more significant in relation to independent–dependent variables. A good example of this is the Scottish Labour Party – Catholic voters are much more likely to vote Labour than for any other party, but the Labour Party in Scotland is not a Catholic organisation (see Seawright 2000: 54). This correlation is the main reason why Britain does not have a more European-style Christian Democratic tradition; the 'cleavage' that Lipset and Rokkan (1967) identified in Europe, while multifaceted (for example, the existence of Catholic and Protestant parties in the Netherlands), was ultimately one of 'faith', not denomination, meaning that like-minded Christians/Catholics organised themselves to oppose secularism.

In the UK, there was no 'confessional' social cleavage, strictly speaking – rather, voting behaviour was distinguished by denomination, which, in turn, was closely linked to socio-economic class. In particular, while Anglicans tended to span all the classes, Catholics, many of whom were descended from Irish immigrants, tended to be predominantly working class in origin. Indeed, in relation to the denominational cleavage, David Seawright (2000) goes further – he makes the point that, actually, not only are such correlations still in existence, they are stronger than ever (2000: 49). In 1992 and 1997, for

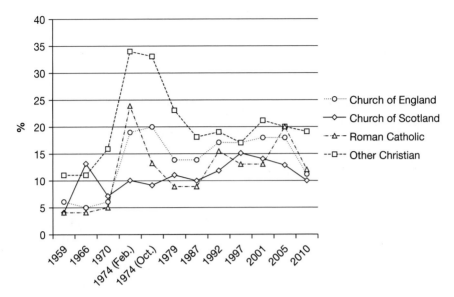

Figure 2.4 Christian vote in British General Elections, 1959–2005 – Liberal Democrats (%)

Note: No data available for either the 1964 or 1983 General Elections; 2010 data are taken from BES pre-election survey (analysis by author).

Source: Denver 2003, 2007; Seawright 2000.

example, Seawright argues that the strength of the link between being a member of the Church of England and voting for the Conservative Party was even more pronounced than in 1979 or the two 1974 elections. Furthermore, Catholic support in 1997 was a 'staggering' 72 per cent – as high a level since the BES surveys began in 1963.

Others are equally emphatic. According to respected pollster Sir Robert Worcester, it was the Catholic vote that actually helped the Labour Party win in 2005:

> As a group, Catholics are among Labour's strongest supporters. Had only Catholics voted, the third Labour landslide would have been of monumental proportions, with Labour gaining more than half of all the votes cast and a majority measured in hundreds of seats rather than tens, while the Liberal Democrats would have almost overtaken the Tories in votes, if not in seats.
>
> (Worcester 2005)

So the first substantial point that needs to be made clearly in this chapter is that the denominational vote is still there – all that has undeniably changed is that the aggregate number of those involved has decreased. However, as we also know, the numbers remain significant enough for social and political scientists to pay attention to their behaviour.

Believing

There is a second, and equally important, dimension to this discussion. Established voting patterns – where 'working-class' voters *identify* with Labour and 'middle-class' voters *identify* with the Conservatives – are in something of a flux, with partisan identification declining and social class being much more complicated to define.

Voters are still prepared to psychologically acknowledge 'possession' of the two main parties – and even confess tacit support for them – but much less strongly. Linked to this, we can note the rise of both 'issue voting' and 'valence voting'. Issue voting concerns the practice of voting for a party not through identification or class or family, but as a consequence of its politicians having addressed a specific policy area in a favourable way. As Heath *et al.* (1991: 33) put it, 'Attitudes have become better predictors of how people will vote'. This approach has been heavily influenced by rational choice theory, and can be also linked to the study of 'valence' issues – that is to say, issues that allow the voter to make an aggregate decision about how to distinguish between the two main parties. It might not be clear to them which party's policies they support ideologically, but they do know which party they trust to run the government efficiently.

Into this more volatile electoral landscape step religious – or 'conscience-based' – issues. If the British voter is much less likely to identify with a party as a consequence of social factors – and more likely to vote on the basis of which party they regard as being the most 'sensible' or 'trustworthy' – the scope for a more 'faith-based' form of religious voting is concurrently much greater. The British voter may now be much less willing or able to make an ideological decision about what he or she thinks about the redistribution of societal wealth due to neither party's social base/bias being especially clear (and the choices available to them in relation to socio-economic and fiscal policy proposals). However, he or she is still able to decide which party could more effectively maintain social order by cleaning up MPs' expenses, telling the truth about weapons of mass destruction in Iraq or curbing the bonuses of bankers.

Questions on church attendance and partisan identification were taken from British Social Attitudes Survey data sets from 1997 to 2007, and cross-tabulated. The church attendance data was recoded into three main categories: 'attends frequently', 'attends occasionally' and 'does not attend'. While partisan identification is not the same thing as voting in an election, the British Election Study has intermittently ignored the important distinction between church attendance and denomination (in effect, the 'believing' versus 'belonging' paradigm). This means we have no usable data from the 2001,

2005 or 2010 British General Elections. There appears to have been a shift in emphasis towards ethnicity questions, with more interest being shown towards issues such as immigration and multiculturalism.

However, the BSAS data are equally informative. The key finding is that if British voters are not religious, they are less likely to identify with the Conservative Party. This is demonstrated over a ten-year period from 1997 to 2007. In each case, a significant chi-square test was produced ($p < 0.05$), and we can draw some reasonably robust conclusions about the wider implications, which fit in with other extant literature on the topic.

This is not to say that if voters are religious, they are more likely to vote Conservative. This distinction is important as observant Catholics and Scottish Presbyterians will be more inclined to vote Labour ahead of the Conservatives – denomination and national identity appear to 'trump' religiosity. However, if a voter has no Christian faith or affiliation at all, it would appear that they are also much less likely to vote Conservative (see Figures 2.5 and 2.6).

In particular, Figure 2.6 shows how non-church attendees are consistently more likely to vote for parties other than the Conservatives. That specific correlation is effectively independent of interference from religious denomination, and therefore more robust than the ones showing a link between religiosity and the Conservatives.

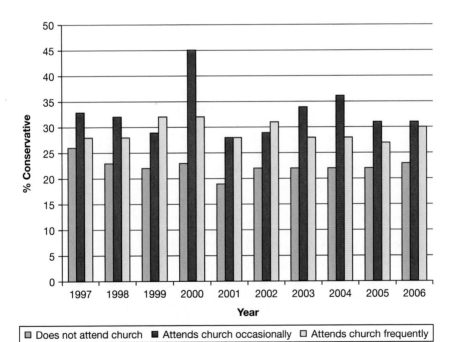

Figure 2.5 Percentage Conservative by church attendance
Source: British Social Attitudes Survey (BSAS).

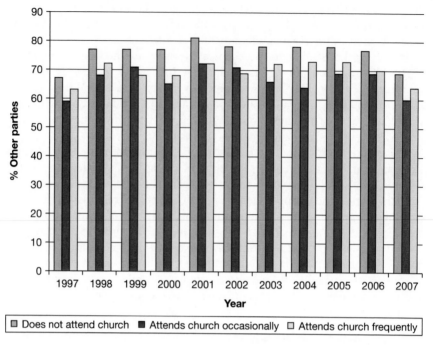

Figure 2.6 Percentage other parties by church attendance
Source: British Social Attitudes Survey (BSAS).

Kotler-Berkowitz (2001: 541) also found evidence from the British Household Panel Study that those who were less religious were less likely to vote Conservative. Similarly, Denver (2007: 184) argues that the non-religious are significantly less likely to vote Conservative, on the basis of his analysis of British Elections Studies. Respectively, the analyses of McAndrew (2010: 100) and Andersen *et al.* (2005: 298) also broadly support this. According to a poll commissioned by the think tank Theos, 20 per cent of Britons would not vote for an atheist (Theos 2008), and there are considerably fewer secularist and humanists in the Conservative Party. Chapter 3 will discuss the reasons for this in more detail but it is worth pausing here to focus upon it also. While the Conservatives under two previous leaders, John Major and Margaret Thatcher, have attempted to tap into this vote in the past, it is much less clear whether or not the British voter either responded favourably, or was of the specific religious profile/evangelical inclination anyway to be especially significant.[4]

Micklethwait and Wooldridge (2009) argue that Britain, along with other Western European states, is experiencing the 'Americanisation' of politics with the emergence of a conservative 'religious right'. They point to the way Tim Montgomerie, an evangelical Christian, and key adviser to the Conservative leadership, has successfully pushed for the party to rediscover its 'moral purpose', and promote traditional family values as the basis for a stronger society. While this journalistic interpretation is difficult to back up with scientific evidence, the present author argues that it is not without merit. There is some evidence, albeit putative, that the 'denominational vote' – or, more correctly, differences between denominational voting – has gradually been augmented by what could be termed the 'alpha vote'[5] – evangelical Conservative Christians who relate their strong religious faith to all aspects of their life, including party politics; in other words, individuals who do not regard themselves as either Catholic, Church of England or Church of Scotland but first and foremost 'Christian' – and who, as a result, have a much more pronounced public Christian identity. The East End of London, for example, is thought to have twice as many Pentecostal congregations as Church of England ones (Micklethwait and Wooldridge 2009: 136).

Fewer Britons may attend church than before but substantial numbers still do – indeed, large numbers continue to both identify with the mainstream Christian Churches and possess an 'evangelical' identity, which means that their Christian faith is much more fundamentalist and all-encompassing. In that context, parties recognise that there are a substantial number of votes to be won and lost if they can send out the right sort of electoral messages to these voters, and it would appear that, in the 2010 General Election, the Conservatives were tempted to do just that, with their emphasis on the importance of the family juxtaposed with Labour's continued predilection for an all-powerful state (Conservative Party 2010).

It is also worth again mentioning Robert Putnam's influential work on democratic engagement in America (2000) – he has found that Christians are much more likely to vote, much more likely to identify with a party, and much more likely to join a political campaign (see also Gerber *et al.* 2008). Putnam is currently leading a joint Harvard–Manchester project on the role of religion in British society, which has its origins in the many similarities he sees between the US and UK. Crucially, David Voas and Rodney Ling do not equate the trend in falling church attendance as being the same thing as the Christian Church ceasing to matter in British society:

> if secularisation means the declining social significance of religion . . . , we would expect religion not to matter much in Britain. As it turns out, these assumptions are not wholly correct. Americans and Britons are surprisingly similar in many of their attitudes.
>
> (Voas and Ling 2010: 83)

The present author would very much agree with this analysis – we will return to the Anglo-American dimension later in this book, but in the meantime, simply focus on the wider point: religion continues to affect people's social and political values, ranging across issues from ethics to party support, albeit with some caveats about its aggregate significance. Questions on church attendance and electoral turn-out were taken from the British Election Study data sets from October 1974 until 1997, and cross-tabulated. No more up-to-date data are available owing to the failure to ask a religiosity-related question after 1997. The same three categories of church attendance were established after data recoding – 'attends frequently', 'attends occasionally' and 'does not attend' – while the BES official verified turn-out question was used.

The key finding to come out of this part of the statistical analysis is that if British voters are religious, they are also more likely to vote. This is demonstrated over a period of nearly a quarter of a century, from 1974 to 1997. Once again, in each case, a significant chi-square test was produced ($p < 0.05$), apart from 1992 which contained missing values. Once more, we can draw some clear conclusions about the way Christian values impact upon voting behaviour. While the most recent of these analyses is over ten years ago, we can still detect a very clear and distinct pattern, and there is nothing that would make us question the continuation of these correlations in the last three British General Elections (2001, 2005 and 2010).

Figure 2.7 was constructed from the cross-tabulation data mentioned above – it broadly reflects a general decline in turn-out at British General Elections, although obviously does not actually show precise turn-out levels for each year.

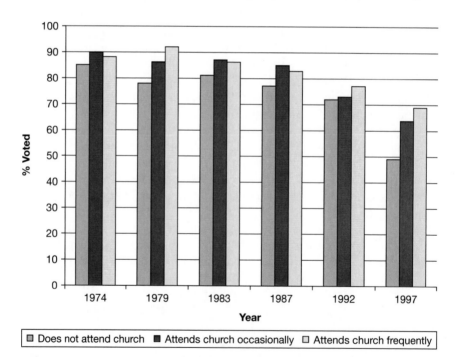

Figure 2.7 Percentage turn-out by church attendance

Note: The 1974 data are taken from the October General Election.

Source: British Election Study (BES).

We can see a less pronounced decline in turn-out among those who attend church either occasionally or frequently. In particular, the 1997 figure shows a big drop-off in turn-out among non-church attendees, while the level for those who do attend remains relatively high.

We would expect this finding – church attendance in the UK matches neatly with age and class, and it could be argued that a more serious analysis is necessary, controlling for the above variables, to try to uncover whether or not religiosity is itself an important, or the most important, factor. However, there is already a great deal of literature on this (McAndrew 2010; Pattie *et al.* 2004; Putnam 2000) that shows the wider links between Christian adherence and democratic engagement, including multinomial logistic regression analyses, so there is no need for this particular study to apply such statistical models for this purpose at this stage.

While Figure 2.8 is effectively a mirror image of Figure 2.7, it nevertheless effectively shows the rise in voter apathy as being especially pronounced among non-church attendees, in the period covered in the analysis. While occasional church attendance can appear to be a better cue for voting than frequent church attendance in some election years, non-church attendance is consistently lower over the period analysed.

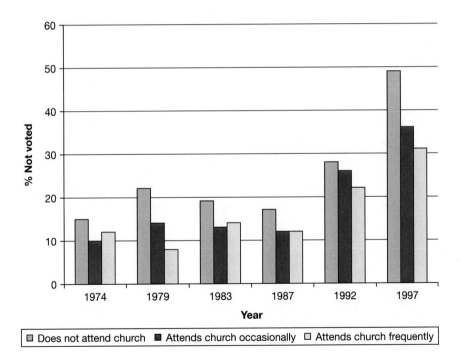

Figure 2.8 Percentage non-voting by church attendance

Note: The 1974 data are taken from the October General Election.

Source: British Election Study (BES).

This finding can be compared with the one on partisan identification discussed in the last section – there, we found that, while being an active Christian did not necessarily correlate with being a Conservative, being a non-Christian correlated with voting for a party other than the Conservatives. It is the same here – while voter turn-out does not necessarily correlate exactly with going to church, not going to church does appear to be a good cue for not going to the polling station either.

Further, as the social statisticians, David Voas and Rodney Ling put it (2010: 84), '[f]ew people are hostile to religious practice per se. Indeed, we have an interest in anything that might make other people behave well'. In one sense, this sort of finding is actually more significant than any other – if Christians are more likely to vote than any other group in society, that has huge implications for parties and politicians. As Berger *et al.* put it (2008: 126), 'In the United States, religion is seen as a resource (the means by which to resolve secular as well religious dilemmas); in Europe, it is part of the problem'.

Conclusions

The religious cleavage remains strong in British party politics – while it is perhaps not as immediately visible as it is in the other Western European countries that Lipset and Rokkan had in mind when they mapped the sociological origins of the party system, it is facile to under-research it; it has always been there, and at the start of the twenty-first century, there is considerable quantitative evidence that it still is.

Clearly, however, we need to be cautious. It would be wrong to suggest that somehow elections in Britain are won or lost on the basis of religious beliefs – as is the case in many US Congressional contests (see also Campbell and Monson 2008). In America, religious faith has gradually become as good a predictor of voting behaviour as socio-economic class, with church attendees significantly more likely to vote Republican than Democrat – regardless of occupation. This is not the case in Britain, and probably never will be either. Indeed, with Christian Democrats still fighting elections on (albeit vaguely) religious policy platforms throughout Europe, the British model does – prima facie – look relatively secularised. Also, the statistics concerning church attendance are quite explicit – active church membership is in decline – so the total number of voters taking their cues for how to vote has also declined since the 1950s, concurrently with class and partisan dealignment. Nevertheless, this chapter has made three key points.

First, it is wrong to assume that religion does not matter at all and ignore it when conducting surveys, or to exclude Britain when looking at politics and religion altogether (in line with the 'secular Europe, religious America' orthodoxy). As has already been mentioned, according to LeDuc *et al.* (2002), Britain lies at the bottom of both denominational and confessional links to voting among global democracies – but that does not mean we should ignore it altogether. Harrop and Miller (1987: 180) state that

'The evolution of electoral choice in twentieth century Britain has been a story of the replacement of religion by class as the principal cleavage'. This book would not seek to contradict this statement but is merely arguing that it is a non-sequitur to then argue that religion has no influence at all. Also, it matters in an interesting way – for example, Catholics vote left rather than right *in spite of* their Catholicism.

Second, and linked to this, it is also clear that Christian Britons are, up to a point, voting on economic and social issues with their faith in mind – and that this tends to favour the Conservatives. While the data is less convincing here, and we need to be very careful not to overstate this – especially given the strength of the denominational vote also in existence – there is evidence of a link between atheists and the parties of the left/progressive/liberal centre, and other scholars have referred to this as well.

More liberal-minded Christians, such as those whose Northern European ancestors were responsible for developing the welfare state (see Van Kersbergen and Manow 2009), clearly exist in Britain – indeed, the development of the Christian Socialist Movement will be discussed in the next chapter, and the way that Catholic voters support the party of the left, rather than the right, in the UK is also well documented. However, from an institutional perspective, that vote is probably not as coherent as the Conservative Christian one – some vote Labour, some vote Liberal Democrat – indeed, some may even vote Conservative, whereas it is the last option that is the only realistic one for evangelicals who are interested in life issues and equalities.

Evangelical Christians place much more emphasis on *individual* personal salvation than on good acts or social work. That is not to say that they do not have any interest at all in the latter – many evangelicals do get involved in this sort of activity – but for most the emphasis is on the spiritual. When they become well off financially, they believe they have been rewarded for their good lives by God, and they deserve to keep their wealth and spend it ('God is good'). Indeed, it is wrong to assume that evangelical Christians have no interest in money – independent churches need to be good businesses in order to survive, much more so than the average Anglican parish church. This phenomenon is very much what Adam Smith was referring to when he noted the desire of the non-conformist ministers to make their congregations grow in a way that did not apply to the established churches, whose clergy had a complacent confidence that they would always be there, regardless of the economic climate (see Chapter 1).

If religious denomination still matters to British voting behaviour, then it is important that scholars recognise that. However, if there is evidence that religious faith also matters – and matters in a new, twenty-first century way – that means that religion is, in some ways, even more important to British party politics than ever before. The fact that the total number of evangelicals has risen hugely is also significant. Voas and Crockett's key conclusion – that Britons are 'neither believing nor belonging' (2005) is ultimately concerned with tracking decline but it fails to give sufficient attention to aggregate figures. The same can be said for Voas and Ling's analysis of decline in 2010 – certainly, the decline in active church attendance since the 1950s has been significant, but that does not mean that Bruce is right that this can be extrapolated to zero people in the future.

Third, the other interesting dimension to all of this is turn-out – the BES data suggest that there is a positive correlation between voter turn-out and religion, apparently confirming Putnam's theory that religion is good for social capital – and also confirming in the process that religion matters to parties. If religious voters are more likely to turn out at elections, then their vote really matters – and should not be ignored. The 'Conservative' correlation is strong but also fluid – similar to the US. While linked to the Republicans at present, there is no reason why it could not go Democrat in the future. It is the same in the UK – the religious vote may be inclined to vote Conservative, but it would be foolish of Labour to ignore that demographic entirely, especially given the denominational dimension already discussed.

Religion still matters to British voting behaviour, which means that, rationally, religion still matters to the British parties – and it is to them we now turn.

3 More Methodism than Marxism?

Christianity and the British party system

The emphasis of this chapter follows directly on from that of the last – after discussing the influence of Christianity on British voting behaviour, we now turn to look at how the parties react, in terms of formulating policy platforms and wider ideological stances. It was Morgan Phillips, the General Secretary of Labour between 1944 and 1961, who said that his party 'owes more to Methodism than to Marxism' – in other words, so sober and buttoned-up was the left in the UK that it took its inspiration not so much from twentieth-century Soviet Russia but from the non-conformist traditions of the English Victorian era. Socialism in Britain was more about 'doing good' than over-throwing the instruments of the State, it was implied. In one sense, this is actually more of a comment on the lack of radicalism in the history of the British left than on its religiosity but it contains, like all amusing lines, an element of truth, and one that can actually be applied to the other parties as well.

The role of Christianity in helping to mould the other two parties – Conservative and Liberal – in the Victorian era has been recognised by historians, and was discussed partially in Chapters 1 and 2.[1] In particular, we have already noted the apparent dispersal of Christian Democracy throughout the British party system, thus avoiding an institutional separation based on anti-clerical arguments surrounding the role of the Church in relation to the State. Table 3.1 on p. 46 is an attempt to categorise the policy areas that the Christian factions of each of the British parties emphasise, when explaining or justifying their perspective on the relationship between their religion and politics. Clearly, a large number of Christians are members of the three parties but have no interest in making that public or formal, and so such a typology does not really apply to them, but for those to whom it does, we can detect three patterns.

The significance of the terms 'fellowship', 'movement' and 'forum' are intriguing. Christian fellowships tend to be evangelical, the word 'movement' has associations with the left, while the 'forum' is a suitably neutral and idealistically constructive Liberal Democratism. For Conservative Christians, the importance of the family is key; for Christian Socialists, it is the pursuit of social justice; for Christians in the Liberal Democrats, it is about moderation and tolerance for religion in a politics free from ideological extremes. This

Table 3.1 Christian party groupings

Party	Grouping	Priorities
Conservative	Conservative Christian Fellowship (CCF)	• Family values • Social order
Labour	Christian Socialist Movement (CSM)	• Social justice • Equalities
Liberal Democrat	Liberal Democrat Christian Fellowship (LDCF)	• Moderation • Religious freedoms

chapter will explore these themes in depth – encompassing them all is the inescapable fact that Christian Democracy did not take root as a political movement in Britain. But is it simply a case of Christian Democracy being 'dispersed' throughout the British party system? After all, Christian Democracy is a notoriously difficult ideology to pin down – of the centre right, but not necessarily right-wing, a 'third way' long before Antony Giddens dreamt up the term (1998). It would appear that this organisational flexibility has simply been taken to its logical conclusion in the UK, with Christianity literally spanning all three major parties. But is it as simple as that? Or is it possible that Christian Democracy lurks more in one party than another, making one of the parties the 'CDU' (Christian Democatic Union) or 'CDA' (Christian Democratic Appeal) of Britain by default, due to disproportionately larger numbers of Christians?[2]

However, before we look at the role of Christianity in the organisation and ideology of the British parties, it is important to be aware of the various models of party behaviour that exist as background. In the same way as Chapter 2 discussed these in relation to voting behaviour, it is helpful to refer to similar theories here.

Models of party behaviour

Scholars with an interest in political parties have developed different terms for the various ways that parties are organised. The central trend that has been documented over time in the context of Western democracies is the shift from 'mass' parties to 'catch-all' parties. Mass parties were first defined by Maurice Duverger (1954), who highlighted, in particular, the 'vertical plane' that provided individual party branches with significant mass memberships. While separate from the partisan identification model mentioned in Chapter 2, the mass party model nevertheless fits neatly with a group or organisational account of political behaviour that sees large sections of society voting for the same party election after election on the basis of socio-economic factors. The emergence of Otto Kirchheimer's 'catch-all party' (1966) challenged this neat landscape – no longer, it was argued, could we say that this was the only way of looking at party structures.[3] It was clear to Kirchheimer that the modern party had evolved into a much more electorally sophisticated organisation, tailoring its policies to appeal to different parts of the electorate, and not just the section of society with which it was traditionally associated. This has also sometimes been called – rather unscientifically – the 'Americanisation' of European politics.

In more recent times, Richard Katz and Peter Mair (1995) have challenged the premise that the mass party is the standard to which all newer models or approaches must refer. Rather, they contend that the origins of the party in Western democracies had as much to do with the way the political elites of states chose to organise, as the party comprised different cross-sections of civil society massing together – partly endorsing Leon Epstein's alternative 'cadre' model of parties (1967). Katz and Mair go on to argue that this process has developed into the creation of 'cartel' parties – parties that are closely linked to the State, through funding and other privileges that make them part of the establishment, regardless of what ideologies or policies they advocate. Crucially, Katz and Mair take issue with the notion that parties are in decline – one of the tacit implications of the 'catch-all' model.

It is not really within the scope of this book to go into detail about which of these models is most convincing or helpful, but in the same way that Chapter 2 argued that the rational choice approach to voting behaviour was the most useful in that context, it is important to clarify that the 'catch-all' model is probably the most relevant to our discussion here. The creation of 'New Labour' under Tony Blair is the epitome of a party modernising and moving away from socialist ideologies with a mass class-based membership to a much more broad voter appeal, and that process has been matched by the modernisation of the Conservative Party under David Cameron – who even described himself as the 'heir to Blair' in 2005 (Pierce 2005). While resisting the temptation to rebrand the party altogether – 'New Conservatives' – the Cameron approach is very similar to Blair's in the mid 1990s: hug the opposition close in relation to policies but make it clear that the party is still 'different' in values and personnel, so terms such as 'progressive' and 'liberal' send out the same signals. That is not to argue that Katz and Mair's cartel model is not helpful, but simply that it is perhaps not as relevant to the focus of this book as the other ones. One could argue that the positive noises that the different Christian factions make towards one another via the 'Christians in Politics' group is evidence of an 'elite' but this is far from being unusual or necessarily significant.

But where does that leave the role of Christianity in British party policy development? Ultimately, the answer is the development of factions within the organisations, illustrating the way that modern British parties are broad coalitions of different views and ideas. In relation to Christianity, we see the three parties develop different groups internally to take into account their different audiences, but this time, in a postmodern/'catch-all' way – this is not the resurrection of the confessional cleavage but instead confirmation that such cleavages are now 'unfreezing' and that there is a need for the parties to respond.[4]

As a consequence, the lack of a mass Christian Democratic movement in the UK has become less relevant and meaningful than it was immediately after the war. The opportunity for scholars to ignore Britain when discussing religion and politics is now less admissible than in the days of the Christian Democrats ruling Western Europe with an overtly 'Christian' set of policy principles, and finding electoral popularity with practising Catholics in Southern Europe and Protestants in Northern Europe. That is not to argue that Britain has become more like America in this respect as that would be far too simplistic – first, the way religion impacts upon US politics is quite specific and modern. Prior to the 1980s, the public role of Christians in America was very limited, and if we leap forward to the second decade of the twenty-first century and an Obama White House, the closeness of the relationship between the religious right and the Republicans is now actually quite strained (see Sullivan 2008). So, to liken the process in Britain to what happened in America thirty years ago would be unhelpful – the 'Anglo-American' model discussed in Chapter 1 pertains much more to the wider political framework in which religion operates, as opposed to specific party models.

Before we look at the three main British parties and their Christian factions, we need to be clear about the methodological framework – for example, is the chapter trying to assess the influence of each faction within each party, or in relation to one another, or both – or not at all? It is methodologically difficult to compare, for example, the power of the CCF with other factions within the Conservative Party – clearly, any modern party is made up of different groups, with policy ultimately formulated by the leadership. The argument that the CCF is somehow more important than, say, the Tory Reform Group is both problematic and pointless. The emphasis that different party organisations place upon certain policies varies and the influence they carry will be commensurate with the focus of the party leadership at different points of the electoral cycle (see Panebianco 1988). Furthermore, an individual Conservative Party member, for example, can also be an active member of a range of different 'factions', and therefore exert influence at different times under different guises.

Equally difficult is to try to assess how the CCF compares with the CSM and LDCF in relation to the above issues. If we were to go down this route, we could examine criteria such as financial resources, size of membership and whether the group leadership enjoys a proximity to the party leadership at a higher level. Again, however, the worth of conducting such a scientific analysis is limited – all of the above criteria will match the relative size of memberships that the parties as a whole enjoy. Even a more weighted analysis taking into account the relative size of the Conservatives and Labour in comparison with the Liberal Democrats (see section on British parties later in this chapter) would struggle to definitely conclude which of the three factions was most influential. The temporal nature of any conclusion would also limit its usefulness, and there is also the question of whether or not it is actually helpful, in any case – ultimately, the CCF, CSM and LDCF are all similar organisations, with similar objectives, who are even formally united under the umbrella group,

'Christians in Politics', mentioned on page 47, which sustains its own website and runs joint events. A similar point can be made in relation to discourse analysis via manifestos (see Budge *et al.* 2001). The problem here is the point-lessness of poring over manifestos when we already know that parties are not going to put in there anything that is anything other than harmless, moderate and designed to win the next General Election. No British party explicitly mentions Christianity in its campaigning literature – indeed, David Burrowes, MP, the Chairman of the CCF, even argues that the organisation is not really all that interested in promoting any sort of policy agenda, nor are there any radical religious objectives: 'We're not on a mission', as he puts it (Interview with author, 2 March 2010).

We will analyse the way this dimension actually impacts upon the three different parties later in the chapter, but it is important to state here that such an attitude does not equate to the subgroups being entirely apolitical – for example, Mr Burrowes founded the Fellowship with Tim Montgomerie twenty years ago as a result of disliking the implication that Christians could not be capitalists or supportive of the free market. It is clear that, for many British politicians, their party politics and Christianity go hand in hand. It is, therefore, very important that these Christian groups exist at all, are active and – rationally – are able to exert influence in different places and at different times, as it supports the public choice assumptions put forward in Chapter 2, in relation to voting behaviour affecting party behaviour.

The global context: confessional parties in the West

In the same way that Chapter 2 provided an overview of the link between Christianity and voting behaviour in order to provide context, and this chapter will do the same, but this time focusing on comparable parties in advanced industrial Western democracies across Europe and North America. This is helpful as it allows us to see, albeit briefly, how the British parties fit in to a more global picture. An obvious place to start is the Christian Democratic movement of Europe – for example, Germany, the third largest economy in the world, is run by Christian Democrats, whose core aim is to demonstrate the 'Christian understanding of humans and their responsibility toward God' (see Der Spiegel 2010). We also need to look at the United States where some argue that the Republican Party has become a quasi-confessional party owing to the strength of correlation that now exists between the many evangelical Christians and the party.[5]

According to Van Kersbergen, Christian Democracy is concerned with a 'religiously inspired model of social reform which is both social and capitalist' (1994: 42). Indeed, he argues that 'religion accords the movement an unparalleled opportunity to adapt to changing circumstances' (1994: 31) owing to its 'bipolar' and 'multidimensional' profile (1994: 37) – something with which the present author would enthusiastically agree. Often accused of lacking ideological clarity, Christian Democrats nevertheless tend to be associated with the centre-right of the political spectrum. In relation to denomination, it is worth reiterating, then, that the UK is therefore the reverse of much of Europe where Catholics empathise with parties of the left, not the right. One does not need to be religious to vote Christian Democrat but party programmes do continue to stress the legacy and values of the Christian Church.[6] As Meny and Knapp highlight (1998: 72), parties continue to place great stress on the values of education and morality, even if Catholic Church law on marriage, divorce and contraception no longer automatically dominates sections of party programmes. Dutch confessional parties, many of which are Calvinist in origin, regard the Bible as a 'direct guide' to policymaking up until the 1960s, and today the CDA 'accepts modern secularised culture only very reluctantly' (Lucardie and ten Napel 1994: 65).

Religious interest groups are also influential voices in the American political system – since the 1970s, religious interests, particularly on the political right, have 'become highly visible forces in American politics' (Guth *et al.* 2007: 55). The two most important religious right organisations of that period, 'Christian Voice' and the 'Moral Majority', were both founded in 1978. The main focus of 'Christian Voice' was campaigning against pornography and homosexuality while the 'Moral Majority', led by the controversial Reverend Jerry Falwell, presented itself as the voice of conservative Christianity throughout America. As Wilcox states, the 1976 Carter Presidential campaign 'mobilized the evangelicals as no candidate had done before' (1992: 11). Carter made his 'born again' Southern Baptist faith central to his campaign, and won many votes as a consequence. However, from a secular and liberal perspective, there was concern over such an uncompromising expression of religious values in politics, and there was also concern from churches that an involvement in politics would lead to a dilution of their moral authority (Guth *et al.* 2007: 58).

By the 1980s, the 'religious right' had become nationally prominent. In 1987, the television evangelist Pat Robertson decided to run for the Republican nomination for President. However, despite spending what Bruce calls an 'unprecedented sum' (2002: 215) he failed to win a primary election. Other religious right figures such as Pat Buchanan and Gary Bauer have also run for the Republican nomination since then, and fared equally badly. In 1994 the Christian Coalition[7] succeeded in delivering the Party's convention nomination for the governorship of Minnesota to Allen Quist, an anti-abortion activist, although he too was eventually beaten in the primary election by the incumbent, Arne Carlson. By the 1990s, the campaign tactics used by religious right groups had become highly sophisticated. As Ivers states, 'the Christian conservatives who came to Washington in the late 1980s were better organised, more sophisticated in their political and legal capabilities, and better financed than ever before' (1998: 294). For example, during the Clinton budget dispute in 1996, the Christian Coalition aired television advertisements in the districts of undecided Democrats. According to Goldstein, viewers 'sick of high taxes' were asked to call a special number that automatically added the name of that person onto the Coalition's list for future campaigns (1999: 67). Callers were also sent out a package of Christian Coalition materials.

After George W. Bush became President in 2000, the political role of religious groups became even more prominent, and also more controversial. Bush is the most overtly American religious leader since Carter, but post-11 September, that feature of leadership now has an added potency. Bush's 'crusade' against terrorism, the 'axis of evil' and Osama Bin Laden – 'a man without a soul' – is heavy with biblical connotations. David Frum, a former Bush speech writer, describes how prayer was a regular feature of meetings at the White House, with Bible studies led by Cabinet members (Frum 2003). Soon after the President took office, he launched a flagship drive to provide public funds for churches and religious organisations involved with social care. He established the Office of Faith-Based and Community Initiatives, as well as faith-based 'centres' in five Cabinet-level federal agencies to assist with its work. He also ordered the removal of 'bureaucratic barriers' regulating public funds for religious groups (Wilson 2003: 30). In implementing these changes, Bush fundamentally altered the way Church and State is traditionally separated in the United States, and opponents of the 'charitable choice' principle, as it is known, argue that this should raise cause for concern (Wilson 2003: 29).

The social context: who joins parties in Britain?

The organisational structure of British parties has changed considerably since the start of the twentieth century – the premise that they represent the interests of large cross-sections of society has been replaced by more elite-led units, marketing themselves effectively in order to win votes from a diverse electorate. One by-product of this development – either directly or indirectly – has been the substantial decline in memberships of parties, and Britain is quite typical in this regard. Ultimately, what is the point – rationally – of joining an organisation if decisions are taken by a small elite grouped around the leader? What is the point of attending annual party conferences each autumn if all the decisions have already been taken? The order in which this happened – parties becoming more hierarchical and then losing members, or vice versa – is perhaps more nuanced but, regardless, the 'anti-democratic' nature of organisations that are pivotal to democracy is one of the great paradoxes of politics.

Certainly, the memberships of all three major British parties are in something of a free fall, and showing no real sign of being able to reverse the trend either. Inevitably, a book of this nature has analysed in depth (see Chapter 2) the decline of church attendance in Britain – and its political significance. However, in many ways it is the decline of the party that this book has a responsibility to chart just as equally, as any analysis of the role of Christianity in British representative democracy requires fully operational parties to provide a context in which to analyse.

Figure 3.1 shows the spectacular decline in British party membership levels over the last forty years – and more than ten General Elections. Admittedly, defining members of parties has been methodologically challenging in the British context. This is primarily because, while the Electoral Commission produces annual reports, it is the parties themselves that are in charge of membership data, and can interpret them how they want. The dual membership set-up that existed for many years with people who joined trade unions automatically becoming members of the Labour Party clearly artificially boosted the party numbers, while the Conservatives' definitions have always been very hazy, even including people who drink in Conservative social clubs up and down England, and also members of the Conservative associations, which is not quite the same thing as being a full party member.[8] Meanwhile, it is also reasonable to argue that the Liberal Democrats would have much larger resources and membership numbers if voters felt that they actually had a chance of winning a General Election.

Linked to the points made on pages 40–1 of Chapter 2 on voter turn-out, this membership decline means that parties need the core voters who partici-pate in the political process even more – older people, the middle class and those who go to church on a Sunday. The power of the 'grey vote', the 'Essex man' vote and the 'Christian vote' is even more vital at British election time

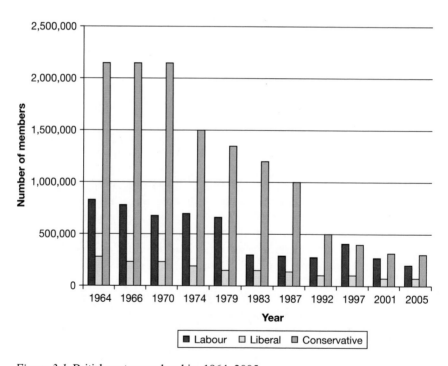

Figure 3.1 British party membership, 1964–2005

Sources: House of Commons Library 2009 (2001–5); Webb 2002 (1964–7).

than it has been in the past. From a supply-side perspective, British Christianity provides a steady resource of individuals who wish to vote and engage in other forms of civic life, in an era of significant partisan dealignment. Using British Social Attitudes Survey data, McAndrew (2010: 100) also shows that Christians are substantially more likely to identify with a party – regardless of which party that is – than non-Christians.

As we can clearly see from Figure 3.1, if the trend continues, the entire concept of party membership will require to be reconfigured in the not distant future. We may be moving towards an American model of registered voters, or something entirely different, if we have not already reached that point. It is not the place of this book to analyse why parties have been in decline in the UK, or whether or not politicians in the parties fully appreciate the extent of the problem, but it is important to note here that representative democracy in Britain is facing a huge challenge, if not quite yet a full-blown crisis.

The Conservative Christian Fellowship (CCF)

There is a very close relationship between the priorities of members of the Conservative Party and traditional British Christian family values. The image of the party has always been bound up with British national identity – however nebulous such a concept is to explain (Hickson 2005; Bale 2010) – much more so than either the Labour Party with its emphasis on international socialism, or the Liberals and their enthusiasm for European integration. The deep importance of national pride in 'Britishness' to the Conservative Party has been consistently prominent in its policies and election manifestos. Perhaps the most powerful embodiment of that is the widespread 'Euro-scepticism' that pervades much of the party to greater or lesser degrees,[9] and it also impinges, albeit relatively mildly, upon immigration policy. As Anglicanism is the national religion of England, the Conservative Party publicly values it, along with the monarchy and the union with Scotland, Wales and Northern Ireland. The party supports conserving the place of Church of England bishops in the upper house of the British Parliament, thereby publicly tying Church and State together constitutionally.

In particular, commitment to the role of the family has been a longstanding feature of party policy through the decades – in the successful 2010 General Election campaign, the party advocated supportive taxation breaks for married couples, and this proposal survived the coalition talks with the Liberal Democrats, who were against it. Party leader, David Cameron, has been unequivocal in his praise for the family as the most important institution in Britain (Conservative Party 2010), but such enthusiasm is merely the modern reincarnation of a traditional party foundation stone. Furthermore, while it has officially updated its manifesto to make it inclusive towards same sex couples in the face of an irresistible tide of equalities initiatives, there remain members who do not support this, or view it as a welcome innovation (Conservative Party 2009).

The Conservatives are, certainly – superficially – the party closest to the Christian Democrats found throughout the rest of Europe, due to the correlation between Christian theology and conservative political ideology. In that sense, there is a neat linkage between secular 'conservative' values and confessional party ideology. Perhaps as a consequence, the Conservative Christian Fellowship is not so much of a 'faction' as it is a social network, as we can see below:

> Firstly we exist to train, equip and support our members. The CCF offers a development programme to those who are under 35 and beginning or thinking of a career in politics. For the past two years, the CCF has offered a Local Councillors' Training Day and encouraged the CCF membership to support all those standing in local and regional elections. The CCF also seeks to encourage those applying for Westminster and European parliamentary seats.
>
> Secondly the CCF provides a relational bridge with the Conservative Party.
>
> Finally, the CCF is a fellowship founded on prayer. The key foundation of the CCF is its relational strength and prayerfulness. Each month, when parliament is sitting, the CCF holds a prayer meeting to pray together for the Fellowship, parliament and the nation.
>
> (Conservative Christian Fellowship 2010)

The above 'mission statement' does really read like a call to action or the sentiments of a faction that wants to exert power over the party. This appears to be primarily an organisation through which like-minded Christians in the Conservative Party can meet one another. It is not at all apparent that the CCF undertake any serious lobbying activities in order to influence the wider party over policy development. Its main calendar of events appears to revolve around prayer meetings and informal gatherings, including those for young Conservative Christians (defined as those under thirty-five years old, perhaps to be expected given the CCF's origins as a student organisation at the University of Exeter). It is clear that the group does not feel the need to actively lobby the leadership for policy direction – in public, at least – but is essentially quite happy that their values fit neatly into the wider party. While this could also be said for the two other parties, as we will see, it is particularly pronounced with the Conservatives.

In many ways, Conservative leader, David Cameron, is the living embodiment of this almost undetectable overlap between the 'Christian' and the 'Conservative'. He is relatively private about his beliefs, describing himself as an Anglican who does not go to church very often, thus placing himself in the mainstream of British society in the process: 'I believe in God and I'm a Christian and I worship – not as regularly as I should – but I go to church,' he said. 'Do I drop to my knees and ask for guidance whenever an issue comes up? No, I don't' (BBC *Songs of Praise*, 15 November 2009). In other words, to paraphrase the former Prime Minister, Tony Blair, 'I do believe in God but don't worry, I'm not a nutter' (BBC News, 25 November 2007).

However, it is the promotion of the family over the interests of the State mentioned earlier that is most significant, that is, the Conservatives argue that no matter what emphasis is placed upon the redistribution of wealth or taxation policy, that should never interfere with the role of the family – a message that appeals equally to non-Christians who want to see a smaller state. Mrs Thatcher's famous quote that there is 'no such thing as society' also went on to say that there were only 'families' (Thatcher 1987). Critics from the left seized upon this selfish, individualistic view of the world but, of course, the full text suggests an altogether more nuanced meaning. Tax breaks for married couples are also linked to this – but this is almost by accident, by coincidence – one does not have to be a Christian to believe in the importance of family, but it just so happens that the two often go together quite neatly.

The most current version of the policy has its origins in research work conducted by the Centre for Social Justice, an independent think tank but one with close links to the Conservatives, chaired by Iain Duncan Smith, the Work and Pensions Secretary. While heavily populated by Conservative Christians, Mr Duncan Smith is adamant that its pro-family recommendations are linked more to efficacy, that is 'the family works', than theology (Interview with author, 4 March 2010). A similar point can be made in relation to another figure close to David Cameron, Phillip Blond, the director of the right-leaning think tank, Res Publica, and a former theology lecturer at the University of Cumbria. His 'Red Tory' and 'big society' concepts may be religious in origin but have a much wider appeal. Indeed, even if we consider Cornerstone, the Conservative subgroup that stands for the promotion of traditional values, that does not necessarily just involve active Christians.

Nevertheless, there is a deeper point – even the modernised Conservative party under David Cameron's leadership has shown a predilection for American-style faith-based initiatives and the concept of giving religious non-governmental organisations (NGOs) more freedom to deliver social services. This is significant as it is evidence that another brand of conservatism can also commend Christianity – if there is convincing evidence from the US that churches are better at providing social care than the State, then that is an attractive option for any Conservative. Anything that reduces the power of the State is a good thing, as far as they are concerned. So while the family provides the centre-point of all of this, there is also the instrumental role that can be played by churches as an alternative to big government.

Linked to this, evangelical Christians have started to make increasingly significant contributions to the party – Bob Edmiston, Ken Costa, Michael Farmer and Sir Peter Vardy have all given generously in recent years. Costa, chairman of the organisation that runs the popular Alpha courses mentioned in Chapter 2, has given the party £113,500 in the time David Cameron has been leader (from December 2005 onwards). Farmer, who is prominent in hedge funds, has given the party more than £1.7 million since then, having been impressed with the Prime Minister's commitment to the aforementioned tax incentives for marriage. The other two men are both car dealers, with Sir Peter having also branched into faith-based schools in the north-east of England in the late 1980s/early 1990s (see Baldwin 2009).

Despite this, there remains a sense that the Conservatives can 'have their cake and eat it' – even those who are not evangelical will still broadly agree with the work of the CCF. Indeed, it is important to remember that the organisation was only set up in 1990 by David Burrowes, MP and Tim Montgomerie (now a key Cameron adviser) when they were students together at the University of Exeter. Prior to this, the party clearly did not feel the need – rationally – to have such an organisation, and again, this can be contrasted with the Christian Socialist Movement with its relatively long history stretching back to R. H. Tawney and Donald Soper. The present author would very much argue that this is a sign of strength rather than weakness – prior to 1990, there was no need for the Conservatives to have a Christian fellowship, any more than there was a need for the CDU in Germany to have an equivalent, as it now does (*Der Spiegel* 2010).

The Christian Socialist Movement (CSM)

The Christian Socialist Movement (CSM) is the Labour Party's equivalent of the CCF, albeit with a slightly different history – existing as an independent society but affiliated to Labour, and sending two delegates to its party conference each autumn.[10] The CSM was founded by R. H. Tawney in 1960, and has developed into one of the Labour Party's largest affiliated organisations. There are presently forty CSM members in Parliament and, unlike the CCF, there is quite an overt attempt to influence policy via party forums and consultations. Issues such as debt reduction, homelessness and poverty are all to the fore on the movement's web page and assorted literature, and it is quite apparent that it is more than simply a prayer network or equivalent.

In terms of policy interests, it is not the case that the CSM necessarily disagrees with the mission statement of the CCF – indeed, there is probably quite a lot of overlap in views. However, perhaps the key policy-related distinction relates more to emphasis. Whereas Conservative Christians prioritise their political aims around family values, Christian Socialists prioritise theirs around social justice – they argue that it is Christian to believe in the redistribution of societal wealth, it is Christian to play an active part in the wider community and it is Christian to help the poorer members of that society, rather than ignore their concerns. The CSM mission statement reads:

- We believe that Christian teaching should be reflected in laws and institutions and that the Kingdom of God finds its political expression in democratic socialist policies.
- We believe that all people are created in the image of God. We all have equal worth and deserve equal opportunities to fulfil our God-given potential whilst exercising personal responsibility.
- We believe in personal freedom, exercised in community with others and embracing civil, social and economic freedom.
- We believe in social justice and that the institutional causes of poverty in, and between, rich and poor countries should be abolished.
- We believe all people are called to common stewardship of the Earth, including its natural resources.

(Christian Socialist Movement 2010)

Given the concern for a progressive social policy, it is worth contrasting Labour with sister parties across Europe. Throughout the European Union, socialist parties, and parties of the left, favour secularism, advocating a separation of religion and politics in every aspect of public life (for example, the French Socialists or the German Social Democrats) and no role of welfare for the Christian Church.[11] Certainly the Nordic social democratic welfare model can be seen to have its origins in Lutheran theology, but only historically. In the UK, however, there exists the Christian Socialist tradition, and, unlike the CCF, it is much more of a policy-orientated lobby group than a social network too.

It is clear that the CSM does have more of the appearance of a 'faction' within Labour than the CCF does within the Conservatives. The formal remit of the director of CSM, Andy Flannagan – who has his own office at Labour Party headquarters on Victoria Street[12] – is to actively recruit both Christians to the party and party members to Christianity, as well as to lobby over relevant issues.

Secular Labour Party members would not agree with many aspects of the above mission statement, and would have a deeper problem with the role of religion in politics. Such misgivings have their origins in socialist/communist philosophy regarding the public role of religion. However, it is also worth noting in passing the fact that the last three Labour leaders have all been identified with the CSM: the former Prime Minister, Gordon Brown (the son of a Scottish Presbyterian minister), has made many public pronouncements suggesting that to be Christian is to help other people via socialist values.[13] His predecessor, Tony Blair, was, by background, a Conservative but due to his born-again Christian faith, became active in Labour circles, after being converted to both simultaneously at university.[14] Prior to Blair, John Smith was an active Church of Scotland member in his local parish in Edinburgh. It would be wrong to read too much into this – indeed, the differences between the three are as significant as their similarities. Blair converted to Roman Catholicism after leaving office, Brown draws a distinction between his religious upbringing and his more contemporary beliefs – which he regards as private – while Smith appears to have started to attend church regularly only in middle life and did not include any Christian references in his speeches.

In much the same way that a Conservative can believe in the family without being a Christian, a Labour Party member can believe in social justice without being a Christian. However, the distinction that probably needs to be made is one of *ownership*. There are a significant number of atheists in the Labour Party who believe that Christians and churches actually get in the way of achieving social justice – for example, wealthy state churches such as the Church of England would be an obvious target. On the other hand, an atheist in the Conservative Party would not argue that Christians get in the way of family values. The role of Christianity in the creation of the welfare state has been increasingly documented (Van Kersbergen and Manow 2009) and the links that exists between, for example, the Lutheran Church – the Nordic social democratic model.[15] But the key point to recognise here is that it is outside the party political realm – indeed, it is almost proof that the State provides better than the Church, atheists would say, as the shift of power from sacred to secular gradually evolved.

The Liberal Democrat Christian Forum (LDCF)

The Liberal Democrat Christian Forum (LDCF) is the third group providing this section's focus. Similar to the CCF, it is formally part of the party's direct organisation – although more akin to the CSM, it clearly has a policy dimension. Here the priorities of members focus upon 'progressive values' and the idea that it would be unchristian not to support the equalities agenda – everyone has the same worth and should be free to fulfil their own potential without any conservative or regressive forces inhibiting them – or so the argument goes. Defending civil liberties, fairness and environmental issues are some of the concerns of the LDCF – the first two can be tied together to core Liberal values, while the emphasis on green issues can neatly link religious and party values.

The LDCF mission statement reads:

> We commit ourselves to the pursuit of just government, which will actively intervene to help the poor, the powerless and the rejected and strive to give all people real liberty and true social justice. To achieve this, we aim to:-
>
> a)   Encourage Christian fellowship among Liberal Democrats and promote the worship of God in Christ Jesus.
> b)   Affirm the relationship between prayer and political action.
> c)   Be a bridge between Churches and the Liberal Democrat Party.

d) Actively encourage and seek to develop Liberal Democrat Christian candidates to stand for public office, and encourage all Christians to become involved in the political process.

e) Support the work of Christian Liberal Democrats who have been elected to public office, as well as those in the House of Lords.

f) To promote understanding and mutual respect between Christians, other faith groups and those of no faith.

(Liberal Democrats Christian Forum 2010)

Furthermore, according to another section of its website, entitled 'Why Christians should vote Liberal Democrat':

In any secular party, Christians will find themselves at odds with some aspects of policy at some times. However, we believe that the extremes of right-wing politics and left-wing politics do not fit with the Christian worldview at all. Centre politics in the UK – despite particular issues where Christians are at odds with their secular colleagues – provide a much better fit than right or left-wing politics. Not of course that the Conservatives or Labour are necessarily extreme – but both move between the centre and the extremes depending on the mood of the day.

In other words, well-meaning Christians should also be Liberal Democrats. Sir Alan Beith, MP (Berwick), perhaps more than anyone, embodies those values – a non-conformist Methodist from Lancashire, he has been associated with 'common sense' northern liberalism for thirty-five years:

Liberal Democrats seek to create a liberal society in which great differences of opinion can be resolved . . . through . . . government . . . in an atmosphere of mutual respect . . . Passion is required to create and defend such a society, and passion to do good based on religious belief is needed within such a society. The tolerance which is a hallmark of liberalism does not rest upon a visionless and lifeless political creed, but on a passion to serve humanity without enslaving it.

(Christian Today 2008)

The idea that liberalism is about freedom from oppression and that that includes religious freedoms is key here. In other words, there is a nod to the American model that people should be free to practise whatever religion they want, without state interference. This can also be tied to wider issues of fairness, progressive values and moderate, social inclusiveness.

An examination of the LDCF literature suggests that they are the group who clearly feel the need to justify their existence the most as they actually go on to state why Christians should be Liberals. They are also much smaller scale than either the CCF or CSM – they employ one part-time staff member who only works two days a week, and whose other job is as a diary secretary for

Chris Huhne, the Energy Secretary. Also, as with Labour, there are Liberal Democrats who believe that churches stand in the way of freedoms and progressive tolerance rather than aid that – for example, Paul Holmes MP or the former prominent Oxford MP, Dr Evan Harris. The internal conflict that exists within Labour and the Liberal Democrats is not matched by the Conservatives. That having been said, the entire Liberal Democrat party organisation is much smaller than either of the other two parties, so everything is relative – it would wrong to assume that the LDCF is any less important to the Party as a whole than either of the other two, and it can count among its leading members Simon Hughes, the party president, and Steve Webb, the party's manifesto group chair.

As it has been argued at the start of the chapter, there is no point in trying to scientifically assess the relative strength of the LDCF in comparison with the other two groups on the basis of resources such as membership or proximity to leadership, as all three broadly reflect the parties that they represent – they all have staff at central office, they all have significant numbers of members and hold various types of events throughout the year. They all try to provide a dual purpose – to recruit Christians to their parties and party members to Christianity. The key point that the chapter is seeking to make, however, is that the Conservative Party appears to be the most natural home for many Christians in modern British politics.

Conclusions

The purpose of this chapter has not been to provide a chronological overview of the way the different parties have advocated religious-slanted policies – not only would such an approach be unnecessarily descriptive, it would also have struggled to produce many cohesive conclusions. Instead, the chapter has been thematic and unashamedly contemporaneous. By analysing the Christian groupings in the three main British parties, we are able to both assess the way that they approach religious or conscience-based issues and gauge the importance that they place upon them. Clearly, the downside to such an approach is that the analysis quickly dates, but the topic is so important that it merits continuous updating in any case.

It is clearly much easier to be a Christian in the British Conservative Party than it is in either the Labour Party or the Liberal Democrats. The secularist strain that runs through leftist or progressive politics makes the latter two parties steer clear of any 'social-engineering' as much as they can and stick to focusing their attention on the more socio-economic affairs. They do have to tackle religious issues from time to time (see Chapters 6 and 7) but that they do not seek them out. Linked to this, the longstanding voting correlation between Labour and British Catholics is as much to do with class as it is to do with the shared values of the left and Christianity. In that respect, the European secular tradition has not been altered in the British context as much as it might be argued. For all that the book will argue that there is a distinctive British model of politics and religion, it will not overstate this particular dimension.

The Conservative Party, on the other hand, is much more comfortable on this territory, even under David Cameron's modernisation agenda. Much of that, in any case, is as much about image as it is about policy – it is about using the right language, talking about the right issues and having the right faces on the front bench. However, it does not necessarily mean embracing an entirely new ideology – which was the case when Labour repealed Clause Four and became 'New Labour'. As Tim Bale puts it (2010: 362), Mr Cameron has been extremely adept at conveying a 'commitment to the pragmatic centre ground without ever moving too far away from the Party's ideological instincts'.

A Christian in the Liberal Democrats could scarcely disagree with the above argument – that it is easier to be openly religious on the right of British politics. Indeed, it would be almost unliberal to do so: the range of ideological views contained within the Liberal Democrats means that it could never seek, as a party, to promote the religious above the secular or indeed vice versa. However, an active Christian Socialist might disagree. He or she may well argue that to be truly Christian is to believe in the redistribution of wealth and to help raise people out of poverty – that such an aspiration is closest to the teachings of scripture about 'loving thy neighbour' and being a 'good Samaritan'. The problem this person has is that, broadly true though that ideal is, they are always going to be neutralised by that other tradition in the party – the Marxist secular ideology that believes passionately in the separation of Church and State, and has no truck with anything that stands in the way or distracts from their core purpose of creating a more equal society – including wealthy state churches. Watching the lord bishops relaxing in style in the tearooms of the House of Lords must irk even the most committed Christian Socialist. While it is possible to be a secularist and a Christian simultaneously – that is, believe in God but not a state church – the in-bred suspicion many on the left of politics have about 'conservative forces' such as Christianity is equally irrefutable, and the most significant from an organisational perspective.

In the Conservative Party, the religious activist does not come up against any real opposition, as by definition, to be Conservative is to respect traditions and institutions. So even if they do not go to church themselves, they still want the Church to be there, doing its job – especially the Church of England which embodies many of the core British values Conservatives seek to promote. The only sort of modern Conservative who would theoretically raise any objection to religious policies would be a libertarian, but that strain of politics has never been entirely at home in the British Conservative Party, in any case.[16] The nature of true libertarianism means that, by definition, its adherents tend not to feel at home in any party or political organisation, and many regard the modern Conservative Party as an organisation that wants to control the organs of the State just as much as Labour, but for subtly different policy objectives (Adam Smith Institute 2010).

So we are left with the Conservative Party to act as the main vessel for Christian policy proposals in the modern UK political system. Public choice principles are present here – modern parties are not necessarily supposed to accurately and respectfully represent the views of their grass-roots members, but instead look towards the next election, and work out the best way of winning office. If a sizeable proportion of the British electorate remains religious, then it goes without saying that the parties will try to tap into that, especially the Conservatives. The modern Conservative Party's clever mix of free market economics and social conservatism (albeit with the latter given a twenty-first century public relations makeover by David Cameron) is the obvious party for a conservative Christian to vote for in 2010. Cameron may make the right noises when it comes to equalities but, where he can, he also stresses the importance of the family.

In other words, he is saying we cannot stop modern society from being plural, multicultural or egalitarian but we can still make sure that our values are also in the mix. We do not want to discriminate against gay people any longer but we do want to make sure that marriage and the nuclear family are still held up as desirable social models (for example, note these types of reasons offered by both the Catholic Bishop of Motherwell, Joseph Devine, and Asian Welsh AM, Mohammad Asghar, when deciding to endorse the party in 2009). The nuances of social legislation are not partisan – issues such as stem cell research, abortion and euthanasia are all subject to free votes in the Commons, and rightly so – but the Conservatives can still create clear blue water between them and Labour by showing how they prioritise the family over the State. The California model – promoting the free market and conservative values in a liberal environment – is one that David Cameron has pursued since visiting the US in 2007.

The concluding chapter will come on to this but, briefly, it is worth finishing by considering this: an interesting dimension exists where many Christians in public life attempt to be friendly towards one another ('I don't care which party people join as long as they join one of them'). This is fascinating for two reasons: there is evidence that it is what the voters want (Putnam 2000; Stoker 2006); second, the idea that the Kingdom of God is more important than party politics has implications for parties. The above can be linked to the last chapter's focus on turn-out and the over-arching themes of this book, that is, is Christianity good for democracy? Cross-party groups such as 'Christians in Politics' are not necessarily new, but their remit is – they have no qualms in stating that their key objective is to get more Christians into politics, and from a rational perspective, this is ostensibly a zero sum game. However, we see the benefits in the way parties regard Christians as 'good citizens' who are natural participants in civic life. In other words, if you went on a 'Make Poverty

History' march, you should consider becoming a Member of Parliament. As Andy Flannagan, the director of CSM, puts it:

> The Make Poverty History generation are starting to realise that it's not good enough just to be shouting from the sidelines. They are seeing that some of them also need to get on the pitch. That's why many of them are starting to join political parties. Members of the organising committee estimated that around 80% of the people who marched on 2 July 2005 were Christians, and up and down the country many of the younger generation bringing the energy to community and global initiatives are Christians. Newly elected MP, 28 year old Gavin Shuker from Luton, is a great example of this.
>
> (Interview with author, 9 December 2009)

Linked to this, the key point to take away from this chapter is the way that all parties – rationally – see the Christian vote as one worth pursuing. They may go about it in different ways, and it may be argued that the Conservatives are the party that does it most naturally, but the fact remains they are all in the same 'office-seeking' business. British party membership is in free fall and suffering hugely from a loss of trust and reputation. The expenses scandal of 2009 was not about voters' outrage at the fact that the niceties of the Westminster parliamentary system were being abused by some MPs – it was about a wholescale public anger at the way the political elite had developed a lack of respect for the people they were supposed to be there to represent. The role of Christianity in relation to this is highly relevant – there is real evidence that voters want to be able to trust their politicians again, and any issues or aspects that involve morality, ethics or religion can help with that process, and make a contribution to it. Churches continue to be trusted public institutions, and again, this has nothing to do with attendance on a Sunday, or belief in God – for so long as that continues, parties will seek to work with them.

For now, however, we turn to perhaps the best evidence of the continued importance of Christianity in British electoral and party politics: the state churches.

Part 2

The Christian lobby

4   Still the 'Conservative Party at prayer'?

The role of Church of England bishops in Parliament

The Church of England has been labelled both 'Marxist', by the former Conservative Party chairman Norman Tebbit,[1] and – more frequently – the 'Conservative Party at prayer', by innumerable political scientists and commentators. While not, strictly speaking, the main remit of this chapter, discussing which view is correct undoubtedly constitutes a theme of this part of this book. Perhaps of more importance, however, is the analysis of how and why the Church involves itself in electoral politics – and the consequences that that poses for the parties. Chapters 2 and 3 have looked at the religious influence within the electorate and within the parties, but it is now time to turn to look at those religious influences in depth from an associational/organisational perspective, and how that poses a 'public choice' challenge for the parties.

Historically, certainly, the institutional links between the Church and the Conservative Party were indeed very close. When voting patterns were primarily an expression of religious denomination – with Anglicans voting Tory and non-conformists voting Liberal in the nineteenth century – the bishops used their seats in the Lords to help conserve British institutions such as the Union with Ireland, the monarchy and their control over the state school system. However, more recently, Lord Tebbit's criticism (he was not intending it as a compliment) was made in the context of an increasing radicalism on the part of bishops, seeing them speak out on a range of contentious and highly political issues such as social justice, poverty and other problems associated with the more excessive side of Western capitalism.

Regardless of whether Lord Tebbit was right or not, the answer to the question of whether the national Church of England is a left-wing or right-wing institution is given substantially more weight by the fact its most senior representatives have a seat and a vote in the British Parliament. As a consequence of the flexible and organic nature of the British Constitution, Church of England bishops continue to sit in the upper house of Parliament at Westminster – the House of Lords. There are currently twenty-six Anglican bishops, known as the Lords Spiritual, who play an active role legislating in the House of Lords – these are the most senior clergy in the Church (out of forty-four), and, alongside this, there also exists the political tradition of granting seats for life to senior retired clergy who have made a particularly significant contribution to British public life – for example, former Archbishops of Canterbury such as Lord Carey and Lord Runcie.

The overtly political elements of the Church of England's established status are as follows: the Queen is head, or supreme governor of the Church – the 'defender of the Protestant faith'. Senior bishops are appointed by the Prime Minister of the day, although Gordon Brown tried to distance himself from this role, and put it in the hands of a committee. Parish councils are influential civic bodies in the lives of local communities, forming the lowest tier of government in England and Wales. Other Christian consequences of having a state church are the requirements that the British Broadcasting Corporation (BBC) airs religious programmes – there is the famous 'God slot' on an early Sunday evening when a traditional religious hymn-singing pro-gramme is broadcast, while radio stations have a 'thought for the day' segment, with a religious – if not exclusively Christian – content. Citizens sitting on juries have to swear a religious oath (or alternative should they wish) before they participate in both criminal and civil trials. Indeed, the Church of England is even represented in the House of Commons, through the Church Estates Commissioner, who is responsible for Church–State relations in Parliament. The Commissioner from 1997 until 2010 was Sir Stuart Bell, the senior Labour MP for Middlesbrough. He makes statements to the Commons on behalf of the Church, and acts as a liaison for any policy proposals related to Church property or employment issues going through Parliament, heading the Ecclesi-astical Affairs Committee in the Commons.

From a comparative perspective, it is important to note that the 'national' Church attempts to embody English values and represent society in a way that goes beyond a simple system of financial subsidies and/or specific legal privileges, along the lines of the systems that exist, or have existed, across Scandinavia, Germany and the Netherlands. There is something inherently political about placing Church representatives in Parliament, and actively encouraging them to speak out on issues related to public policy and society – it cuts deeper than allowing them certain ceremonial or royal privileges. Nevertheless, England, and Britain's reformed tradition of Protestantism, is broadly in keeping with the religious values that spread across Northern Europe from the sixteenth century onwards. Nation states such as the UK, Sweden, Norway and Denmark became more 'distant' from continental Europe – more Euro-sceptic – as a result of their Protestantism, and there are other politically relevant features of this, too – for example, the Anglo-American economic system of economics undoubtedly has a Protestant origin.

The creation of the independent Church of England came about after King Henry VIII objected to interference from the Vatican over his marital arrangements – while some may argue that there are very little liturgical or theological differences between Anglicanism and Roman Catholicism, the political and nationalist dimensions were very much the former's *raison d'être*, and continue to be so. While there is no need to get into those here, not least because of the author's total lack of theological credentials, we should nonetheless acknowledge the Christian religion's contribution to the political culture of both England and Britain.

There are two important dimensions to this chapter: first, the fact that these bishops still operate at all within a highly political context is testimony to the fact that voting behaviour and public opinion still very much signal – rationally – that they should be there. Party politicians steer clear of 'rocking the boat', knowing that there is no great electoral mandate out there for upsetting the Constitution even further. It is one thing to reform the House of Lords (a *vote neutral* policy) or grant devolution to Scotland (a *vote-winning* policy) but quite another to abolish the monarchy or disestablish the Church of England. Public choice theory dictates that politicians are perennial office-seekers who try to maximise votes at all times, and not take any unnecessary electoral risks.

The second aspect is that it is vitally important, if we are to get a 360-degree picture of the role of Christianity in British party politics, to examine both sides of the dynamic – that is to say, the churches *and* the parties; the interest groups *and* the policy organisations. We already know how the parties accommodate Christians in both their membership ranks and in their policies – but how do they relate to Christians from outside, Christians acting effectively as interest group campaigners? This chapter will try to answer that question – how do the parties respond to this sort of political influence?

Churches as interest groups

Before we can answer that central question, however, we need to consider a more preliminary one. Is it actually legitimate to look at the political activities of a state church as if it were merely a 'cause' or 'sectional' pressure group? The present author argues emphatically that it is, but understands why some criticise this approach on the grounds that churches are unique institutions. Nevertheless, according to Wyn Grant, when the established Church attempts to apply pressure on government over a certain issue, it is a 'secondary' pressure group. Its 'main purpose is that of a religious organisation: to provide facilities, buildings and clergy for worship and the administration of the sacrament in accordance with its doctrinal beliefs, and to propagate its interpretation of the Christian gospel' (2000: 16). When it does speak out, however, it is both a 'promotional' group, in the sense that it makes pronouncements on social and political issues, and a 'sectional' group, when, for example, it criticises the Government for not exempting its ministers from the Community Charge. The prime purpose of the Church of England is, then, 'a religious one, but it has a secondary function as a pressure group seeking to influence public policy' (Grant 2000: 16).

Have there been any scholarly attempts by political scientists to look at the Church in this way before now? In his 1985 study of the Church of England and public policymaking, *Church and Politics Today*, George Moyser makes no attempt to assess the overall influence of the Church in his case studies, choosing instead primarily to describe the nature of its political behaviour at the time. The chapters are more concerned with describing how the Church of England goes about trying to influence policy in these areas, rather than attempting to evaluate its effectiveness. In other words, they are not critical analyses of how effective the Church of England is when it tries to exert political influence – more a chronicling of its political activities. However, Chapter 4 of the first part of the book – 'Lambeth Palace, the bishops and politics' – co-written by Moyser, does critically assess the way senior figures in the Church, notably the Archbishop of Canterbury, act when they involve themselves in politics and whether or not they are effective in this role. In more recent years, Timothy Blewett, Adrian Hyde-Price and Wyn Rees have provided an international relations analysis of the behaviour of the Church in their edited volume, *British Foreign Policy and the Anglican Church* (2008).

On the other hand, Carolyn Warner's analysis of the political behaviour of the Catholic Church in Europe is one of the few contained studies that analyses a mainstream church as if it were a 'conventional' pressure group. *Confessions of an Interest Group: The Catholic Church and Political Parties in Europe* (2000) starts from the same two premises as this book – that this specific aspect of religion and politics interacting is important, and that it is possible to apply interest group characteristics to churches. In the same way that this chapter analyses the political behaviour of the Church of England, Warner's research is 'a study of the Catholic Church's strategic behaviour' (2000: xi). She argues that 'the Catholic Church is an interest group whose actions can be modelled as if it were a firm in a market seeking a supplier of goods' (2000: 4). Warner uses interest group theory but has not chosen the Catholic Church in Europe simply to *test* an interest group theory. Her motivation is the same as the present author's – in her words, to rectify the fact that the 'Church's actions in the context of democratic political systems are poorly understood' (2000: 4).

Warner adopts a different approach from this book in some ways – her study spans different countries and its main focus is how the Catholic Church impacts on the electoral behaviour of the Christian Democrats. Nevertheless, her approach justifies the idea of evaluating the role of a church as it tries to achieve influence in the political system. Once again, it is important to note that this is not the same as attempting to accurately measure political influence – it is assessing whether or not the Church can be said to be effective in this assumed role. Individual chapters on the Catholic Church's 'mobilisation techniques' and its close 'alliance' with Christian Democrats attempt to do this. In Warner's words,

> the Church has lobbied democratic governments, via political parties and other means, to retain its monopoly over education and to have the costs of it paid for by governments; it has lobbied them to impose its morals on society through legislation; it has lobbied governments to gain or retain

preferential tax status; and it has lobbied to keep some of its employees from being conscripted . . . . To put it bluntly, the Catholic Church is, in addition to being a religion, an interest group.

(Warner 2000: 6–7)

Meny and Knapp's analysis of 'church and society' also looks at the way churches try to convert their values into political action but it is a very brief section of their text on West European politics and concentrates mainly on the Catholics in France, Italy and Germany (1998: 29–32). Bakvis's *Catholic Power in the Netherlands* (1981) takes a similar approach to Warner (2000), although he restricts his focus to the Dutch political system. While Bakvis places significantly less emphasis on interest group literature, like Warner, he also focuses on the relationship between the Catholic Church and the Christian Democrats. Truman's *Catholic Action and Politics* (1959) looks at the political behaviour of the Catholic Church in Australia. While not a European text, it is worth mentioning in order to emphasise the lack of up-to-date literature on the political activities of churches in Western political systems outside America. Truman's text is now some forty years old but was written for those 'who are bemused by the partisan and sectarian controversy concerning the relation of the Catholic Church to politics and would like the subject illuminated by an objective enquiry based on evidence' (1959: vii).

Models of interest group behaviour

In Chapter 2, we looked at models of voting behaviour, concluding that a rational choice framework was the most appropriate for this research; in Chapter 3, we examined models of party behaviour, concluding that the 'catch-all' party was the most relevant; in this chapter, we will look at models of interest group behaviour, concluding that the related 'public choice' model, developed by Mancur Olson, works best for the purposes of our analysis here.

Grant states that 'the study of pressure groups is the study of organised interests'. A pressure group is an 'organisation which seeks as one of its functions to influence the formulation and implementation of public policy . . .' (2000: 9). Essentially, pressure groups aim to bring about some form of social change, without becoming part of government themselves. The great American pluralist scholar, David B. Truman (1951: 37) disliked the term 'pressure group', preferring 'interest group' – a 'shared attitude group that makes certain claims upon other groups in the society. If and when it makes certain claims through or upon any of the institutions of government, it becomes a political interest group'. Some organisations also dislike the term 'pressure group' because it somehow implies an improper exertion of influence. When it is suggested that churches do not have much political influence, there is a tendency for leading figures to say that they have no desire to be viewed as pressure groups anyway, as if it somehow implies something negative. Many groups would prefer the title 'non-governmental organisa-tion', but as Grant points out (2000: 8), 'other than they are independent of government, it is difficult to give a precise definition of what a non-governmental organisation is'. Terms such as 'faith-based organisation' (FBO) and 'faith-based initiatives' have also been introduced to the UK. In 2002 for example, the Labour Government appointed a 'faith tsar', John Battle, MP, to act as an 'extra channel of communication between faith groups and the Prime Minister' (July 2002), although this role has now disappeared.

The American literature generally uses the term 'interest group', only referring to organisations that exist solely to influence political decisions as 'pressure groups'. However, British writers use 'pressure group' more generically and this book will generally follow this approach, although not exclusively. In any case, as more and more groups have been drawn into politics in order to protect their interests, the American distinction has become less meaningful. Nevertheless, Stewart's categorisation (1958: 25) of 'sectional' groups and 'cause' (or 'promotional') groups remains important. While sectional groups represent a section of the community, cause groups represent some belief or principle (Stewart 1958: 25). As Jordan and Richardson explain (1987: 21), sectional groups tend to advance more limited, specific objectives, and hope to avoid public controversy, while cause groups require a wider public participation in order to achieve their aims. Another approach is Grant's insider/outsider distinction (1978), which focuses more on the receptivity of government to the aforementioned strategies. Insider groups are regarded as legitimate by government and consulted regularly, while outsider groups do not receive, or do not wish to receive, the same recognition. There also exist numerous definitions of 'power' and 'influence', with Grant (2000: 193), for example, arguing that 'power may be said to refer to the exercise of authority', while influence 'rests on the power to persuade'. Grant's distinction is undoubtedly helpful in clarifying the sort of political activity interest groups are involved in and so in this sense, it is 'influence', more than 'power', with which this book is concerned.

By analysing the Church of England from a pressure group perspective, this book accepts the premise that pressure groups have a significant role to play in the British political system, if not necessarily a consistently influential one – the plurality of views in modern party politics means that there exists an equality of opportunity for many groups, if not necessarily an equality of power. Smith describes pluralism as an 'enigma' (1995: 209) of a theory – and the limits to its use have been well documented – although it must be added that this does not mean it is entirely without coherence. Broadly, much of the pluralist case rests on the premise that access to the political system is relatively straightforward and that forming a pressure group that will have some sort of influence is not especially difficult. While flaws can be found in these assumptions (more so in Britain than in the United States, where government is more fragmented), the theory still has aspects to recommend it, particularly in its neo-pluralism form, which has gone some way to update the original principles as well as making them more applicable to the UK. Pluralists such as Polsby and Dahl typify the dominance of American literature in the field but their central theories can still be applied to the British political system. Polsby (1980) rejects Hunter's stratification argument (1953) that in any one community, a single group must necessarily dominate due to its economic superiority. From his classic New Haven study (1961), Dahl also determined that the distribution of influence was not determined solely by economic wealth. Pluralism tends to focus on the exercise of power, rather than its sources. Polsby argues that policy outcomes must be studied empirically in order to determine the real patterns of influence (1980: 113). This view follows on from Dahl's fundamental assumption that power only truly exists when it is exercised (1961: 272).

Neo-pluralists such as Lindblom (1977) and more recently Lowery and Gray (2000) argue that there is much to be recommended in the pluralist approach, albeit in a form that takes into account elitist, Marxist and New Right criticisms. While Lowery and Gray (2000: 13) concede that this new perspective is a 'pale reflection' of Truman's original form of pluralism (1951), they also contend there exist sufficient similarities to merit comparison. According to Lowery and Gray, there are six distinct characteristics of neo-pluralist perspectives on policymaking: emphasising the importance of analysing a wide range of *institutions* (2000: 15); acknowledging the different types of *competition* that exist between groups (2000: 15); analysing the *context* of the particular policy process (2000: 17); acknowledging the existence of *uncertainties* in policymaking (2000: 18); being aware of *linkages* between the different stages of the policymaking process (2000: 19); and emphasising the *two-way* nature of the flow of policy (2000: 20). As with classical pluralism, all these features can be contrasted with the economic/elitist view that government will always be captured by organised or corporatist interests regardless of the specific circumstances. There may well exist state bias towards business interests and economic policy in the neo-pluralist model, but it also continues to stress the importance of groups and competitive policy areas.

The most compelling criticism of the pluralist approach in the context of this study of Christianity and British politics comes from Mancur Olson (*The Logic of Collective Action*, 1965). Applying a public choice approach, Olson meticulously picked apart the established pluralist orthodoxy that had been embraced by scholars by pointing out that the aggregate balance of different pressure groups fairly neutralising one another was not entirely watertight – in fact, individuals only join groups or associations if there is some sort of private benefit to them, and are essentially neutral when it comes to the wider public good (see McLean 2001).

This rational theory is ultimately the one that fits most neatly into this study – churches only act as interest groups when they see something at stake that they care about and want to influence directly. They are not full-time political campaigners – indeed, they are often at pains to protest the absence of a partisan agenda from their more policy-orientated activities. Nevertheless, they do not baulk at involving themselves in politics if their Christian interests (broadly defined) are challenged. In particular, the disconnect between church members 'free-riding' and therefore being at odds with what their church leaders want, lies at the heart of this interpretation. Churches get involved in party politics because it is rational to do so, but they are often reluctant players and do not always take their members with them.

A related theory will be expanded upon in Chapter 7, when we focus partly on the Catholic Church and its ability to keep some items off the political agenda. Here, Bachrach and Baratz (1962, 1970) also criticise the pluralist approach for simplistically ignoring what they label the 'second face of power' (1970: 3). Their 'non-decision-making' model (1970: 9) sees controversial items being deliberately kept off the political agenda by political elites. Lukes (1974: 23) goes even further than Bachrach and Baratz, arguing that the power can also be exercised by 'influencing, shaping or determining' the entire political climate, so that individuals are not even aware they are being influenced. Christianity can be said to have this effect on British electoral and party politics – there is an unwritten rule that says politicians do not meddle with the churches. In particular, this is a position acknowledged by the most vocal opponents of the churches – the secular lobby – which is the most convinced advocate of the institutional power of the churches in Britain (despite the decline in active church attendance – see focus group interviews with the author later in this chapter).

Of course, measuring political influence precisely is problematic, but gaining an overall picture of the effectiveness of a particular pressure group is not. As Baumgartner and Leech put it, scholars 'may be right to avoid questions that cannot be answered, but then again it would be preferable to rephrase the questions so that they could be answered' (1998: 14). The Church of England consistently attempts to exert political influence and so it is a valid question for a political scientist to ask 'does it succeed?'. The conclusions of this chapter do not reveal the precise level of political influence of the Church of England – its objective is more to illustrate a) the way it operates politically via its 'special status' and, linked to this, b) the way its leadership can often pose serious challenges to rational, vote-seeking party politicians who wish to avoid irrational or controversial moral issues.

Even this type of approach, however, is difficult and, as Grant points out, often depends on perspective and context (2000: 194). For example, the Confederation of British Industry (CBI) had much more interaction with the Labour government of 1974–9 than it did with preceding and succeeding Conservative administrations, but only because the organisation viewed Wilson and Callaghan's policies as more threatening and so tried to do more to influence them. Coxall agrees with Grant (2001: 160–1), arguing that the 'nature of government, as well as the multiplicity of goals pursued by many groups, hinders attempts at objective assessment'. He also states that the success or failure of groups can be partially explained by the 'prevailing political culture' (2001: 160). For example, if a government is committed to increasing economic growth, the goals of environmental groups, for example, will be moved down the list of priorities.

Writers in the field have tried to address the difficulties involved, although as Paul Whiteley and Steven Winyard argue, 'the question of interest group effectiveness is probably one of the least adequately researched aspects of the study of pressure groups' (1987: 111). As Grant correctly states, it is often easier to assess the ineffectiveness of a pressure group, or a change in its levels of effectiveness, than its effectiveness per se (2000: 211). In other words, while we cannot definitively sum up how influential the Church of England is, we can draw conclusions about whether it is as influential as it should be, based on its resources and assets. Whiteley and Winyard also argue that it is important to speak to the pressure groups themselves to ask them whether they think they are effective, even if that is only a second-best solution to directly observing the decision-making process (1987: 114). This has been done in the book, although the potential is always there for individuals to exaggerate their own importance within the Westminster village.

Anglican bishops at Westminster

The 'Bishops' Bench' is an interesting constitutional inheritance in Britain and one packed with political resonance – both metaphorical and real. For a book focusing on party politics and Christianity to have two chapters on Christian churches might, at first, appear a little indulgent. Should the emphasis not be on the parties themselves, rather than on the organisations that apply pressure on them, one might ask? But of crucial importance here is the fact that these churches have a direct and central role to play in British parliamentary democracy. In the mother of all parliaments, church clergy sit and vote alongside parties, and often on highly politicised issues. That is hugely significant, and unique among all advanced democracies in Western Europe and North America. Sitting in the chamber in their robes of state, they also provide a very vivid symbol of the power of Christianity in the British political system.

Church figures are keen to point out that the twenty-six bishops[2] in the Lords are not 'whipped' on votes in the same way as the party political peers are – nevertheless, there is a convener of the bench, presently the Bishop of Leicester, the Rt Revd Tim Stevens, who acts as the Lords Spirituals' representative in cross-party meetings and other political arenas:

> It entails chairing meetings of the Lords Spiritual to review forthcoming legislation and debates and to co-ordinate the presence of the Lords Spiritual. Also, keeping in regular touch with the Party Leaders and the Chair of the Crossbenches in The Lords. Further, there is a role in terms of servicing discussions with Government and the Opposition in relation to Lords' Reform. The role of Convenor is not equivalent to a Party Leader or a Party Whip and there is no comparable discipline for the Lords Spiritual.
>
> (Correspondence with author, 5 March 2010)

However, this is a new development, and he is not the formal 'leader' of the group. The fact that the bishops are also required – by convention – to wear their clerical garments in the chamber, serves a practical purpose that transcends the more symbolic one mentioned in the last paragraph – in order to show that they are not full Lords with seats in their own right, but are there as institutional representatives of the established Church.

Bishops sitting in the Lords has its origins in the rather complicated British system of government, with its many colourful and ostensibly anachronistic features the direct result of its unwritten constitution. So different parts of it evolve flexibly, while others remain constant. It is not within the remit of this book to discuss the merits or otherwise of that, other than to say that, once again, rational choice theory can be brought into play, with public opinion able to exert much more leverage over the political establishment than in countries such as the US where it takes a lot of pressure to amend the Constitution. Prior to 1539, most lords were bishops before the dissolution of the monasteries and the civil war gradually restricted their role and number. Linked to this, a point that will be returned to can be highlighted here – one of the more persuasive arguments that bishops have seats in Parliament is that they were there at the origins of Parliament, helping to set it up in an era of a divine right monarchy. They are not newcomers or there only because a government of the past decided it would be a good policy idea.

While always careful not to be directly party political, today's bishops nevertheless actively seek to involve themselves in issues that are not necessarily simply 'conscience based' – for example, abortion, human genetics or same sex marriage (see Chapters 6 and 7). Indeed, the Church has often shown itself to be highly progressive over social issues such as poverty and homelessness, for example, and willing to use its 'independent' leverage for positive effects, almost as if its leadership knows – rationally – that the privileged position it continues to enjoy in twenty-first century Britain comes at a price, and that its territorial domination should be used to good purpose. Equally, the Church is very circumspect when it comes to more controversial issues – for example, it tends not to enter debates over ethnicity, immigration or foreign policy lightly (see Blewitt *et al.* 2007). The Church did have a position opposing the Iraq war but it was communicated very diplomatically and unobtrusively.

Obviously, there are lots of examples of churches in other countries speaking out on these types of issues also – however, the difference with the British model is the way in which the Church of England can have a direct effect on public policy, having twenty-six permanent seats and votes in the House of Lords – albeit, out of 742, this only equates to 4 per cent (Edge 2006: 100).

The fact that Church bishops choose to use their seats at Westminster to highlight matters such as some of those listed in Table 4.1, as well as promoting that attention be paid to developing countries with deep social problems, illustrates that they do not view their role as one motivated solely

Table 4.1 Political interests of the Lords Spiritual

Bishop	Countries of interest	Political interests
Bath and Wells	Brazil; Central America; Iraq; Palestine/Israel; Zambia; Zimbabwe	International affairs
Bradford	Not listed	Not listed
Canterbury	Not listed	Children and family issues; Middle East
Carlisle	Not listed	Not listed
Chelmsford	Not listed	Development; housing; constitutional affairs
Chester	Not listed	Not listed
Chichester	Turkey; Europe	Not listed
Durham	Not listed	Coal; farming; education; constitutional reform
Ely	Not listed	Agriculture; rural affairs; energy; education; historic buildings
Exeter	Solomon Islands and Vanuatu; Middle East; Kenya	Rural affairs; education; aid and development
Leicester	Not listed	Not listed
Lincoln	Not listed	Not listed
Liverpool	India; Nigeria; Honduras; USA	Urban regeneration; voluntary sector and community renewal; family and social cohesion; Christian faith and contemporary culture; environment and sustainable development
London	Europe	London; environment; Europe
Manchester	Pakistan; Namibia; Tanzania; Zambia	Broadcasting and communications; Interfaith
Newcastle	Botswana; India; Norway	International relations; environment
Norwich	Not listed	Rural issues; broadcasting; education and training
Peterborough	Kenya	Education; rural affairs
Portsmouth	Denmark; Scandinavia	Education; health; Europe
Ripon and Leeds	Sri Lanka	Social, educational and ethical issues; asylum; combating racism
Rochester	Pakistan; Iran; Israel/Palestine; Nigeria; Egypt; Gulf	Sufism; South Asian Middle Eastern history and politics; languages
Salisbury	Not listed	Heritage; international trade; rural affairs
Southwark	Not listed	Science; technology; education; development
Southwell and Nottingham	Kenya; South Africa	Heritage; environment; charity law
Winchester	Uganda; Rwanda; Burundi; Congo; Burma	Education; local government; poverty; welfare; marriage; gender issues
York	Not listed	Legal; community; young people; faith

by cold self-interest. Nevertheless, there is no question at all that running through all these contributions lies a consistent Christian message, and an attempt to bring the values of the Christian faith to the policy proposal being debated and make them politically relevant.

An analysis of the speeches made in the Lords by the two most senior bishops – the Archbishops of Canterbury and York – shows a similar pattern. Out of twelve speeches made by the Archbishop of Canterbury since taking his seat in the Lords, six were about purely political issues: the Good Childhood Inquiry; the global economic downturn; young people in prison; immigration detention centres; conflict in Africa; and criminal justice. The Archbishop of York's speech followed a similar pattern (three out of six): House of Lords reform; human trafficking; and Zimbabwe. In addition, more recently, in December 2008, a group of senior bishops openly criticised the then British Prime Minister, Gordon Brown, in relation to condoning materialism in modern society (Kirkup 2008).

This is all of interest not because of what the bishops have to say about such matters but simply that they speak out in the first place – all of the afore-mentioned policy areas have very little to do with pure theology, morality or matters of conscience, yet there is clear evidence of Church leaders viewing their national responsibility to comment on such matters regardless and, crucially, able to do so. Indeed, as Haynes puts it, '[as] the political landscape in Britain converges, mainline Church leaders are saying things elected politicians, anxious not to irritate the middle-class electorates, dare not utter' (1998: 71). It is important to note the difference in levels of trust that churches continue to have as institutions, in comparison with parties. As Voas and Ling state, '[t]here is a widespread view that religion is functional for both individuals and society' (2010: 72). Their analysis of the BSAS 2008 data shows that half of respondents – the largest group – regard the influence of British life to be 'positive' (2010: 73). Meanwhile, public trust in government has collapsed: in 1987, 37 per cent of respondents said that they trusted government at least some of the time – by 2007, this figure had dropped to 29 per cent, and had been as low as 19 per cent in 2006 (Butt and Curtice 2010: 7). Both may be suffering from declining membership figures but only the latter is suffering from anti-party sentiment (see Dalton and Weldon 2005). Data show that even many British atheists continue to show public support for the good that religion/Christianity does. Chapter 8, in particular, will draw together this finding as evidence for the positive relationship between democracy and Christianity in Britain. It would be highly irrational for an unpopular party politician to try to take away power from a well-respected Christian Church leader.

Brown (1994) gives a good account of the role of the Lords Spiritual in the period 1979–87, and makes the important point about the range of participation that exists across the bishops – some contribute a great deal to the life of Parliament, others less so. Indeed, technically, they are individuals in their own right, and can vote however they choose. The Convener of the Bishops' Bench states:

That is a matter for individual judgement. The Lords Spirituals' responsibility is to relate issues of current political interest to the Judeo-Christian tradition. Sometimes this will appear as radical, sometimes progressive, sometimes conservative. But the political compass of the Lords Spiritual is not partisan but Gospel based.

(Correspondence with author, 5 March 2010)

While it would be wrong to make overly normative statements one way or the other about the content of these contributions, what is clear is that the bishops are prepared to get involved in hard policy debates, and speak out on non-religious matters – and frequently in a progressive and radical way too. Table 4.2 details the number of contributions made by each bishop in 2008.

A more in-depth time series data analysis would help to establish patterns of behaviour – how often do they contribute, and so on, which is not too vital to this book – we are not really interested in how much influence the churches have per se, but more how the parties and the politicians react to them. The tables are designed to show the sort of activities the Lords Spiritual address, and the next section will analyse the political consequences of them. In any case, the difference in contributions – while significant – are not necessarily relevant; some bishops clearly regard their seat in the Lords as more important than others, but there are likely to be other factors at play here. For example, some of the lower end participants come from dioceses geographically remote from London (Durham, Newcastle and Carlisle). The temptation to rank the bishops in order of contributions in the table was therefore resisted. As the Convenor of the Bishops' Bench states,

There are no Church rules relating to frequency of bishops' attendance, but increasing expectation that bishops will try to attend as frequently as possible. Bishops are expected to attend for two weeks per annum to read the prayers and to act as the 'Duty Bishop' being ready to speak on relevant matters as required.

(Correspondence with author, 5 March 2010)

We also have to be careful here about being too charitable to the Lords Spiritual – the fact that the bishops only appear to speak out on apparently innocuous subjects does not mean that what they say is innocuous. A more detailed discourse analysis of speeches using the political rhetoric literature might be useful in the future (see Kettell 2009b). Nevertheless, it is actually quite difficult to find examples of bishops speaking out in an overtly conservative way, even on more conscience-based issues. In relation to issues such as abortion and euthanasia, while the Church collectively – in very measured tones – might release a statement that is critical – there is no scope for individual bishops to stand up in the House and be openly negative. Some (Biggar and Hogan 2009) go as far as to argue that democracy is good for the churches, and vice versa – because the Church is an insider, there is no need

Table 4.2 Contributions to debates in the House of Lords
by bishops, 2008–9

Bishop	Total number of speeches and questions*
Bath and Wells	6
Bradford**	n/a
Canterbury	5
Carlisle	5
Chelmsford	21
Chester	31
Chichester	3
Durham	5
Ely	1
Exeter	11
Leicester	9
Lincoln	6
Liverpool	43
London	6
Manchester	6
Newcastle	6
Norwich	9
Peterborough	1
Portsmouth	15
Ripon and Leeds	19
Rochester	6
Salisbury	1
Southwark	12
Southwell and Nottingham	29
Winchester	23
York	21
Average	**12**

Information taken from They Work For You/Public Whip
(www.theyworkforyou.com)

* Tracking voting behaviour is less informative as bishops
  conventionally abstain owing to diocese commitments but
  this does not detract from their active and non-partisan
  contribution via questions and speeches.
** Only appointed in January 2009.

for it to be either controversial or outspoken, as it is part of the establishment. Second, the ability of an outspoken cleric to become a bishop is much more difficult as they have to show that they are the 'right sort of person' for public life in parliament.

So far, we have discussed the role of the bishops in Parliament – what they do and how they do it. But what about the key first question – the argument that they continue to be there in the second decade of the twenty-first century because of public choice pressures? Is the role of bishops in parliament now under threat? After all, the New Labour government, elected in 1997, was the most reforming of modern times, introducing devolution to Scotland, Wales, Northern Ireland and London, a Supreme Court, a Freedom of Information Act, and proportional representation for some parts of local government. The government that replaced it in May 2010 has also revealed plans to introduce a proportional voting system to the upper house as part of what Deputy Prime Minister, Nick Clegg, has labelled the 'biggest shake-up of our democracy in 178 years' (BBC News, 19 May 2010).

Crucially, despite this, neither Government produced plans for abolishing the place of the Lords Spiritual. Indeed, in a document leaked just before the 2010 General Election, the Justice Secretary, Jack Straw, outlined his justification for this, in his plans for an elected upper chamber:

> The Lords Spiritual . . . have always held a special and different position in the House of Lords . . . The nature of establishment has changed over the years to reflect changing circumstances, but a presence in the Lords has been a constant manifestation . . . The Government proposes that a fully reformed second chamber, in recognition of the enduring importance of the established Church in national life . . . should continue to allow a role for the established Church. So the continued role of the Church would be guaranteed.
>
> (*The Guardian*, 20 April 2010)

The paper goes on to explain that the number of bishops in the Lords may be reduced, but only subject to talking with the Church, and that other faith group representatives may also become members – an increase in the role of Christians and other religious figures in British party politics, not a decline. Meanwhile, the Liberal Conservative coalition government has set up a commission to examine the way the new Lords will look, but it is far from clear whether the Church of England's presence there will end, as the Government has still not committed to a 100 per cent elected upper house, and it is interesting to note the lack or urgency in relation to the Lords in comparison with some of the other political reforms mentioned. In particular, the Conservatives are publicly committed to retaining the establishment of the Church.

According to Baroness Whitaker, a Labour peer and leading member of the All Party Parliamentary Humanist Group (APPHG), 'it is a rash government who takes on the Church of England' (Interview with author, 3 March 2010). Meanwhile, Lord Macdonald, the APPHG chair, argues that 'after its battle to remove most hereditary Peers, the Labour Government had no appetite for a fight over further reform of the House of Lords' (Interview with author, 9 December 2009).

Two respected British political scientists, Iain McLean (Oxford) and Philip Norton (Hull), the latter also a Conservative peer, have turned their attention to the role of bishops in the Lords. Norton (2010), in a fairly neutral way, via his blog has written: 'I am struck by the extent to which the Lords Spiritual continue to fascinate people'. McLean, in a much more critical way in his text, *What's Wrong with the British Constitution?* (2009), argues that there is no intellectually defensible case for maintaining an established church. As a scholar of rational choice, the present author fully respects his views but, in this case, respectfully disagrees: if there is no great public groundswell in favour of disestablishing the Church, then there is no need – rationally – to allocate parliamentary time to doing so. British voters do not decide elections on whether or not there is a state church, and that means that the parties leave the issue alone.

The General Synod and party politics

The last section discussed the way the established status of the Church of England is directly linked to public opinion – this section will analyse the second dimension, that is, the way the Church acts as an interest group, pressurising politicians. The Church of England – as the state Church – does not just restrict itself to parliamentary politics inside the Westminster village. It also involves itself directly in party politics outside of the Palace of Westminster, as opposed to relying on its distinguished bishops making meas-ured speeches in the Lords. Its General Synod – the national decision-making body of the Church – will often, through its committees, make statements about public issues – many of which are essentially party political. The interesting distinction that needs to be borne in mind here is between a bishop speaking on behalf of himself in a considered speech in the Lords and the Church as an institutional whole launching a campaign over a national issue, such as the environment, pay conditions or development aid, that is not necessarily the result of a piece of legislation or bill going through Westminster. While the Church is always keen to make clear that it is not making a party political point, it nevertheless enters party political *issues* on a regular basis, posing huge challenges for party politicians in the process.

Fairness and consensus are values that also lie at the root of the Church's position on social justice – a highly political and highly partisan issue or concept – but one that churches love to get involved in with an almost evangelical enthusiasm, and the Church of England is no exception. While it has nothing to do with religion, it is very much linked to 'loving thy neighbour'. The next chapter on the Church of Scotland also focuses on these issues – poverty, social care, homelessness. The Church's website has a section on 'Social and Public Issues', and these types of issues are crucial: capitalism, homelessness, poverty and taxation policy are all frequently addressed. In February 2007, the Government was defeated in its attempts to pass its new 'super-casino' plans through Parliament – it lost by three votes in the House Lords and – intriguingly – three bishops voted.

In the run-up to the 2010 General Election, the Archbishops of Canterbury and York urged people to vote 'hopefully and compassionately': 'The deepest challenge is how the wealth we possess collectively is to become a real "common wealth", wealth that serves a whole population, not just the powerful and privileged'. They also argued that it was crucial to eradicate economic inequality, as it caused 'grave social and psychological problems' in British society (BBC News, 30 April 2010). Indeed, social justice has also been a constant theme of the primacy of Dr Rowan Williams, the Archbishop of Canterbury. A self-confessed 'hairy lefty', Dr Williams talks about redistribution of wealth, and does not shy away from making forceful political points. In his 2003 Christmas sermon, he warned that a more secure world would only be possible if the developed countries shared their wealth with the poorer ones. He even accused some countries of concentrating on terrorism rather than focusing on the importance of halving world poverty by 2015 (BBC News, 21 April 2004).

But has it always been thus? Certainly, what we see is a traditional concern for social justice that can be traced back to Victorian times, and also predates the term even being invented, but also a dramatic shift to the left during the 1980s, and Margaret Thatcher's Conservative government. Perhaps, ironically, Mrs Thatcher was herself the product of a strict religious upbringing in provincial Lincolnshire, and believed her capitalist ideology to be entirely in keeping with her reformist Methodist values. This did not stop many leading Christians having grave concerns about her government's prioritising of the City of London making money ahead of displaying any concern for the welfare of those less fortunate.

Interestingly, however – as was hinted at on page 73 – there is evidence of a real institutional, Olsonian disconnect between the average Church member and the Church leadership. The average Church member is not as radical as the average Church leader. So Archbishop Runcie may well have disliked Mrs Thatcher's politics, but that does not mean that the average Anglican sitting in pews up and down the country felt the same – hence the rather fractured image of the Church mentioned at the start of the chapter, and also the logic of Olson's 'free rider' theory. Churches are notorious for having people who attach themselves nominally to them but rarely attend or contribute financially – yet the organisation itself is committed and motivated politically.

The big challenge for parties is how to respond to all of this (Kettell 2009a). For example, given their secularist strains, are Labour and the Liberal Democrats more critical of clergy when they try to get involved in politics? Probably not, as that strain is not especially mainstream and certainly not all that prominent. Indeed, the fact that this is the case is itself a sign of rational choice/public opinion. Linked to this, there is no evidence that the Conservative Party responds critically to the Church, given that it is capitalism that is on the receiving end a lot of the time – while this may appear to be somewhat ironic, given the traditional voting links that were charted in

Chapter 2, it is actually quite easily explicable: first, while the message is often quite extreme, the presentation is consistently measured, moderate and crucially non-partisan – when the Church complains about the excesses of Western capitalism, it is not perceived to be motivated by any sustained anti-Conservative sentiment. After all, it is not advocating a socialist/leftist economic model either. Second, it is a good example of the complex and multidimensional aspect of party politics – there may well be a difference of opinion over socio-economic policies, but not necessarily over more ethical or equalities-related issues.

In any case, an institutional relationship that is close does not necessarily always have to be friendly – and a broader point can be made here. The capacity for the Church to make often quite controversial statements on socio-economic issues is unquestionably facilitated by its role at the heart of the British establishment – senior bishops know senior party politicians by name, mixing with them in Parliament, so there is no need for them to act as an outsider interest group, 'rent-seeking' from the party of the day holding power. Rather, they act in a way that does not need to be overtly self-interested as it has nothing immediate to lose – its place at the top table of influence is basically assured, and it can speak out on whichever political issues it likes, but primarily in a friendly and collegiate fashion. That delicate balance of honesty mixed with politeness and respect is a very successful recipe for political influence at Westminster.

There is real evidence that British politicians respond differently to Church leaders when they engage in political issues. With other parties, they are ruthless and rude; with other interest groups, frequently dismissive and high-handed. But when the General Synod of the Church of England speaks out on poverty or global warming, the political establishment listens respectfully. The premise seems to be that the Church – while rational and probably self-interested – also speaks from an unparalleled position of authority and knowledge. Somehow, the same rules do not apply to it – that being a vicar or bishop is a calling to public service that deserves respect. The way that dimension has been lost from British electoral politics – and indeed from many comparable Western industrial democracies – is something that has been written about at much length. For reasons linked to *trust*, the Church of England has managed to hold on to its influence over British society, retain its seats and votes in Parliament, and gain respect for mounting campaigns on the basis of helping the many, not the few. For that reason, it is a very powerful British interest group.

Conclusions

First, we have discussed the very strong evidence for the sort of arguments put forward in Chapters 2 and 3, that is religion still matters to British politics owing to voting behaviour and the way British political parties continue to recognise an electoral market for Christian values. In short, public opinion would not stand for the disestablishment of the Church of England – clearly, there are many British voters who would not care about the issue, as well as many who would support the move, but that does not detract from the fact the Church would portray it as an attempt to marginalise further the Christian tradition, and also link it to issues of religious freedoms and rights. While bishops voting in the Lords is not necessarily the same thing as the establishment of the Church, that is to split constitutional hairs. Ultimately, it sends out the wrong political signals. Rightly or wrongly, it looks like a powerful State saying to a weakened Church 'there is no place for you in modern Britain', and the way the New Labour Government (1997–2010) consciously held back from tackling the issue is the best example of this. The issue is a bit like the one related to the republican versus monarchy debate – while the average British subject (citizen) does not care too much whether there is a royal family or not, try to get rid of them, and suddenly, people react. In 2007, a BBC poll found that 78 per cent of respondents favoured retaining the monarchy, with only 19 per cent arguing that it should be abolished (BBC News, 28 December 2007). Similarly, the presence of bishops in the House of Lords is a very powerful symbol of the continuing importance of Christianity in modern British party politics.

The second dimension that is of interest to us is the way this piece of the British constitutional jigsaw fits in with the rest of the puzzle. The Church acts politically – subtly, diplomatically but nevertheless politically and even partisan, up to a point. This causes challenges for the parties – how do they respond to a bishop criticising their socio-economic policies? They cannot simply use the same tactics as when they are responding to opposition politicians – they have to be more respectful, they have to be more conciliatory, and they have to show that they are prepared to listen to voices from outside of the political and media bubble. The evidence would suggest that parties and politicians tend simply not to get involved too much. Indeed, even politicians from the left show the Church respect – there is no public narrative along the lines that churches should 'stay out of politics' (Kettell 2009b).

The political role of Church of England bishops in the British parliament is important, unique, influential and worthy of further attention from political scientists. Indeed, the longer they continue to sit and vote in the House of Lords, the stronger their position becomes in the medium term as there is unlikely to be such a busy period of constitutional reform again in the UK as the first two decades of the twenty-first century. The way the Liberal Conservative coalition government chooses to include the bishops in their future plans will be extremely insightful, when it comes to judging how the new British political establishment considers the importance of the Christian Church.

5 A Presbyterian conscience

The Church of Scotland, the Labour Party and the politics of social justice

In the midst of the expenses scandal that engulfed British party politics in the spring of 2009, the then Prime Minister, Gordon Brown, made the following comment in a BBC interview: 'To be honest, what I've seen offends my Presbyterian conscience. What I've seen is something that is appalling' (BBC News, 31 May 2009).

The religious upbringing of Mr Brown has already been mentioned in Chapter 3, and there is probably no need to return to it. However, the term 'Presbyterian conscience' is worthy of further attention: while there are plenty of examples of Conservative Scottish Presbyterians – Adam Smith, John Buchan and Lord Reith, to name but a few – Mr Brown does, nevertheless, rather personify modern Scotland's love affair with the Labour Party, and values such as social justice and fairness. Chapters 2 and 3 argued that there was a correlation between atheism and not voting Conservative – of course, while true, this does not take into account areas of the UK where there are very few Conservatives (elected as MPs to Westminster, at least – see voting behaviour in Chapter 2). In Scotland, it is the Labour Party that has been the overwhelming choice for voters from the 1959 General Election – with the Conservative vote going into apparently terminal decline from 1983 onwards – and there is no sign of that changing any time soon.

Indeed, while it is only in the last twenty years that Labour has truly cemented an unassailable position as the top of Scottish politics (an SNP minority administration in Edinburgh serving from 2007 aside), the non-conformist roots of the Labour movement had always found a natural home North of the Border. The first Labour Prime Minister, Ramsay MacDonald, came from Lossiemouth in the north-east of Scotland, and the size of the country (only five million people concentrated mainly in the Central Belt cities of Glasgow and Edinburgh) meant that communitarian values and an emphasis on redistributing wealth, rather than wealth creation, were embraced comprehensively (see Keating 2007).

In particular, the Conservative Government of the 1980s had a divisive effect on the unity of the United Kingdom in this respect – ironic, given Mrs Thatcher's predilection for British national pride. During this period, the voters of Scotland, Wales and the north of England entrenched their support for Labour, while ever more cooling their enthusiasm for the Conservatives – and this continues today. Indeed, the Conservatives actually won more votes than Labour in England in the 2005 General Election, but lost due to a lack of support from the Scottish and Welsh electorate. Linked to this, Mr Brown's comments also rather neatly encapsulate the approach that Britain's other state Church – the Presbyterian Church of Scotland – has taken towards politics and public affairs for many decades, especially post-war, acting as the 'national conscience' by speaking out on issues via an unusual combination of radicalism and conservatism.

This chapter will adopt a broadly similar approach to the last one, focusing first, on the way the Scottish establishment continues to regard the Church as an important part of it, primarily for rational reasons, and second, on the way the Church acts as an interest group. There is much more to British party politics than the 'beltway' of the Westminster village – the rise of Scottish nationalism in the 1990s and creation of a modern Scottish Parliament has been of huge importance to the way the previously overly centralised British system functions, and while we can note very similar themes that fit with the broader framework of this book, we should also note some interesting departures. The absence of a strong Conservative presence in Scotland makes some of the previous statements less relevant – however, that does not contradict them, nor does the public choice framework of this book become irrelevant either.

Indeed, in some ways, scholarly literature on the role of the national Church in Scottish politics has actually been more extensive than that on the Church of England – due perhaps to the radical policy positions the Church has consistently adopted over a much longer period than the Church of England. Of perhaps most significance is the 1990 book co-edited by Walker and Gallagher, *Sermons and Battle Hymns: Protestant Popular Culture in Modern Scotland*, including a chapter written by the editors on the place of 'Protestantism' in Scottish politics (1990: 86–111). Boyle and Lynch's *Out of the Ghetto: The Catholic Community in Modern Scotland* (1998) can be compared with the Walker/Gallagher study – it is also an edited volume but this time the chapters focus on the place of the Catholic Church in Scottish society and politics. Forrester's 1993 article – 'The Church of Scotland and public policy' – is the only other comparable piece of academic political research on one of the mainstream churches in Scotland – the approach adopted here was more methodical than the one adopted by Walker and Gallagher, using case studies of the Church and Nation Committee to evaluate its role in six different areas of policymaking.

Some writers have touched on the topic in the course of wider studies. Bennie *et al.*'s *How Scotland Votes* (1997) devotes a whole chapter to the topic of religion and politics, arguing that religion continues to matter to Scottish voting behaviour, which it clearly does. While the focus of this book is on electoral behaviour, the chapter is wide-ranging in its scope, and covers the history of the relationship between religion and politics in Scotland. Kellas's *The Scottish Political System* (1989) approaches the topic from a more traditional institutional perspective, the Church of Scotland being one of his 'holy trinity' of pillars of the Scottish system. In fact, both the political behaviour of the Church of Scotland and the Scottish Catholic Church are included in the chapter on 'organisations and interest groups', which gives examples of issues on which the two institutions have lobbied, for example licensing laws, divorce laws, abortion laws.

Kellas (1989: 179) argues that Scotland has historically been more morally conservative than England, as a direct result of the alliance of Presbyterian and Catholic lobbying impinging on the legislative process. Midwinter *et al.* agree (1991: 10), stating that 'Presbyterian and Catholic influences have converged to make Scotland less of a "permissive society" than England'. Divorce and abortion rates are traditionally lower on average in Scotland than in England, although more recent reports suggest that this is no longer the case (NHS 2009; ONS 2010). In terms of licensing laws, however, there can now be said to be no real difference between Scotland and the rest of the UK. While there used to be a distinction in opening hours, the liberal tide of the 1960s and 1970s was too much for the Church of Scotland to cope with, with the 1976 Licensing (Scotland) Act opening pubs on Sundays, and granting new hours of business to off-licences (Carnie 1986: 57). However, there is some evidence that the residues of difference continue to exist between Scotland and England over 'observing the Sabbath'. When it emerged in July 2002 that the high street retailers, Argos, were forcing their staff in Scotland to work on a Sunday, the Church of Scotland wrote to the then Scottish Secretary, Helen Liddell, asking her to intervene in the matter. Robin Cook, the then Leader of the House of Commons, stated that he 'deeply regretted' Argos's decision, and in November 2002, the superstore agreed to review their decision (BBC News, 6 November 2002).

Scotland's historic status as a nation is well documented, as are the various 'political' institutions that have survived intact since the Act of Union with England in 1707 – the legal system, the education system, the royal burghs, and the Presbyterian Church (the focus of this chapter). Taylor writes that there are 'obvious institutional examples of the perseverance of Scottish identity: the Church of Scotland, deliberately protected in the Act of Union and now providing temporary shelter to Scotland's new Parliamentarians in the General Assembly building on the Mound in Edinburgh . . .' (1999: 16). Before significant political power was devolved to a new national Parliament in 1999, these political institutions provided the evidence that home-rule campaigners pointed to, in order to show that Scotland was more than just a northern region of England and required its political system to be complete once again. So what of one of the pillars of the Scottish political system – the Presbyterian Church? Exactly what kind of political institution is it?

The Church of Scotland is a very different kind of state Church from others in Western Europe: it is free from all state interference, and has full autonomy over the running of its affairs, including legal exemption from certain Acts of

Parliament concerning employment rights. The 1921 Church of Scotland Act stipulates that the Church alone can fully adjudicate in all matters of doctrine, worship, government and discipline in the Church, and is therefore 'subject to no civil authority' (Linklater and Denniston 1992: 80). Its links with the State are therefore essentially symbolic, rather than political – the contact is with the Crown, in the person of the monarch, not her Ministers of State. Unlike the Church of England, the Church of Scotland is free from such practical political interference. Dyson describes it thus: 'the Church of Scotland's constitution has been ratified and confirmed, rather than conferred, by the State, and establishment . . . is compatible with complete spiritual autonomy' (1985: 299).

There are four fundamental features of the Church of Scotland's national status: first, it is the 'public' religion of Scotland, according to parliamentary statute – the British monarch is Anglican when he or she is in England, and Presbyterian when he or she is in Scotland. Every year at the General Assembly of the Church, HM The Queen is represented by her Lord High Commissioner, a distinguished politician or person in public life, who has links with the Church. However, to symbolise the Church's political independence, he or she is only permitted to watch proceedings from the gallery, and has to enter and leave by a side entrance. Nevertheless, for General Assembly week, he or she holds the status of a King or Queen of Scotland. Occasionally, the Sovereign will appear in person, for example The Queen in her 1977 Jubilee year, and for her Golden Jubilee in 2002. In 2000, the Prince of Wales was the representative of the Crown. All royal chaplains in Scotland (the Ecclesiastical Household) are ordained Church of Scotland ministers – no other denomination is included. The Dean of the Order of the Thistle is always the minister of St Giles' Cathedral in Edinburgh. All local authorities have a civic service held annually in a local parish church to dedicate the work of its councillors. In 2002, the serving Moderator of General Assembly said prayers at both HM The Queen's Golden Jubilee thanksgiving service in St Paul's Cathedral, and the funeral service for HM Queen Elizabeth, the Queen Mother in Westminster Abbey.

Second, the Church operates a territorial parish system – local ministers have responsibility for everyone in their congregation's geographical area, regardless of what denomination they belong to. Its parish system does not just depend on where members of the Church happen to live. While the Catholic Church operates a similar system, the boundaries of a Church of Scotland parish have their origins in local government organisation. Until the late nineteenth century, the Church of Scotland had a substantial amount of influence administratively – local authority boundaries actually grew out of parochial borders, but the 1929 Reorganisation Act modernised local government. Third, Church of Scotland ministers are not allowed to be Members of Parliament, without giving up their ordained status. In other words, they must cease being ordained clerics permanently, and give up the right to call themselves 'Reverend'. Fourth, the Moderator of the General Assembly ranks above the Prime Minister and the Dukes, and equal to the Lord Chancellor, in matters of constitutional precedence, for the duration of General Assembly week in May.

Crucial to any understanding of the political nature of the Church of Scotland is a knowledge of its internal organisation. As the government of the Church is Presbyterian and not Episcopal (hierarchical), there are no permanent leaders or bishops to impose their personality on the way the Church is managed. However, every year, one minister is nominated to chair the proceedings of the General Assembly, the annual decision-making forum of the Church. The Moderator, as he or she is known (there have already been two female Moderators), also provides the Church with ceremonial leadership throughout his or her year in office, representing it at public events at home and internationally. However, while the internal government of the Church dictates that all ministers are equal, there does exist a hierarchy of Church courts or governing organisations. The lowest court is the Kirk Session, the ruling body of every parish church, which ranks below Presbytery, the ruling body of a group of churches in an area. The General Assembly is the highest court of the Church, and meets once a year in May for a week – it is the Church's law-making body, passing motions, or 'deliverances' as they are known, for the year to come. Every presbytery sends commissioners to the Assembly, who must be either ministers or elders ('ordained' lay men and women, who sit on the Kirk Session).

As the Church has no leader to assume control of any public campaign, how does it 'speak out' politically, if not through a national head? The answer is through its national committees and boards, and in particular, the various conveners of these arms of the Church. The Church of Scotland has within it a wide range of theological views. In terms of doctrine, it places less emphasis on the ceremonial or symbolic (e.g. Communion) than the Roman Catholic or Anglican Churches, and substantially more on reading scripture and preaching. While Presbyterianism has its origins in Switzerland, where the Reformed leader, John Calvin, lived, it was the type of church order which John Knox carried to Scotland that is now practised around the world. The Church of Scotland is the original Presbyterian Church, and St Giles' Cathedral in Edinburgh the mother Church of Presbyterianism worldwide. St Giles' categorisation as a cathedral is a misnomer, a legacy of its time as an Episcopal place of worship – in Scotland, medieval cathedrals nominally retain their Episcopal title even though they are no the longer seats of bishops.

Only three churches have ever had any formal links with the Scottish political system – the Catholic Church (pre-Reformation, if one excludes denominational schools), the Episcopal Church (post-Reformation–1689), and the Presbyterian Church (1689–present). Indeed, there is some debate over whether the present Church of Scotland can be described as 'established' due to the nature of its structure, and the way it is linked to the British State – its correct designation is simply the 'national Church' of Scotland. However, the religious historian, Callum Brown, goes further, talking of the 'myth of the established Church of Scotland', and arguing that it was effectively disestablished by four Acts of Parliament between 1921 and 1933 (Brown 2001: 50). As Bochel and Denver put it (1970: 210), the Church of Scotland 'cannot be regarded as "established" in entirely the same way as the Church of England'.

Thus, the public profile of the Church of Scotland is one of ambiguity – part of the establishment, but free from political interference simultaneously. However, like the Church of England, its privileged political status owes much to the fact that Scottish politicians have no rational interest in taking away its special position. Scottish politicians from across the party spectrum hold the Church in respect, and acknowledge the unique role it has to play in the public life of the nation. For Scottish Nationalists, the very existence of the Church helps to justify their claim that Scotland is a historically distinctive entity, and, along with its universities and laws, capable of being even more independent from London (and closer to Brussels). For Scottish Conservatives, the Church embodies tradition and core national values. For Scottish Liberal Democrats, the Church is part of a wider non-conformist sphere that is especially popular in the Highlands and Islands. And for the Scottish Labour, similarly, it is about a radicalism and a social conscience that has helped Scottish society in different ways for a long time.

When he addressed the Church's General Assembly in May 2009, the First Minister of Scotland, Alex Salmond stated:

> This is the place – and you are the people – that do so much to give expression to the heart of Scotland . . . The Church of Scotland has filled this role so many times in our nation's history. It continues to do so today and let no one doubt your ability – as a reformed church to continue to promote reform . . . This Church, this Assembly, are part of the foundations of Scottish society . . . Today this church and our other institutions – spiritual and secular are the walls of Scotland – the rocks on which reform and renewal will be built . . . And as we seek to rebuild our economy, to renew our political institutions, to build the new Scotland, we will continue to draw on this Church as a source of wisdom.
>
> (Salmond 2009)

While spoken by a nationalist, these words could actually have been articulated by a politician from any of the parties in Scotland – they embody the deep respect that exists for the Church, but crucially, not for spiritual or theological reasons but for political reasons – the reformed Church that is still trying to reform society, and does so in an inclusive and progressive way that politicians respect. That means that its place at the heart of the political establishment is secure, but also as we are about to see – that its political influence is equally significant.

A new covenant: the Church and Scottish devolution

As one might expect, the Church of Scotland does not endorse any political party – however, nor does it shy away from getting involved in party politics, and its influential Church and Society Council (previously called the Church and Nation Committee) has been especially prominent in this area. Its longstanding remit, which dates back to its establishment in 1919, is to 'watch over developments of the nation's life in which moral and spiritual considerations specially arise' and to 'consider what action the Church from time to time may be advised to take to further the highest interests of the people' (Church of Scotland 2001a: 12). 'Church and Nation Day' at the General Assembly continues to be attended by the 'great and the good' of Scottish political and civic society, who sit up in the Lord High Commissioner's gallery, and follow the proceedings of the most high profile standing committee of the national Church. For example, when the former Moderator, the Very Revd Dr Andrew McLellan, was appointed HM Chief Inspector of Prisons in July 2002, BBC News online reported that he had often been critical of the privatisation of prisons when he had been 'convener of the Kirk's influential Church and Nation Committee' (BBC News, 22 July 2002).

Interestingly, the Conservative-run Scottish Office of the 1980s and 1990s was frequently irritated by what it perceived to be the 'left-wing' pronouncements of the Church. Linked to this, if one issue epitomises the involvement of the Church of Scotland in politics, it is its strong support of the creation and growth of the modern Scottish Parliament in Edinburgh. The Church had officially supported the cause of Scottish devolution for some fifty years before it finally came to fruition in 1999, grounding its support for the cause in reformed theology, and argued that the reconvening of the Parliament would bring power back closer to the Scottish people – thereby supporting the premise that it would provide 'Scottish solutions to Scottish problems' (see Bromley *et al.* 2003). According to Brown (1992: 74), there was a 'growing trend [from the 1950s onwards] for clergy of the Church of Scotland to see themselves as upholders of Scottish identity', which may explain why its Church and Nation Committee was so in favour of devolution at a time when many Scots were still undecided. In a similar vein, Marr (1992: 33) offers the explanation that the 'Kirk's [Church of Scotland] struggle to define its own role, which has a real input on the rest of the Scottish political establishment, [was] also about rediscovering its own history'. The Church and Nation Committee made regular contributions to the ongoing constitutional debate, particularly around periods when calls for reform were at their loudest – the late 1970s, the late 1980s and the mid 1990s.

In 1989, the Church and Nation Committee began to make a concerted effort to root its devolutionist stance in some sort of theology, and the official Church of Scotland approach generally became more unified. That year, the Committee presented a major report to the General Assembly, entitled *The Government of Scotland*, which talked of the need to create a 'stable rational ground for our Scottish democracy'. It called for a referendum on the issue so that there could develop the 'democratic control of Scottish affairs through a Scottish Assembly established with the support of the Scottish people' (Church of Scotland 1989: 151). The report promoted the view that over-centralised power went against the democratic Calvinist tradition.

After 1989, the Church's influence in this area grew tangibly. The inaugural meeting of the Scottish Constitutional Convention in March 1989, which launched the document *A Claim of Right for Scotland*, took place in the General Assembly Hall, was opened with a prayer, and included a contribution from the Revd Maxwell Craig, the then convener of Church and Nation. The 1989 Assembly instructed the Church and Nation Committee to continue its 'reflection in co-operation with the other bodies which are discussing the consti-tutional future of Scotland, including the proposals set out in *A Claim of Right for Scotland*' (Church of Scotland 1989: 138). The Convention returned to the Assembly Hall on St Andrew's Day in 1995 to launch 'Scotland's Parliament, Scotland's Right', where again, the serving convener of Church and Nation made a contribution. The convener at the time was the Revd Andrew McLellan, who formally welcomed the members of the Convention to the Assembly Hall. When the Convention agreed to appoint a Constitutional Commission to look into various future recommendations, a former Church Moderator, the Very Revd Prof. James Whyte, of St Andrew's University, was appointed one of its members.

Regardless of how much political influence the Church and Nation Committee exerted on the devolution process, the campaign for home rule drew heavily upon Scotland's Christian heritage, although there is some ambiguity over how intentional this was. Paterson (2002: 118) argues that the 'religious origins are unmistakable, and indeed Church of Scotland theologians in particular were eloquent in their contribution to the debate, modernising the Knoxian idea that the people have the right to overthrow unjust rulers'. Meanwhile, Brown and McCrone (with Paterson) highlight the Constitutional Convention's intention to 'evoke the radicalism of the religious reformers who issued the two previous claims: the Free Church . . . in 1843, and the Presbyterians . . . in 1688' (1998: 66). Furthermore, the repeated use of the Church of Scotland Assembly Hall for a set-piece Constitutional Convention resulted in it also being used as the temporary home of the Parliament, until the Holyrood site was completed – something the BBC's Scottish Political Editor, Brian Taylor, labels 'neat symmetry' (1999: 46). In both 2000 and 2002, Members of the Scottish Parliament were happy to vacate the Hall for General Assembly week, with no public criticism being made that the Parliament was 'more important' than the Assembly. During the official opening ceremony of the Parliament by the Queen in June 1999, the 129 new parliamentarians sang the Old Hundredth Psalm, 'All People That On Earth Do Dwell', the archetypal Scottish Presbyterian hymn.

The Church of Scotland was centrally involved in the most important contemporary Scottish political issue of the 1990s – and one not without partisan controversy. The Scottish Conservatives were opposed to the project, while the Scottish National Party (SNP) only agreed to come on board at the last minute. While it was not a government-led exercise until after 1997, the Labour and the Liberal Democrat parties, the main driving force of the Constitutional Convention, realised that a wide range of organisations had to be involved in the process, if it was going to be viewed as democratically legitimate. However, the fact the national Church was so committed to the concept of home rule was significant, and emblematic of the sort of 'quality of democracy' issues in which its leaders have consistently involved themselves.

'Scottish solutions for Scottish problems': homelessness and social care

The Church did not simply support devolution because of nebulous concepts such as 'quality of democracy'. The key to much of the above lies in the concept of 'Scottish solutions for Scottish problems'. The Church of Scotland retains what Callum Brown describes as the 'legacy of collectivism and democracy in its internal organisation' (1992: 72). It was the mid 1980s that witnessed the beginnings of what is now an annual activity for the Church – producing reports on issues of social justice, and what it perceives to be the unfair distribution of wealth in Scottish, and British, society. The tone of its pronouncements changed dramatically when the Revd Maxwell Craig took over as convener in 1984. Mr Craig, then the minister of Wellington Church in the West End of Glasgow, was an Old Harrovian with radical left-wing views. He shaped the ethos and image of the Church in a way that can still be seen today, and this remains an area of social policymaking where it invests considerable time and effort in trying to influence.

One of the central concerns the Church has had in the area of social policy is the issue of social care in Scotland – and it provides an excellent case study of the relationship between the parties and the Church in devolved Scotland. This section will focus both on the way the Church has actively campaigned against homelessness, using the Housing (Scotland) Act 2001 as its main instrument, and on the battle the Church has had to keep its extensive range of care homes for the elderly open in an increasingly tough economic climate. Both provide us with excellent examples of the way the values and priorities of the new devolved political system in Scotland are much more in keeping with those of the Church, once again confirming public choice assumptions.

The Church of Scotland's stance on poverty and injustice in society has always been politically controversial, because its pronouncements have often been interpreted as left wing, even though it would not recognise that description of itself. The most vivid example of this came in 1988, when the Church of Scotland demonstrated it was still a major national institution with which politicians had to deal. The Prime Minister, Margaret Thatcher, came to the General Assembly to deliver her now famous 'Sermon on the Mound', following a long line of premiers such as Wilson, Heath and Callaghan. It is worth considering whether she would have bothered to do so if the Church of Scotland was a political irrelevance, and her choice of 'sermon' was interesting. Unlike her predecessors, who talked about vague political matters, Mrs Thatcher decided to tell the Church how she interpreted her faith as a Christian. Quoting St Paul, she stated 'if a man shall not work, he shall not eat', and concluded that it was not the 'creation of wealth that is wrong, but the love of money for its own sake'.

The response of the assembled theologians' was mixed. Marr (1992: 168) called it the 'great symbolic non-meeting of minds', because as Callum Brown explains, the Church of Scotland really did 'attack the policies of the Thatcher administration after 1979 as alien and inappropriate for Scotland', and Mrs Thatcher was not entirely unaware of this (1992: 9). The Moderator that year, the aforementioned Professor James Whyte, decided simply to present the Prime Minister with her own copy of *Just Sharing: A Christian Approach to the Distribution of Wealth, Income and Benefits.* This book was produced after the 1984 General Assembly had called for a major study of the distribution of wealth in Scotland. Its basic tenet was that the distribution of wealth in society was just as important as the creation of it in the first place, and called for higher taxation to reduce the levels of poverty in Britain. This book received considerable coverage by the media, got a number of mentions at Westminster, and resulted in two Scottish conferences to discuss the recommendations being held in Glasgow and Edinburgh. This may have been on Mrs Thatcher's mind.

Clearly, parallels with the last chapter's section on the Church of England can be drawn here – we have already mentioned that the Anglican Church has periodically spoken out on the excesses of the free market. However, there is something quantifiably different about the approaches of the two churches here – with the Church of England, such pronouncements are fundamentally about some members of the leadership of an establishment institution politely reminding its political colleagues in London that they have a duty towards the less fortunate; with the Church of Scotland, it was – and is – much more about a democratically grounded representative assembly articulating the majority view of a nation that the values of social justice should take precedence over the values of individualism or greed.

In 1993, the central bodies of twelve Christian denominations in Scotland came together to set up the Scottish Churches Housing Agency, subsequently (Scottish Churches Housing Action). Homelessness in Scotland is an archetypal Church and Nation concern, and the fact the Agency Chairman for many years was the Rev Maxwell Craig, the former Church and Nation convener, is significant. The personal influence of Mr Craig over the work of the Agency is considerable, and he took his job of chairman as seriously as he took his term in charge of Church and Nation – but this time, he had the resources that allowed him to do more than simply speak out against policies.

From the start of 2000 until June 2001, the Scottish Churches Housing Agency was actively involved in the Scottish Executive consultation process over its new Housing Bill, still the largest and most complex piece of legislation yet to go through the new Scottish Parliament. The Agency made clear its belief throughout the process that 'more thorough changes [were] needed if homelessness is to be a thing of the past'. During the passage of the new Act through the Parliament, the Agency campaigned to:

1. Abolish the priority homelessness rule, which means that 'non-priority' homeless people get little or no help.
2. Abolish the 'intentionality' rule, which means that some homeless people suffer from mistakes they made in the distant past.
3. Give councils the job of assessing people's need for support, as well as for accommodation when they are homeless.

(Scottish Churches Housing Agency 2010)

The Agency gave evidence at a session of the Social Justice Committee of the Scottish Parliament on 22 November 2000. Members of the Committee spent forty-five minutes asking representatives from the Church of Scotland and the Salvation Army to justify their written response, submitted during the Bill's consultation process. The delegation emphasised their main priority was to have the notion of 'intentional homelessness' removed from the Bill. The Scottish Churches' Parliamentary Officer, the Revd Dr Graham Blount, a former secretary of Church and Nation, helped the Agency prepare for the session.[1]

Throughout the consultation process, the Agency's position was that the Bill should not be a 'missed opportunity', and that too much of the legislation was concerned with peripheral housing issues, and not enough with the immediacy of the problem facing people who were already homeless. In January 2001, the Agency shared a public forum with Johann Lamont, MSP, Labour convener of the Social Justice Committee in the Parliament, where it again reiterated the idea of legislation that tackled homelessness on its own, and not as a side issue. Maxwell Craig also had a meeting with the Homelessness Task Force, set up by the Executive and chaired by the Social Justice Minister, on 25 June 2001, where they concentrated on the issue of intentionality. Craig realised the importance of having a clear message, but not too many unrealistic demands, when he was lobbying MSPs. He also appreciated he had to approach the issues from a perspective where they had expertise, in order to make their position distinctive from other interest groups such as Shelter and the Scottish Federation of Housing Associations. He gave a presentation at the meeting, but was disappointed that no discussion followed. In April 2002, the Agency Executive met with David Belfall, the senior Scottish Executive civil servant, two months after the Task Force had published their report.

The central question for us is this: is there any evidence that the new, devolved Scottish Parliament, which the Church had done so much to bring about, listens to the influence of the Church more closely than the old London-run Scottish Office? Was the Scottish Churches Housing Agency successful in its objectives? While ultimately, the Scottish Executive did not do what the

Agency wanted, it was happy to listen to the opinion of the Churches, and take on board their views and criticisms. According to a civil servant in the Homelessness Team at the Development Department of the Scottish Executive, the Agency's emphasis on homelessness, as opposed to other housing matters, was significant as 'certain amendments tabled by backbenchers reflected the arguments of the Agency' (Interview with author, 1 August 2003). While the civil servant was not suggesting that these MSP amendments were definitely influenced by the churches, he felt it was worth noting that this was certainly a possibility.

Furthermore, the former Labour Social Justice Minister, Jackie Baillie, MSP, hinted at a meeting of the Task Force that the concepts of intentionality and priority will be phased out in due course, while the longer-term aims of the Task Force Report were welcomed by the Agency. Also, when the Executive published its second Housing Bill, this time based on the work of the Task Force, in September 2002, the Churches Housing Agency enthusiastically endorsed it. As Grant (2000: 18) points out, when trying to assess the political influence of a pressure group, it is important to consider the status a group has in the political system, as well as its own objectives.

On the other hand, prior to devolution, the success of Church of Scotland campaigns on homelessness was rather mixed. In 1985, the Committee was instructed by the General Assembly to establish an 'independent and detailed investigation of Scotland's housing', and a commission was set up, chaired by Mary Millican (Forrester 1993: 78). Its 1988 report was well received in professional quarters, and the Scottish Office, as it then was, saw fit to prepare a detailed response, which both contested some of the wider recommendations of the report, and acknowledged much common ground. As in 2001, the Committee was critical of the Housing (Scotland) Act of 1988, for not doing enough for the homeless, but despite the discernible contact between St Andrew's House and the Church of Scotland, the evidence suggests that the latter's input to the Act was ultimately negligible. The reaction of the Committee to the passing of the Act suggests that it did not feel it had been successful in its influence itself (Church of Scotland 1988: 86). In 1990, a report was produced entitled *The Church and Scotland's Poor*, following on from where *Just Sharing* left off, but it was not as widely read or examined by politicians as the 1980s equivalent.

In this sense, the Scottish Executive (now the Scottish Government) clearly regards the Church as an important organisation in their devolved 'issue network', to use Heclo's (1978) and Rhodes's (1988) terminology – much more so than the old Scottish Office. There is an intimate policy 'community' regarding housing and homelessness in Scotland – the network has a wide range of opinions contained within it, and executive consultation is not automatic but the Scottish Executive has shown in the decade of devolution that it values the views of the Churches in this area of policy, and is happy to listen to their practical experiences when consulting over legislation. In June 2002, for example, a church representative was appointed to sit on an advisory group for research into rent and deposit guarantee schemes commissioned by the Scottish Executive. According to a member of the Homelessness Team at the Scottish Executive, the Scottish Churches Housing Action (SCHA) is in 'fairly regular contact with the Team. We receive their newsletter and have had specific contacts during the Homelessness Bill over issues they wished to pursue' (Interview with author, 1 August 2003).

This approach is perhaps a consequence of the very inclusive way the Scottish Executive now consults on relevant policies. According to a policy adviser in the Civil Law Division of the Justice Department at the Scottish Executive, civil servants will tend to first contact the two umbrella organisations – ACTS (Action of Churches Together in Scotland) and SIFC (Scottish Inter-Faith Council[2]) – rather than individual denominations, if they feel their input is appropriate (Interview with author, 2 May 2003). The type of consultations mentioned above do indicate some level of 'influence' in terms of policy formulation at earlier stages than pre-devolution, even if the more public campaigns produced little in the way of positive 'results'. Any substantive policy changes as a result of meetings between the Scottish Executive/ Government and the Church are an unrealistic aim, but the potential for less fundamental, but still significant, alterations always exists. The Church has the advantage of being considered by politicians and civil servants to be an important 'player in the game' in Scotland in this area, and generally receives political respect. It is a major Scottish care provider, employing over 1,600 people nationwide in its homes for the elderly and the terminally ill, and centres for drug addicts, alcoholics and the homeless. It has a multimillion pound budget, as well as its own headquarters in the north-east of Edinburgh.

The question of how society looks after its older members has become another important political issue in recent years, with greater numbers of elderly people living longer, and less state funding available for their care. In Scotland, there has been an ongoing public debate in this area of policymaking, since the Sutherland Report recommended in March 1999 that there should be free state provision of care for the elderly in long-stay nursing homes. This was the main proposal of the Royal Commission, which was set up by the Scottish Executive, and chaired by Lord Sutherland of Houndwood, the then Principal of Edinburgh University. Controversially, however, the Executive took until June 2001 to accept the Report's recommendations, and the subsequent legislation did not come into effect until July 2002. As the new Act applies only to Scotland, there now exists a significant difference between the component parts of the United Kingdom in the way old people are cared for. The new proposals led to private care home organisations, of which the Church of Scotland is by far the largest, raising concerns over its future levels of government funding.

The Church's largest area of care provision involves the elderly – it runs thirty-three homes for 1,300 older people across Scotland. The Scottish Parliament's new legislation will have a major impact on its work, as local authorities and the Scottish Executive try to determine the boundaries of their responsibilities towards caring for the elderly. According to its 2002 annual report to the General Assembly, the Board regarded itself as being 'in the midst of one of the greatest periods of change in recent social care history'. It goes on:

> In recent years, it has not been possible to report to the General Assembly without a major comment on the Financial Care Gap that arose because local and central government failed to fund properly the residential care of older people. As has been explained regularly, the only resolution to the problem was a major review of the funding provided through the public purse; the alternatives to such a review were that the Church was required to carry the deficit or decide to close the Board's homes, making up to 1,000 old people homeless and up to 1,600 staff unemployed'
> (Church of Scotland 2002: part 1, section 2)

For some time, the Church of Scotland decided to 'accept the deficit while protesting to government and trying to secure a change in funding'. However, in June 2001, the Board decided that the Church had 'fulfilled more than its responsibility and that the deficit funding at the existing level could not continue' (Church of Scotland 2002: part 1, section 2). Another piece of legislation, the Regulation of Care (Scotland) Act (2001) stated that individuals once in care should not be moved out, if their care needs increase, and this had further financial implications for the Board. In September 2001, following threats to withdraw residential care opportunities by the private sector, the Scottish Executive set up a National Review Group, consisting of representatives from the NHS in Scotland, the Convention of Scottish Local Authorities, Scottish Care (the private sector umbrella organisation), the Voluntary Sector and the Scottish Executive. The Group aimed 'to conduct a review of the costs associated with providing nursing and residential care for older people in Scotland and to determine appropriate fee-funding levels for application from 1 April 2002' (Church of Scotland 2002: part 1, section 2). As part of the Scottish Care delegation, Church representatives were involved in the work of the Group, which eventually produced a 'Report on Care Home Costs for Older People in Scotland'. The report was presented to the then Labour Minister for Health and Community Care, Malcolm Chisholm, MSP, in November 2001.

In January 2002, the Church wrote to Mr Chisholm, stating that it could no longer afford to subsidise its care home residents, and that its homes were threatened with closure. It argued that it required an extra £2.5 million a year to keep them open and functioning. This made the front pages of a number of national newspapers, with its director of social work, Ian Baillie, telling BBC Scotland: 'I am optimistic that there will be a resolution, although we can't say whether they will come up with all the money . . . But if the government does not resolve this issue then homes will have to close' (BBC News, 13 January 2002). He argued that the Church of Scotland had been supporting local and central government for the last decade by paying about

£100 of the weekly cost of each of their resident's care. His tactics worked. He involved the media, and spoke in drastic terms of the future of his organisation's care provisions. The Scottish Executive responded quickly, stating that it was 'doing everything possible to bring this matter to a satisfactory conclusion'. Malcolm Chisholm stated that 'action will be announced soon'. A few weeks later, in February 2002, following a meeting of the Scottish Executive and the Convention of Scottish Local Authorities, Mr Chisholm wrote directly to the Church:

> I understand that there will be frustration within the Church of Scotland that progress has not been quicker . . . However, the Executive's commitment to resolving this, in terms of both effort and finance, is considerable. Raising care homes fees is a priority for us and I wanted to see that reflected in increased fees for care homes in both the voluntary and independent sectors, and a secure future for older people, as soon as possible . . . There was a commitment by everyone round the table to ensure that funding for care homes, for the future, is sustainable . . . Furthermore the fee levels recommended by the National Review Group on which we are all agreed, suitably uplifted, will be paid in full from 1 April 2003.
>
> (Church of Scotland 2002: part 1, section 2)

The Scottish Executive decided to commit an additional £24 million to be applied as from 1 April 2002. In addition, £11 million was added to an earlier £10 million in order to pay a level of back-dated fees to 1 July 2001. While, in April 2002, the Church was forced to close eight of its homes, still blaming a lack of central and local government funding, it can be pleased with the campaign's overall success. As with the previous case study on homelessness, we see the Church was heavily involved in the policymaking process, an 'insider' group working closely alongside government. The Scottish Executive met regularly with it, and other interested parties, to try to resolve the disagreement in policy formulation, with the Church very much at the heart of the policy community. This section shows the Church leading a successful and unified political campaign to receive better government funding for its care homes, and central to the negotiations throughout. Some cutbacks have had to be made, but significant concessions were made by the Scottish Executive, which responded to the Board immediately when approached. Ian Baillie states quite perfunctorily that whenever he had a concern over any issue as Board Social Work Director, Malcolm Chisholm and Susan Deacon (Mr Chisholm's predecessor as Health Minister) would always 'make themselves available' (Interview with author, 31 August 2001). According to a senior officer in the Community Care Policy Branch of the Health Department at the Scottish Executive, the Board was 'very professional' in the way it put forward its case against the closures to civil servants, and can be favourably compared with other 'stakeholders' in this respect (Interview with author, 13 August 2003).

This section has outlined the way the Church of Scotland mixes its role as a key provider of social care, and a campaigning emphasis on speaking out on social issues. Similar case studies could have been used in relation to the Church of England, with Chapter 3 alluding to this. However, the strength of focus of the Church of Scotland, and the way it consciously seeks to tie its priorities to those of devolution and a new type of politics is worthy of note. The Church leadership took the decision in the 1990s that it would beneficial to Scottish society if power were devolved to Edinburgh – that decision had very little to do with the teachings of scripture (nowhere in the Bible does it say that there should be a Scottish parliament) but rather had everything to do with the reformed Presbyterian values of democratic accountability and egalitarianism.

Linked to this, the evidence from this section would also suggest that – rationally – it made sense for the Church itself to support devolution. It is now part of a much more intimate policy community on these types of issues as a direct result of its practical expertise. The pre-1999 system of administrative devolution, with policy formulation centred in London (and operated by Conservative party politicians increasingly rejected by voters in Scotland), was not so conducive to these types of aims. The General Assembly of the Church may have lost its status as Scotland's parliament, post-devolution, but there is evidence that it achieved a greater victory. Devolved Scottish politicians have listened because their values are ultimately very similar – in particular, Labour, the Liberal Democrats and the SNP all share social democratic principles, which means that the Church can cooperate fully with them, and in a non-oppositional way. Rationally, the Church needs the parties in order to get its ideas implemented via policies, while the parties need the Church for its wider credibility linked to expertise in social care.

Conclusions

While it is – prima facie – anomalous that Anglican bishops continue to sit in the House of Lords and vote on matters of public policy, and that the Church of Scotland continues to hold a 'special place' in the Scottish political system, this aspect of the British unwritten constitution also allows the churches to flexibly and informally develop a public role for themselves. This role does not involve narrow interest groups and single issues but equally it does not involve keeping a dominant church separate from politics or financially maintaining it because of a centuries-old constitutional amendment. Rather, it embodies the idea that the national churches somehow constitute the national guardians of British (both English and Scottish) democracy and values. There is still a tacit consensus on behalf of political actors which regards the Christian Church – Scottish and English – as being an important part of civic Britain – even twenty-first century secular Britain, and thereby sustaining 'multiple modernities' in the process (Eisenstadt 2000).

However, more to the point, while it is the British Constitution that provides the original base for national churches, it is British public opinion that sustains them. The way the Church of Scotland aligns itself with ordinary Scottish voters, campaigns for them and offers support to them, makes it a politically acceptable ally with whom Scottish party politicians want to be associated. The argument was made in Chapter 4 about the occasional 'Olsonian' disconnect between ordinary Church of England members who have a tendency to vote Conservative and – at least some – leading bishops, who will speak out quite vociferously about the excesses of capitalism. This free-riding game was explained in terms of churches being large organisations involving different levels of individual participation. In Scotland, however, it can be argued that that type of disconnect simply no longer exists owing to the overwhelming pro-Labour voting patterns north of the border – it is much easier to refer to the relatively homogeneous Scottish voters than to the more diverse English ones.

However, this is also testimony to the successful way the Scottish Church's General Assembly has been able to see its role as representing democratically the views of ordinary Scottish people living in its parishes across the country. While this role is much diminished owing to the creation of the new Scottish Parliament, that democratic base continues to live on. For example, poverty is an issue about which the Church has campaigned consistently now for over thirty years, despite making itself unpopular with more Conservative-minded politicians, and saying things that other parties would like to say, but cannot. With budgets to balance and a broadly centre-right consensus in London, the radical pronouncements of the Church of Scotland at times seem unrealistic, but their impact comes from the role the Church plays as a social care provider with extensive expertise in the field. The Scottish parties pay attention because, ultimately, it is rational to do so.

More generally, the Church of Scotland case study shows that the relationship between Christianity and party politics in Britain is not one-dimensional or based solely in and around the Palace of Westminster. It also has a massive contribution away from London, in the devolved nations, as well. After leaving 10 Downing Street for the last time on 11 May 2010, Gordon Brown stated in a speech at Labour Party headquarters: 'One thing will not change: I am Labour, and Labour I will always be' (Brown 2010).

For the best part of thirty years, much the same can be said for Scotland, along with its national Church. This is not to argue that the Church explicitly advocates voting Labour but there is no question at all that, institutionally, it is broadly sympathetic to the social justice priorities of Scottish voters and their parties.

Part 3

The religious issues

6 Little wonder 'We don't do God'

Ethics, life issues and the power of the Christian lobby

On the occasion of his fiftieth birthday in May 2003, the then British Prime Minister, Tony Blair, gave a suitably glamorous interview to the American magazine, *Vanity Fair*. The wide-ranging topics that were discussed included both the political and personal, but when the interviewer, David Margolick, asked Mr Blair about his Christianity, the Prime Minister's Director of Strategy and Communications, Alastair Campbell, stepped in immediately: 'Is he on God? We don't do God. I'm sorry. We don't do God' (Brown 2003).

It is perhaps unnecessary to discuss at length the merits of Mr Campbell's comments, given the content of this book and what has already been argued. However, it is a suitable place to start this third part as, given the focus of some of the policy areas involved, Mr Campbell's intervention seems decidedly rational. Issues related to the sanctity of life – abortion, stem cell research, euthanasia – are not only extremely sensitive and challenging for politicians, they also represent areas of society where Christian values, embodied by the churches, continue to exert a great deal of influence as a consequence.

Shmuel Eisenstadt's influential sociological theory of 'multiple modernities' will feature both in this chapter and the next one – we will look at how different values coexist alongside one another in British politics, but in the process, cause significant challenge for the parties and their leaders. As Newton and Van Deth put it (2005: 212), '[w]hat makes the existence of persistent religious differences all the more interesting and important is that politicians in secular societies usually try to push religious issues, such as abortion or matters of faith, off the political agenda'. In the UK, while, generally, conscience-based or life issues are not 'whipped',[1] there is still very much a *partisan dimension* to them, and crucially, there is no sign of such issues disappearing from the political agenda either.

Indeed, quite the contrary – rather perversely, as active religious observance has declined, the ethical and moral challenges faced by society have concurrently multiplied. Issues related to human genetics are all postmodern issues, born in the twentieth century, and ever evolving. The advances of science are matched by the challenges of how society legislates those advances, and for that reason, the place of religious and moral interests in relation to the policymaking process, and political parties, is assured. The development of the practice of cloning animals by the Roslin Institute at Edinburgh University made Dolly the Sheep a global celebrity in 1997, while the growth in production of genetically modified foods has been continuously in the media spotlight. Never before has science been able to do so much, and never before have politicians had so many complicated ethical questions to consider, when legislating.

As Chapter 1 discussed in detail, the scholarly literature from social scientists on religion has shifted quite significantly since the new orthodoxy arrived in the 1960s proclaiming that religion was no longer of interest – and in many ways, it is Shmuel Eisenstadt who has gradually come to personify that shift, arguing that in modern advanced industrial democracies such as the UK, different sets of values coexist alongside one another, and disagreeing with the idea that secularisation is an irreversible and inevitable trend. As a political scientist, applying a rational choice framework within an analysis of the relationship between religion and democracy, the content of Eisenstadt's inherently sociological approach is not going to be referred to in much detail. Nevertheless, its main thrust is very much in keeping with one of the overarching themes of this project – that we ignore religion as a social variable at our peril.

Eisenstadt criticises scholars who 'assumed, even only implicitly, that the cultural program of modernity as it developed in modern Europe and the basic institutional constellations that emerged there would ultimately take over in all modernizing and modern societies' (2000: 1). Grace Davie also points out 'the importance of taking the religious factor seriously, and in public as well as private life' (2007: 109). The present author would concur – as we will see, particularly in relation to life issues, there is no evidence that British politicians or parties have ever really stopped taking the Christian Church seriously.

The central role of the British Constitution

The United Kingdom is well known for not having a codified, written constitution that encapsulates British national values or civil rights – indeed, Israel is the only other nation state considered to operate on the principle of conventions and statutes. Clearly, in recent years, the role of the European Union has become more relevant to the lives of British voters,[2] with the incorporation into British law of the Human Rights Act, and the establishing of 'European citizenship'. Nevertheless, the constitutional legacy of English and Scots law continues to have a massive impact upon the way Parliament at Westminster deals with issues and policies related to rights and life.

In the United States, for example, the political parties are only one set of actors in the field of human rights and religious liberties. The Constitution protects the rights of Americans by stipulating in black and white what they can and cannot do; while inevitably, interpretations of those rights are constantly open to revision, the power of either the Democrats or the

Republicans to actually amend the Constitution and/or introduce a new law that goes against the Constitution is extremely limited indeed. The Supreme Court operates as a guardian of those rights and values, many of which are defined as being intrinsic to what it means to be American. Freedom, for example, is a value that has become synonymous with the US – rightly or wrongly. A similar picture can be painted of Western European states such as France, Germany or the Netherlands – there, national constitutions created at the birth of their modern political systems continue to provide a base for their political behaviour.

But what of Britain? What exactly are British values? What is a British citizen's rights? If there is no written constitution, how are British rights protected? In the UK, the government of the day makes the law – and that government is traditionally formed by a single party, Conservative or Labour (although there has been a coalition government since May 2010). The majoritarian electoral system (also something of a relic from the Victorian era) means that it tends to be only one of two parties that forms the government and, assuming it has a workable majority, it can basically do whatever it wants, simply by passing a bill into law, and creating a new Act of Parliament. Even manifesto pledges are of limited value – while parties attempt to stick to many of them, they must also revise many others. If the Government of the day wanted to ban abortion, it could; it does not need to refer to Supreme Court rulings or any other document – it could just do it. Admittedly, it would be heavily criticised in the media, and many of its backbenchers would rebel, but the principle stands.

Such an example is fanciful, but there is a more realistic one: if we take twenty-first century life issues such as stem cell research – the only thing that stands between British scientists being able to use whichever methods of research that they wish is the party that happens to be in power in Downing Street, usually Labour or Conservative. While it is too simplistic to argue, therefore, that the UK has taken a different approach to regulating conscience-based issues from other Western countries, what is clear is that the pressure is much more on the *parties* to have views, one way or the other, or at the very least, to be clear about giving its members a free vote in the House of Commons and Lords, as bills pass through Parliament. In America, there is no need for either the GOP or Democrats to have a thought-out policy position on these matters – while individual Congress men and women may well come to views that reflect their conservative/liberal backgrounds, that is as far as it has to go. In the UK, the Conservative Party has actually maintained a policy stance of formally banning euthanasia in the past, while the current Labour Government whipped its MPs over the Human Fertilisation and Embryology (HFE) 2008 Bill owing to the pressures that potentially losing a vote in the Commons would have posed at the time of the debate to the long-term survival of Prime Minister, Gordon Brown. However, it should also be pointed out that this is not the norm, and for rational reasons that will be discussed later in the chapter – nevertheless, the point is made now to illustrate the centrality of the party in all of this.

The present author is not arguing that the rather unusual nature of the British Constitution in itself provides a different environment for the treatment of life issues – a detailed analysis of where Britain is on academic research into human genetics, for example, is unlikely to discover that British scientists either lag behind or pull ahead of, say, American colleagues as a result of some sort of ethical black hole at the heart of the political system. Many of the differences between having a written constitution and an unwritten constitution are essentially academic, and ones for constitutional lawyers to mull over. However, the impact upon *party behaviour* is very clear – Parliament is the sovereign law maker, and parties run Parliament. They have to decide on a regular basis how they handle best these types of issues.

In modern, Western politics, the 'holy trinity' of life issues are 1) stem cell research/human genetics; 2) abortion (both contained in the HFE Bill) and 3) euthanasia/assisted dying. This section will examine their role in contemporary British party politics in an attempt to show how vital it is that parties cope with them effectively, despite the decline in church attendance or secularisation of society. There remain substantial numbers of votes to be won and lost in relation to the way a government handles such fundamental issues.

The rise of issue politics was touched upon in Chapter 2, but it is worth reiterating that such peculiarly late twentieth-century/early twenty-first-century issues are symptomatic of the phenomena – stem cell research, in particular, is a great example of how the decline in religiosity of voters does not concurrently transfer into a decline in the importance of religious issues to politics and parties. The rational choice-inspired theory of 'valence voting', that is, the perception of how parties *perform* (see Clarke *et al.* 2010), argues that governments win and lose as much as a result of their competence as over socio-economic ideological affairs. While the UK is not at the stage that the US is, where single issues can effectively swing elections owing to the collection of different interests that make up the whole, nevertheless parties have to be sensitive to a huge gamut of different challenges.

A very similar high profile case was the proposed introduction of ID cards by the Labour Government (2005–10) – such an issue is almost impossible to place on a traditional left–right scale. It was originally dreamt up by John Major's Conservative government in the 1990s, but taken on by New Labour. The Conservatives under David Cameron opposed it, as did the Liberal Democrats and the Scottish National Party, and it was scrapped when the new coalition entered Downing Street in May 2010. Ultimately, it is up to the individual voter to decide on whether or not they think it is a good idea, but that same voter can potentially cast their vote based on their preference. Issues such as human fertilisation are very similar – while the Labour Government could never be accused of politicising the issue, the scope for voters to judge them on it remains, nevertheless, large, while the lack of a written constitution allows the issue to become more politicised in the first place.

The next two sections will examine two excellent examples of this phenomenon where religious issues can be used to apply pressure to British party politicians, ultimately forcing them to alter policy or to simply step back from the issue altogether and allow their MPs and peers to vote in whichever way they wish. First, we look at the way the Labour Party has made various attempts to appease its Catholic support base over issues such as human fertilisation and abortion; second, we will look at the way the Church of England bishops in the House of Lords were able to help block a bill on assisted dying by collectively voting it down. Both are highly visible cases of the continuing latent power of the Christian lobby in British politics.

Weak parties, strong churches I: life issues and free votes

In modern, twenty-first century Britain, it would be patently wrong to try to argue that social policy in the area of life issues has been successfully influenced by the more conservative wing of the Christian Church. Abortion is legal and commonplace across the UK, while scientific research in the field of human genetics is constantly testing the boundaries of both ethics and technology. However, what is interesting from our perspective is the way the parties collectively remove themselves from these areas of policy, and make them much more of a parliamentary rather than a partisan debate. There are two dimensions to this that help confirm our public choice analytical context: first, the fact that the parties choose to act in this way, while entirely rational (clearly, such issues are not overtly partisan, in any case), nevertheless causes them substantial organisational challenges – after all, sometimes governments have to bring forward legislation for medical or scientific reasons that are then politicised and linked to the wider popularity/unpopularity of the party in power; second (as the next section will focus upon), the present author would actually go further and argue that parties are acutely sensitive to British public opinion in relation to issues such as abortion, euthanasia or human cloning, so rationally acknowledges that it is wise to try to de-politicise debates whenever possible.

The Human Fertilisation and Embryology (HFE) Act of 2008 provides us with an excellent example of this. The Act constituted the culmination of a major review of how modern Britain deals with matters such as abortion and stem cell research. Often, these issues can be thought of separately – one more associated with the highly emotive politics of the US and one linked to the more rarefied world of science and universities. In fact, both belong to essentially the same policy area – the question of where we draw the line between an embryo and a fully fledged human being. The HFE Bill was born primarily out of a need for parliament to legislate over where that line is drawn – a difficult yet necessary requirement. It was drafted because of a feeling that the existing law, passed in 1990, had become increasingly outdated and irrelevant to scientific advances made in the prior twenty years.

In particular, the Bill caused major problems for Catholic Labour MPs who objected to being whipped by the party to vote in favour of three of the main proposals contained within it. First, to allow the practice of scientists working with hybrid embryos (half human tissue–half animal tissue) in order to study genetic defects; second, to abolish the role of the 'father figure', the stipulation that IVF (in vitro fertilisation) clinics take into account the welfare of any future child; third, to permit 'saviour siblings' – babies born only because they are a tissue match for a sick older brother or sister with a genetic condition. In essence, all three of these proposals concern the question of whether or not it is right for doctors to 'play God' and interfere with nature, manipulating human DNA and genetic cells.

Owing to low public opinion ratings, the Labour Government attempted to whip its MPs, arguing that the Bill was simply the result of scientific evidence. In a letter to all Labour MPs in March 2008, PM Gordon Brown wrote:

> The Human Fertilisation and Embryology Bill will update the legal framework that governs assisted reproduction and embryo research, bringing this into line with recent scientific developments and equalities legislation. It will reform the regulatory framework in which embryo research is conducted, ensure that all human embryos outside the body are subject to the best regulation, create a ban on sex selection of offspring for non-medical reasons, and update the rules around entitlements to IVF. Stem cell research is important because it makes it possible for this generation to contemplate new and effective treatments and cures for diseases that have afflicted mankind from time immemorial – from leukaemia and Alzheimer's to conditions affecting every family such as cancer and heart disease.
>
> (BBC News, 25 March 2008)

Under pressure from Catholic colleagues in the Cabinet like the Defence Secretary, Des Browne, and the Education Secretary, Ruth Kelly, Mr Brown allowed his party's MPs a free vote on the above three aspects but whipped them for the rest of the Bill. There were sixty-eight 'publicly' Catholic MPs in the House at the time – sixty-four if the three Sinn Fein members who do not attend were not counted – all of whom were seen to be potential rebels in relation to the Bill (Elliott and Hurst 2007). Conservative and Liberal Democrat members, meanwhile, were permitted a free vote (with both parties having a good record of allowing this in past similar policy debates). Such an episode demonstrates first, the political problems that issues of this nature can cause, and second, the influence of the Church as a consequence.

A brief look at the historical context is insightful also: it had been the arrival of Dolly the Sheep in 1997 that first signalled the start of intense media interest into the practice of cloning animals. However, the production of Dolly was not the main aim of the work of the Roslin Institute at Edinburgh University, merely a by-product. The main aim of the research programme, under the leadership of Professor Sir Ian Wilmut, was to find better ways of genetic modification using fewer animals, by growing a living creature from genetically modified cells. Nevertheless, it was Dolly who made the front pages of the newspapers, and a public debate began on the ethics of cloning living creatures, as this had implications for similar research concerning human genes.

In December 2000, MPs voted two to one in favour of allowing the 'selective' use of embryos for research, leading the Church of Scotland to conclude that 'Parliament has agreed that humans may, in principle, be cloned' (Church of Scotland 2001: 24/43). The month before the House of Commons debate, the Church's Human Genetics Group had written to all British MPs, asking them to consider delaying voting for this raft of fresh legislation recommended by the Donaldson Report, conducted by the Government's Chief Medical officer (Church of Scotland 2001: 20/16). While that did not work, and the recommendations became law in January 2001, the Church was 'heartened by the responses from some MPs, who had clearly thought hard about the ethical issues and had come to a conscientious decision' (Church of Scotland 2001: 24/18).

While the churches failed to stop MPs voting for the Donaldson Report recommendations at the end of 2000, its standing in the eyes of government departments, national ethics bodies and the cloning research community became high. According to the 2001 Report, it has been given numerous opportunities to give a Christian view to these organisations at the 'highest levels', and has twice been invited to speak to MPs at the House of Commons. In the Donaldson Report, for example, specific responses are made to issues highlighted by the Church of Scotland, which claims to have earned a 'rare position of trust, both as to the understanding of the science and the ethics' (Church of Scotland 2001: 20/16). Crucially, at no point did any of the above process become overtly politicised – the various points were discussed within the context of the merits or otherwise of the scientific research, not in a partisan way. The Public Health Minister at the time, Yvette Cooper, even went so far as to say that it has been 'the most thoughtful and considered debate she had witnessed in the House' (BBC News, 19 December 2000).

A few years later, it was the issue of abortion that returned to the fore of Westminster politics. In the run-up to the 2005 General Election, the Conservative leader, Michael Howard, stated that he personally supported a reduction in the legal abortion time period from 24 to 20 weeks (BBC News, 14 March 2005). While Mr Howard stressed that Conservative MPs would not be whipped on the issue in the future, and that this was a personal view only, crucially, he also made clear that he would allow a vote to take up floor debating time in the next Parliament should his party win. In the process, he forced the then Labour Prime Minister, Tony Blair, to make a public statement about his own stance on abortion, and why he did not feel there was a need to revisit the issue. The important point to note here is that while Mr Howard was unquestionably trying to tap into his party's socially conservative base, discussed in Chapters 2 and 3, he was not prepared to go so far as to make it an explicitly partisan issue and official Conservative party policy. Once again, we see party politics at play here, but with the strength of the individual party substantially weakened.

The Conservative backbencher, Nadine Dorries, tried to introduce Mr Howards' preferred time limit via an amendment to the HFE Bill; however, she failed to win sufficient votes. Cowley and Stuart (2006) noted the partisan division that took place on the amendment, with 96 per cent of Labour MPs and 80 per cent of Liberal Democrats voting down the amendment and 81 per cent of Conservatives voting in favour. They also state that this 'was perhaps a sign that the issue [abortion] is about to return to the political agenda'. Meanwhile, in an interview with the *New Statesman*, Ms Dorries herself claimed that her party was becoming increasingly populated by Conservative Christians: 'I can think of half a dozen Conservatives that don't agree with me, but they're leaving at the next election – people like Andrew MacKay and David Curry. The new MPs that are coming in are all social conservatives – people like Fiona Bruce, Philippa Stroud, Louise Bagshawe' (Hundal, 26 April 2010). Interesting as such arguments and statistics are, in relation to the points made earlier in this book about the differences between the parties and their vote, ultimately, they do not detract from the fact that this was a free vote, without a formal partisan dimension. Indeed, David Cameron himself spoke out against the Catholic Church 'misrepresenting' embryo research ahead of the HFE Bill being debated (Hurst and Henderson 2008) so it is a complex picture overall. Such is the influence of religious groups and public opinion over this type of issue that the politicians prefer to play safe, and leave their party labels behind when entering the Commons lobbies.

In relation to assisted dying, or euthanasia – while this area of policy is connected to the HFE Act, it is also fundamentally different. Here, scientific advances are less relevant, as are the intellectual definitions of what constitutes a human being, with the emphasis much more on the practical implications of allowing hospitals to end/not prolong the lives of patients if they so wish. Nevertheless, it too has featured increasingly in recent years in British party political debates as the mobility of British patients to travel abroad to countries such as Switzerland where the practice is legal has increased. Indeed, it is an ongoing debate in the UK – for example, Church of England bishops blocked Lord Joffe's Bill in the House of Lords in 2006, while Margo Macdonald, MSP is currently trying to win support for a bill in the Scottish Parliament to legalise assisted dying.

Chapter 4 discussed the role of Church of England bishops in the House of Lords, arguing that this represented the weight of public opinion being supportive, and also the responsibility the Church felt to reflect that opinion. This section will offer an excellent recent example of this – the role of the Lords Spiritual in the passage of the Assisted Dying Bill through Parliament.

In February 2003, the Labour peer, and human rights lawyer, Joel Joffe proposed the 'Assisted Dying for the Terminally Ill Bill' in order to legalise medical-assisted dying. After deliberation by a House of Lords committee, the Bill was debated on 12 May 2006, but an amendment to delay its introduction by six months was carried by a margin of 148–100, effectively kicking it into the political long grass. All fourteen bishops in attendance voted that day, adding substantially to the body of opposition. Meanwhile, in 2009, a slightly less significant amendment introduced by Lord Falconer intended merely to clarify the law surrounding the procedure of going abroad for assisted dying was also defeated by 194 to 141 votes, with five bishops voting on that occasion.

According to Richard Chapman (Interview with author, 4 March 2010), the Church of England's Secretary for Parliamentary Affairs, many within the Church of England, not least the Lords Spiritual themselves, realised that the bishops needed more coordinated support for their work in the House of Lords, and so a parliamentary office, based at Church House, was created in 2008. This move was also motivated by an increasing number of MPs and Lords asking 'What is the Church's view?' on a range of contemporary political issues. There is no question that the capacity for the bishops to organise effectively when necessary is greatly facilitated by the secretariat at Church House, who monitor the various relevant policy developments very closely. It would be wrong to claim that they do so in a superior way to the past as there was not as much need for such a structure in a previous era (see discussion in Chapter 7 on the way state churches have been forced to function to a new political environment). However, it is clear that the Church has adapted to its new role as 'one interest group among many' in a relatively sophisticated fashion, and for that reason, it is wrong to dismiss it or ignore it as a significant British political actor.

At the time of the second debate, Britain's three most senior religious leaders expressed their joint concern about 'back door' attempts to legalise euthanasia. Rowan Williams, the Archbishop of Canterbury; Vincent Nicholls, the Roman Catholic Archbishop of Westminster; and Sir Jonathan Sacks, the Chief Rabbi, signed a joint letter to the *Daily Telegraph*, stating that such a move 'would surely put vulnerable people at serious risk, especially sick people who are anxious about the burden their illness may be placing on others' (29 June 2009).

This is not a partisan issue in the first place – the first was a private members bill and, in the second, MPs and Lords were allowed a free vote. However, as has already been argued, that in itself is an admission by the parties that they do not want to get involved in this type of delicate issue. Indeed, governments have to decide to give parliamentary time at Westminster for bills of this nature to pass through the Commons and the Lords – clearly, a calculation has to be made about whether they regard it as such a serious issue that it needs to be debated, and potentially legislated on. British public opinion is uncertain and broadly conservative when it comes to such matters of life and death, and it is a very brave politician indeed who enters this sort of territory lightly. For example, a 2008 poll for *The Times* newspaper found that, while 58 per cent of British men felt stem cell experiments should take place, only 43 per cent of British women thought so (Clements, 2008). While some surveys show support for assisted dying, others do not, and the bishops know that, at the very least, they would not lose anything by intervening.

A related point – the present author is not arguing that the bishops make up their minds about issues because of rational choice concerns such as popularity. Clearly, this is not the case – what is being argued, however, is that they are *allowed* to do so because the parties do not get involved, and they are willing to do so quite unashamedly because they know they have that sort of endorsement and legitimacy. So the rational choice theory (RCT) dimension is not about the Church's stance on assisted dying but on the political elite letting the Church dictate to it what it thinks.

Linked to this, it would still have been a very controversial thing if the bishops had blocked a popular proposal. The fact the Church knows when to enter public policy debates at the right time, and exert its influence is a very important dimension to British parliamentary politics. It is no coincidence that such situations happen rarely – on the majority of issues, the bishops do not vote as a bloc and this is because they understand that there is no public appetite for a group of twenty-six Anglican bishops continuously voting in a certain way, and/or blocking legislation on a regular basis. In particular, on a socio-economic matter, the bishops will often abstain, or vote in a diverse way. But when they feel that they are in line with wider society, and the fears or concerns of ordinary voters, they act decisively.

Public opinion allows this – the Church instinctively knows that it is in line with the views and fears of wider British society, and the parties know not to interfere with that important dimension of British politics. As Steven Kettell puts it:

> what is demonstrated by these events [the HFE debate] is both the increasing organisation of faith groups and individuals, and their willingness to mobilise in order to press their case. While their battle on this occasion may have been lost, pressures for a greater role for religion in the public sphere are likely to remain a key feature of the British landscape for some time.
>
> (Kettell 2009a: 74)

Weak parties, strong churches II: the power of the Catholic vote

So far, the point has been made that political debates in life issue policy areas are effectively 'de-partied' owing to rational considerations, but it is possible to go further and examine the way by far the most vocal interest group in the field – the Roman Catholic Church – has an influential role to play. While the highly conservative views of the Church on these issues are not at the mainstream of modern British society, they nevertheless provide a visible and powerful symbol of the concern normal voters have about politicians trying to 'play God' or turn ethical issues into political ones.

Conveniently, as we already know from Chapter 2, there exists in Britain a very tight correlation between Catholics and Labour, much stronger than any link that Church of England voters have with the Conservatives. It is therefore legitimate to talk – albeit with many caveats – of a Catholic vote in Britain.

The caveats include the fact that the basis of that vote is socio-economic class, as opposed to moral stances, as well as the question of how cohesive – long-term – that voting bloc will remain, but the point stands. While Chapters 2 and 3 argued that religious people voted Conservative, that does not preclude other, longer-standing correlations based on social cleavages, as they are clearly still around too, playing the same game.

This electoral correlation meant that there really are votes to be lost if parties, and in particular, the Labour Party, get things wrong. While Labour is, more often than not, able to wash its hands of such affairs, and claim that it allowed a free vote, it does not preclude the Catholic Church using often quite sophisticated tactics to call Labour's bluff. The consistently biggest irritant to the insider networks of Westminster is the Catholic Church, and its interest in life issues. The Catholic Church has a very different sort of remit from the Church of Scotland or Church of England – it has no need to embody British values or be inclusive to minorities. In fact, its only mission is to uphold the principles of its faith that have survived for over 2,000 years – and that obviously includes sanctity of life issues. While the reformed Anglican and Presbyterian Churches embrace a much more tolerant approach to these issues (in general), the Catholic Church regards itself as the main defender of ethics against the overly swift advances of science.

This is helped by the fact that a number of formal links between the Catholic Church and the British political system continue to exist. The most obvious of these are denominational primary and secondary state schools, but the Church has other political dimensions to it, particularly at a British level. First, as the Vatican State is an independent nation state, it has an ambassador to the United Kingdom – the Pope is thus not just a church leader – he is also a head of State, and the Catholic Church often holds a unique 'political' place in many nation states around the world. Constitutionally, the Catholic Church holds a distinct and recognisable place in the British political system, more so than any of the other 'non-established' denominations. In terms of the British State, the Catholic Church in England and Wales is considered a 'Privileged Body' by the Crown, which means its senior bishops have audiences with HM The Queen at Buckingham Palace – other privileged bodies include local civic dignitaries, the ancient universities, the armed forces, and both established churches. So the institutional power of the Catholic Church is not entirely dissimilar to that of the established Protestant churches.

The more recent emollient attempts by Cardinal Basil Hume to put a rather charming face on an essentially conservative and entrenched organisation should not be allowed to cloud the fact that the Catholic Church has a very different approach to politics from either the Church of Scotland or the Church of England, and his two successors, Cardinal Cormac Murphy O'Connor and Archbishop Vincent Nicholls, both represent a return to a more conservative position. For by far the best example of the Catholic Church in Britain flexing its political muscles, and using political methods to advance its interests, we can look to the Archdiocese of Glasgow under the leadership of Cardinal Thomas Winning. Coxall (2001: 147) states that, in the context of British politics, 'good leadership matters to the success of pressure groups' and that the 'internal organisation of a group may be a key factor in accounting for its relative success' (2001: 161). Another British politics scholar, Baggott (1995: 58) agrees, stating that 'good leadership is essential if a pressure group is to make maximum use of its resources'. As well as his influential work on the Protestant work ethic, Weber's writings on authority are helpful to this discussion, with his description of 'charismatic' leadership particularly relevant to the analysis of the role of the late Cardinal Winning (1978 translation: 1,111–17).

While Winning was originally made Archbishop of Glasgow in 1974 at the age of 49, and was known to hold strong views on a variety of issues, it was only from 1994 onwards, after he was elevated to the College of Cardinals, that his public recognition factor rose significantly. The new Cardinal, only the second in Scotland since the Reformation, was a different type of prelate from his predecessor, Cardinal Gordon Gray of Edinburgh, who had died a year earlier. An unassuming man, Cardinal Gray made few public pronouncements in the media, and having not been reared in the west of Scotland, was also more ecumenically minded than Cardinal Winning. After the death of Cardinal Hume in 1999, Winning became the most senior and recognisable Catholic in the UK.

Winning may have been a Prince of the Catholic Church, but he also had a 'common touch' as well as the 'self-imposed inner determination' of a 'natural leader' (Weber 1978 translation: 1112). He realised that the Scottish press listened to his public pronouncements – 'a very savvy media operator', according to Douglas Fraser, BBC Scotland's economic editor (Interview with author, 24 June 2003). He was the most recognisable clergyman in Scotland – in many ways, the public face of Christianity in the nation. Parry describes him as the 'overwhelming religious presence in recent years' (2002: 145). By the time he died of a heart attack in June 2001, he was one of the best-known public figures in the UK – his recognition level was higher than most Scottish politicians, particularly after devolution. It was a significant achievement for the 'leader' of such a conservative institution to achieve celebrity in a secular Western European country – however, in a sense, he was the voice of the past, the voice of conservative Christianity, and the personification of opposition to liberalism. He was the 'man of the people', who spoke out on political issues others dared not to, able to channel his 'gift from above' into providing direction and leadership to his 'organisation' (Weber 1978 translation: 1112).

By far the biggest campaign Winning mounted in his period of office as Archbishop of Glasgow was the Pro-Life Initiative he set up in 1997. Highly controversial at the time, it involved the Archdiocese of Glasgow paying mothers to keep their babies, and not have abortions, as well as providing financial support to bring the child up. It was a revolutionary scheme, and one that Winning's successor as Archbishop vowed to continue to support. In March

2002, Mario Conti opened the Pro-Life Centre in Glasgow which helped to continue the work that has already been done. Hundreds of women gave birth to children after approaching the Church, including a twelve-year-old girl who was given financial support after falling pregnant. The issue of abortion is one that the Catholic Church has always involved itself in passionately – it is one of its most sincerely held beliefs, and in contrast with the reformed churches' position, significantly less equivocal. According to its 1985 deliverance, the Church of Scotland accepts that there are occasions when abortion is the only answer for the mother after the 'exhaustion of all alternatives' (Church of Scotland 1999: 24/19).

Since much of Catholic teaching is contained in the *Catechism*, there is little room for deviation from the official Catholic position. When Cardinal Winning spoke out on an issue, his view was often based on what was written in the *Catechism*, and his press office had the simple task of telling the media about it. For example, on abortion, article 5.1 of the *Catechism* states that 'human life must be respected and protected absolutely from the moment of conception', and that 'from its conception, the child has the right to life'. On the issue of human sexuality, part three (section two, chapter two, article 6) states that 'among the sins gravely contrary to chastity are . . . fornication, pornography and homosexual practices' (Roman Catholic Church).

While the *Catechism* clearly does not have the capacity to go into depth or detail about contemporary British political issues, the moral principles that are outlined do give a clarity and conviction to the public pronouncements of leading Catholic clergy. While bishops' conferences meet six times a year to discuss a variety of issues, the basic 'moral laws' of the Church remain unchanged. Also, even if a policy issue arises that is not specifically mentioned in the 1992 *Catechism*, for example, genetic engineering, it is still possible for Catholic leaders to refer back to it for general guidance on 'respect for human life'.

It would be wrong to overstate the importance of the Catholic Church actively campaigning on life issues – clearly, the actual influence of the Church on social policy in Britain has been essentially quite limited. However, it does, once again, reiterate the point that British party politicians will not get involved in these types of affairs, if they can possibly avoid them. Cardinal Winning, as the most senior cleric in the British Catholic Church, provided firm leadership to his clergy and community, and was a personality with whom politicians and civil servants could engage. In political pressure group terms, Winning was a very effective chief executive of his organisation. Grant (2000: 199) argues that pressure groups 'have to develop decision-making structures that take account of the different interests and viewpoints of their members whilst being able to develop effective policies and to respond to changing events'. While the Catholic Church does not attempt to represent the views of its members, it does have a very effective leadership structure, and this is a more important factor. Grant gives the example of the CBI which suffers from 'stifling breadth' because it attempts to represent everyone who comes under its auspices – small firms, large firms, manufacturers, financiers and retailers. He compares this to Greenpeace's internal structure which is very hierarchical, with the 'rank and file' excluded from all decision making, but which maintains a very unified public face (2000: 199).

British politicians still recognise that there continues to be a 'Catholic vote' of some kind, and that it is important not to alienate potential voters. Winning enjoyed a close personal relationship with a number of leading political party figures, most notably Alex Salmond, the former leader of the SNP. That friendship is credited with helping to make the SNP more 'Catholic-friendly' in the 1990s, leading to a rise in the number of Catholics in favour of independence.[3] One incident in particular exemplifies the closeness of the relationship between Salmond and Winning. When preparations were being made for the funeral of Diana, Princess of Wales, in 1997, Cardinal Winning was not invited onto the chancel, as Cardinal Hume was, but instead had to sit in the congregation. Alex Salmond publicly criticised the exclusion, arguing that Winning was equal to Hume, and not subordinate to the 'English' Cardinal. While the pair's friendship was genuine and sincere, it was also expedient for both parties. Winning gained the ear of one of the most influential politicians in the country, while Salmond drastically changed the image of his party from being 'anti-Catholic', to being the party for 'New Scots', including Catholics and Asians.

As Paterson *et al.* point out, it is interesting to note that the long-established correlation between being Catholic and voting Labour in Scotland has not yet been severed by the 'new politics' of devolution (2001: 63). Indeed, a number of writers believe that the decline in active attendance of Church of Scotland members is one of the main factors in the decline in fortunes of the Scottish Conservative Party since the 1960s (e.g. Seawright and Curtice 1995; Brown *et al.* 1999: 61). In 1965, the Unionists changed their name back to 'Conservative', but it is unclear if that accelerated its decline, or was merely a symptom of it. This can be compared with Labour's prolonged capacity to hold on to middle-class Catholics, whose social and economic circumstances had improved, but who remained loyal to the party.

Meanwhile, the Scottish National Party has always been viewed with some suspicion by the Catholic community. It was perhaps no surprise in the mid twentieth century that the SNP's early brand of Scottish patriotism found no favour in a community that still viewed itself as essentially Irish, and the Labour Party, with its brand of international socialism became the party most Scottish Catholics felt comfortable with. This lack of trust in the SNP by the Catholic community lasted until relatively recently. In 1989, Kellas wrote that the 'Catholic voter contributes in no small measure to the continuity of Labour support in Scotland and to the weakness of the SNP' (1989: 110).

In interviews, two back-bench Labour MPs stated that they disliked the tactics used by the Catholic Church to try and influence them, and resented the implication that being a Labour MP in Central Scotland meant that they were expected to listen carefully to the views of the Catholic Church. Furthermore, one Catholic Lanarkshire Labour MSP explained how he considered changing his mind over repealing Section 28 (see the next chapter) – he had previously been in favour of retaining it – after feeling the Catholic Church was trying to tell him what to do (Anonymised telephone interviews, October 2001, March 2002). The 'latent' political influence of the Catholic Church was very apparent among the responses. A majority of politicians felt that the SNP had deliberately targeted the Catholic vote in the last decade, something a number of leading nationalists also admitted, but that the party continues to deny officially. One experienced Labour MP felt that the SNP, under Alex Salmond's leadership had 'unquestionably tried to attract Catholic voters'. Another agreed that Alex Salmond had made an attempt to attract Catholic voters to the SNP, by writing in *Flourish*, the Catholic newspaper, and that Salmond 'articulated' Cardinal Winnings' views on many issues. A senior Labour MSP argued that the SNP had a very 'definite strategy' to attract Catholic voters in recent years, because they realised they had to 'get that constituency of support in west central Scotland', and that a secret memo existed urging members to try to recruit more Catholic voters. When Salmond spoke openly about his faith around the time of the Glasgow East by-election in July 2009, it was widely interpreted as an attempt to appeal to Catholic voters (Allardyce 2009).

While the last section focused on the way parties try to avoid life issues altogether, this section has focused on the way the major interest group in the field – the Catholic Church – has been able to use different strategies to exert influence, if not necessarily successfully in relation to social policy, unquestionably in relation to party politics and electoral behaviour. When the Conservative leader proposed cutting the time for a legal abortion from 24 to 20 weeks, Cardinal Cormac Murphy O'Connor commented:

> There has been a notion in the past that Catholics would be more in support of the Labour Party because they were working-class people who felt that the Labour Party stood for many of their needs. I'm not so sure that would be quite as true today.
>
> (Gledhill and Charter 2005)

That sort of veiled threat speaks volumes about the disappointment the Church has that its own party, the Labour Party, has lost its way so radically.

Conclusions

The first section was designed to offer an overview of the way that party politicians are happy to take the 'party' out of the 'politics' in relation to life issues and allow their MPs and peers to vote in whatever way they choose, even to the point of allowing Church bishops to block legislation that is not government or party-backed. Meanwhile, the second case study explored in depth the rational game that is in play when the parties are actually forced to legislate over life issues – an awareness of the Catholic vote means that they have to be careful in this area of policy formulation and delivery. This is epitomised by the Scottish context where we see a very overt correlation between votes, seats and policies – and, as a consequence, a game played out between the different self-interest and rational actors.

While a free vote is often the reward from party leaders to their MPs and Lords when it comes to voting over life issues – British politicians often talk about how 'this is not a partisan issue', and that they do not want to make their members vote in a way that offends their individual consciences – the only problem is that other rational choice factors frequently come into play. The premise of removing the parties from the debate altogether and letting politicians act unilaterally is ostensibly innocuous and reasonable, but there are other rational dimensions to it that do not always secure such consistency. With no document to work from – no supreme court prior to 2009, no constitution, no formalised British tradition of human rights – the parties also risk public opinion if they are perceived to be getting something wrong. It is a brave MP who gets up in the Commons and argues that stem cell research should not be funded, for example.

Prime Ministers never like to lose a vote at Westminster, regardless of whether or not it is overtly partisan in its detail. The HFE Bill was an excellent example – because it was a government-backed bill, introduced as a result of scientific advances and the sorts of real-life 'events' that Harold Macmillan used to fear, it became politicised. Gordon Brown, struggling to remain popular, whipped most of the vote, with all the consequences that went with that. This chapter has demonstrated that this is not so much an example of how the churches have lots of power but more an example of how difficult it is for parties to cope with this sort of sensitive issue. Church attendances may be falling but the influence of religion on party politics is not.

The other point that needs to be made is that this sort of issue is not going to disappear – the ethical debate surrounding stem cell research and human genetics is only going to intensify. The issue of assisted dying is also one that is going to remain prominent. While political careers are not going to be made on the basis of such issues, the role of the party in relation to them remains pronounced in the UK, and for that reason, the study of Christianity in British party politics is vital and timely. There is no Constitution, no supreme court or other body that can take the pressure off elected politicians, and the way the Catholic Church has quite pointedly cooled its institutional relationship with the Labour Party is perhaps the best rational example of this. We have already noted that elections can be won and lost by religious voters – a party that is not seen to be taking these types of issues seriously could be made to suffer at the polls.

7 Still fighting a losing battle?

Equalities and the weakness of the Christian lobby

Chapter 6 examined the relationship between British party politics and ethical issues such as abortion, stem cell research and euthanasia. This chapter has a similar remit, but with a slightly different emphasis, examining the impact of equalities policy on the lifestyles of British voters, rather than 'sanctity' of life issues, that is, human sexuality, gender rights and policies related to the family, often grouped together under employment and education legislation. Clearly, there is an overlap with this chapter and the last one, but what we see very quickly is a quite different power dynamic existing between the parties and the churches. In Chapter 6, we saw how influential the Christian lobby is, and how parties and politicians do everything they can to avoid controversy, by allowing free votes and generally taking the advice of church representatives as experts in the field of ethics. In the area of equalities, however, we see a rather different picture – here, the balance of influence is effectively reversed, with the relevant issues very much taking on a partisan dimension, and the churches effectively powerless to do very much in the face of an irreversible tide of equalities and civil liberty advances.[1]

Linked to this, rather than look to the British Constitution for our context, we instead assess the role of the European Union, and Britain's membership of it. There is no question at all that much of the equalities legislation that passes through Parliament at Westminster has its origins in Brussels and Strasbourg – attempting to introduce uniformity in human rights across Europe has been one of the core aims of the integration project, and the UK has often been forced to implement directives that it might not have initiated itself at that time, had it not been an EU member state. The Conservative Government's hard-fought opt out of the social chapter and accompanying minimum wage package in the mid 1990s is an excellent example. Europe is the main driving force behind the equalities agenda, and it has had a huge effect on the British churches, and the way they function.

However, it must also be stated that the vitally important role of British public opinion is of equal value here – as with the issues discussed in Chapter 6, the reality is that concepts such as equal pay for men and women, equal rights for same sex couples and equal freedoms for non-Christian citizens, are all broadly supported by the vast majority of British voters (for example, see

Eurobarometer opinion polling (European Commission 2010)), making the battle that churches sometimes have to fight to protect their various centuries-old privileges all the more challenging. The parties know that they are on safe ground introducing legislation, as it is merely formalising in law the wider modernising of British society, which started in the 1960s. One of the more prominent 2010 General Election manifesto commitments from the Conservatives was to replace the Human Rights Act 1998, which enshrined European fundamental rights with a British 'Bill of Rights', in order to provide a more libertarian emphasis – but this was quickly shelved when the Liberal Democrats made clear that they did not support the proposal. As Meg Munn, MP, the Labour Minister responsible for introducing much of the equalities policies related to same sex couples and women, commented in an interview: 'The vast majority of Britons do not discriminate in their own lives, in any case, so introducing legislation that formalises that is not really a problem' (Interview with author, March 2010).

Public choice theory dictates that the parties will adhere to the equalities agenda if there are votes to be won or lost, and the evidence would very much appear to support that theory. Much more than life or conscience-based ethics, equalities has a much more partisan dimension – the left or progressive parties, Labour and the Liberal Democrats, inherently embrace the values of the agenda much more enthusiastically, whereas the Conservatives are less programmed to consider such issues to be a priority and/or correct. However, as David Cameron's modernisation of the Conservative Party demonstrates, there is an acknowledgement that he has to fight the battles that he can win, and the Conservatives have conceded a huge amount in the last decade about the merits of a 'progressive' values system.

All of this means that this chapter has a much more simple – on the face of it – purpose than the last: Labour and the Liberal Democrats support the promotion of gay rights and gender balance in employment and education, while the Conservatives traditionally do not, and have to battle internally to deal with the issues. However, in reality, the debate is much more nuanced, and the way the British parties deal with the challenges is not always uniform. Many MPs in the Labour Party, for example, are very 'conservative', and even within the Liberal Democrats, there is a moral/non-conformist strain that is actually quite illiberal (see the Scottish Highland tradition of voting Liberal, for example).

Before we focus on the issues, let us start by looking at the context – and in particular, that means looking at the European context.

The role of the European Union

The role of the European Union (EU) in all of this is somewhat multifaceted: first, while the Amsterdam Treaty protects the right of the individual citizen to freedom of religious expression, the EU is an inherently secular body with no mention of Christianity in any of its other treaties or directives. Within this context, the harmonisation of fundamental citizen's rights in policy areas such as education and employment has led to a situation in which a standard equalities norm has been introduced in the UK. Second, the transfer of power from national level to Brussels has meant that the territorial political influence of national churches is no longer clear: the wider impact of European integration is proving to be as significant as specific directives. Thus 2006 witnessed a controversy over a British Airways flight attendant not being permitted to wear a cross, following a debate in 2004 over the place of religious symbols or clothing in French classrooms – both issues that transcend the boundaries of the traditional nation state. These trends also reflect the wider debate about the role of religion in an enlarged and secular EU: does integration inevitably mean a less certain – if not necessarily less influential – political role for individual Christian churches in relation to national party politics?

EU member states are increasingly integrated, with supranational legislation now taking precedence over national laws. Brussels offers a specific policy focus where a wide variety of different types of interest groups can lobby: supranational political institutions such as the European Commission and the European Parliament have become more central to decision making, working in conjunction with the intergovernmental Council of Ministers. The development of different tiers of multilevel governance – supranational, national and subnational – has created a constantly evolving legal and political framework with which interest groups and political organisations must engage. Against the backdrop of 'ever closer union' (Dinan, 2005), centuries-old traditions of national or state churches being given special political rights or status in the domestic societies of their respective member states are inevitably affected.

Fourteen EU member states continue to maintain a formal link between Church and State (Madeley and Enyedi 2003: 13), and as a result sustain official channels between religion and politics. As Mirjam Künkler and Michael Meyer-Resende explain, 'the relationship of the state to religious institutions in established democracies takes such a variety of forms that it is impossible to speak of one general pattern' (2007: 2). Yves Meny and Andrew Knapp highlight the European tradition of a 'dominant' church or religion 'marking' the political systems of both Italy in Southern Europe and the UK in Northern Europe (1998: 26). All the Nordic nation states – so often perceived to be socially liberal – have a tradition of sustaining the work of their respective Lutheran churches via taxation, although this practice is now much reduced in practical significance. In Denmark, for example, the Lutheran Church is still supported by the State under the Danish Constitution, and there is a minister for ecclesiastical affairs, that is, a cabinet member who handles the political side of Church affairs. Meanwhile in France there exists a strict separation of Church and State, but one Church – the Catholic Church – continues to 'dominate' what is still a relatively homogeneous society with 82 per cent of the population continuing to claim adherence in 2000 (Bale 2005: 25; Barrett *et al.* 2001).

One of the consequences of the dynamics of European integration is a challenge to justify the 'established' place of traditionally held values – and in two key ways. First, the development of supranational legislation in policy areas where emphasis is placed upon the shared and uniform fundamental rights of citizens across the EU has had a significant impact on the nature of this role. Churches are finding it increasingly difficult to justify their automatic right to unique political privileges such as state funding or legal exemptions – particularly in policy areas relating to education and employment where EU legislation seeks to ensure equal opportunities. Second, the wider 'hollowing out' of the conventional parameters of the nation state has led to Europe-wide political issues in the twenty-first century rendering the conventional model of Church and State relations more peripheral.

The contemporary debate concerning the nature of Europe's 'common values' is not merely theoretical. On a practical level, 'ever closer union' has involved the harmonisation of human rights and civil liberties across the EU. For example, British people are no longer simply 'subjects' of the Queen – they are EU citizens, with their freedoms protected by pan-European legislation, enshrined in the EU Charter of Fundamental Rights, and safeguarded by both the European Court of Justice and the European ombudsman. In policy areas such as education and employment, 'equal opportunities' are an important component of European law. As integration has advanced, European directives on laws in the workplace and schools have tightened up practices across different member states.

The issue of harmonising 'common values' goes to the very heart of the European integration project as it focuses on the sensitive political issue of 'foreign' values being 'imposed' upon traditionally independent territorial areas. For example, the British Conservative Party's enthusiasm for the type of free market economics represented by the EU is substantially tempered by its dislike of what it perceives to be the centralising and overly bureaucratic aspect of the Single Market. Euro-sceptics argue that there exists a quantifiable difference between conceding aspects of sovereignty for tangible economic benefits and an undemocratic body imposing unfamiliar laws (Holmes 2001). Supranational EU laws are at their most contentious when they are perceived to be alien to the values of an individual member state – for whatever reason. Defining the limits of human rights – and the nature of civil liberties – is a difficult and a delicate task, where compromise and harmonisation are not always easily achieved.

This problem was highlighted in 2004 when the Italian Christian Democrat politician Rocco Buttiglione was nominated to become the new EU commissioner for justice, freedom and security. His nomination was blocked by a group of Socialist, Green and Liberal/Democratic MEPs (Members of the European Parliament) who expressed 'reservations' that his devout Catholicism was incompatible with the role of promoting and protecting equal opportunities across Europe, with its distinctive 'union of values' (Charlemagne 2004). This was despite Buttiglione's assurance that he drew a clear distinction between the theological concept of a 'sin' and 'crimes' recognised by European law, and that he would feel entirely comfortable implementing the EU Charter of Fundamental Rights. In this context, we should note that the European Parliament maintains an all-party 'Platform for Secularism in Politics', originally known as the 'Working Group on Separation of Religion and Politics'. Its aim is to:

1. Identify issues pertaining to the intersection of religion and politics in which the political values and principles of the European Union are at stake;
2. Identify ways MEPs and civil society can work together to raise awareness of these issues;
3. Promote knowledge, understanding and acceptance of freedom of religion and non-religion, and the impartiality of the EU regarding organizations of faith and conviction;
4. Take action, where appropriate, to counter any attempts to undermine democracy, human rights and in particular women's rights and minority rights, sexual and reproductive health and rights, pluralism and the rule of law.

(European Parliament 2008)

The language used in the group's mission statement epitomises the wider debate over the role of religion within the EU: the Group is ostensibly concerned with maintaining a healthy balance between religion and politics, but also makes pejorative references to democratic values potentially being 'at stake' or 'undermined' by religious organisations.

In contrast, European leaders seem to ask for official recognition of the place of religion – and particularly Christianity – in the political development of the EU. German Chancellor Angela Merkel has backed Pope Benedict's call for the EU Reform Treaty to make reference to the importance of Europe's Christian values and heritage (Traynor 2007). In November 2007 Donald Tusk, the new Polish prime minister, announced that his government would refuse to sign the EU Charter of Fundamental Rights, as a result of concerns that some of the provisions relating to 'moral' or 'family' policy areas, namely same-sex marriages, would contradict domestic law in Poland.

Can there ever be compromise between such polar viewpoints, or is this type of conflict an everlasting process within the EU? Is it possible for a 'third way' to be developed between those who believe in moral relativism and those who stand for objective truth? Secular values are not necessarily being promoted as a consequence of antireligious sentiment – more as a consequence of the practical need for uniformity and consistency. The Buttiglione case was really more of a political dispute between the integrationist values of those serving on the European Commission and MEPs arguing for the safeguarding of individual freedoms, rather than between liberal, secular northern Europeans and conservatively religious Mediterraneans. Philosophical debates on the relationship between the State and the secular also have practical consequences for policymaking – and this applies to the wider debate on the role of religion in the new Europe. Churches are directly affected by new legislation and directives particularly when these challenge their right to hold a special status as the 'national' Church. In addition, churches are influenced by a change in 'political culture' (Almond and Verba 1963) initiated by the EU: the prevalence of equal opportunities, and a change of political status which means that the role of the nation state is no longer central and links between Church and State are also less important.

Strong parties, weak churches I: a decline in special privileges

The equalities agenda is prominent in the UK, and there are two dimensions to this – first, the general context of passing laws that ban discrimination on the grounds of sex, sexuality, race or disability. Second, the more specific application of those values to the way churches function and operate – the Christian Church has existed for over 2,000 years, and it existed long before terms such as 'gender balance' or 'progressive values' were developed, so it should come as no surprise that it often has difficulty adapting to the new policy environment where departing from a broad consensus in favour of equalities can sometimes appear hopelessly outdated. This section will examine the first dimension and the next section the second.

The special status enjoyed by the state churches is under constant challenge. In the spring of 2010, the Labour Government succeeded in passing into law its Equality Bill, one of its key 2005 manifesto commitments to harmonise and strengthen the various parts of anti-discrimination legislation that had already been introduced in the UK. One of its main objectives was to close the pay gap that continues to exist between men and women, which is also a key aim of the European Commission. The legislation also sought to entrench the equal rights of gay and transsexual employees, and it was this dimension that led both the Church of England and Catholic Church to be critical of the Labour Government's proposals. Indeed, in a rare victory for the Church in this particular area of social policy, Anglican bishops in the Lords succeeded in rejecting an amendment (216–178 votes) to the Bill proposing that religious organisations did not have the right to resist employing people whose personal lives did not comply with core Christian values. Meanwhile, the Pope reportedly urged his Catholic bishops in England and Wales to fight the entire Bill with 'missionary zeal' – his Church had lost a battle to continue its adoption agencies' practice of rejecting same sex couples as potential parents. Much of the Bill's content had its origins in the EU's Equal Treatment Directive (ETD), which came into effect in November 2000, and established a general framework for equal treatment in employment and occupation. The ETD prohibits discrimination against individuals in the workplace on the grounds of disability, sexual orientation, age or religion: 'Employment and occupation are key elements in guaranteeing equal opportunities for all and contribute strongly to the full participation of citizens in economic, cultural and social life . . .' (European Union 2000).

Our first example involves the Church of Scotland: in December 2005, referring to the ETD, the House of Lords ruled that the Revd Helen Percy, a minister in the Church, could take the Church to an employment tribunal after she was suspended from her post in 1997. The ETD covered working conditions, pay and dismissals as well as recruitment. Church lawyers had argued that because of the content of the 1921 Act, which stipulated that the Church alone can fully adjudicate in all matters of doctrine, worship, government and discipline in the Church, and that it is therefore 'subject to no civil authority', ministers were not protected by employment law in the same way as employees in other areas of work; that is, they did not have the same rights of procedure and appeal. The House of Lords interpretation of European law did not accept the legitimacy of that argument.

The Scottish legal system is distinctive from its English equivalent, which means that British-wide bills often have to be amended or revised before they can become law in Scotland. One of the consequences of this is that the Church of Scotland has full autonomy over the running of its affairs, including legal exemption from certain acts of parliament concerning employment rights. Traditionally, the Church's principal clerk (who, as well as being an ordained minister, is legally trained) acts as the Church's 'chief executive', setting up ad hoc courts to deal with cases such as that of Revd Percy. However, while the Percy case was eventually settled out of court in October 2006, a new legal precedent was set, with the Church's automatic exemptions from standard elements of employment law being challenged. The concept of national churches being able to conduct their affairs without any interference from the State was judged to conflict with the spirit of the ETD.

A second example of EU employment legislation impacting upon a church comes from the area of education – as a consequence of the 1918 Education Act the Catholic Church possesses more de facto importance in Scottish society than at national level. The main teachers' union in Scotland, the Educational Institute of Scotland (EIS), has regularly shown signs of frustration that Catholic teachers have an inherent advantage over their non-denominational colleagues when applying for promoted jobs in Catholic schools. Appointments of teachers are made in accordance with the wishes of the representatives of the Catholic Church on the local authority education committee. Non-Catholic teachers can be hired to work in Catholic schools; however, they cannot be promoted as they are not allowed to teach Religious Education or to handle related pastoral issues. In May 2007 the EIS publicly cited the European Convention on Human Rights as the basis for arguing that no teacher should be denied a job on 'religious or moral grounds' (Denholm 2007). The issues involved are also relevant to the ETD, which specifically refers to equal opportunities in relation to promotion, as well as recruitment and dismissals. The EIS stance dates back to 1979, when a motion was passed at its annual conference calling for religious integration in schools. However, employment rights lawyers have continued to show an interest in the case, and since 1999 the EIS has resolved to 'formulate a policy on campaigning for denominational schools' abolition – subject to the consent of churches and parents' (Devine 2000: 163). There have been various tribunals involving teachers who have been blocked from promotion in denominational Scottish schools as a consequence.

In the context of EU politics, both churches' special status is being challenged by individuals or groups who believe they should be brought 'into line' with other employers – and they are responding accordingly to protect their interests. EU 'fundamental rights' are having a practical impact upon everyday life – and the advancement of equal opportunities and civil liberties do not always sit particularly comfortably with traditional religious values. Constitutional anomalies are inevitably going to be ironed out as member states grow ever closer. New political institutions promulgate new laws and the place of older values is re-evaluated in the process.

In November 2006 the decision of British Airways to stop one of its flight attendants from wearing a cross prominently around her neck prompted senior figures in the Church of England, including the archbishops of Canterbury and York and the bishop of London, to speak out strongly in her defence. The debate was particularly intense because it involved Britain's 'national carrier', with many of the subsequent criticisms focusing on the country's Christian heritage and traditions. Dr John Sentamu, the archbishop of York, stated that 'British Airways needs to look again at this decision and . . . at the history of the country it represents, whose culture, laws, heritage and tradition owes so much to the very same symbol it would ban' (BBC News, 21 November 2006). Ultimately the Church won the argument and in January 2007 the airline dropped the ban. The British Airways case represented a challenge to the traditionally prominent political role of the Church of England similar to the challenge in the Scottish case to the political status and behaviour of the Scottish churches.

The Church of England exerts considerable power among the British political establishment, as we know – however, in the context of the British Airways row, the established Church became a rather less powerful interest group. Its most senior clergy were compelled to speak out on behalf of Anglican communicants in the modern workplace to defend the right of people to wear the most recognisable symbol of Christianity while working for British Airways. In contrast to the Percy and EIS cases in Scotland, European law was not directly involved. The airline did not seek to justify its ban on the grounds that it was adhering to EU legislation. Nevertheless, a very similar pattern can be identified here in that a traditionally dominant church in an EU member state was compelled to take radical political action in order to 'defend' its place in its own domestic society, with the harmonised and secular political values of the EU again playing a prominent role. Indeed, in April 2010, a similar case involving a nurse wishing to wear a cross concluded less successfully, with the employment tribunal finding in favour of the NHS Trust, on the grounds that it went against health and safety regulations.

The fact that British Airways took a decision of this nature is itself a statement about the role of religion and/or Christianity in modern Europe. The decision reflects a wider trend across Western Europe: churches are no longer automatically powerful. It suggests that the values of churches are not as important as the secular equal opportunities or civil liberties expounded by the EU. The political power of the Church has been substantially altered. The 'non-decision making' model of Peter Bachrach and Morton Baratz (1970: 9) sees controversial items being deliberately kept off the political agenda by political elites. Steven Lukes (1974: 23) goes further than Bachrach and Baratz, arguing that power can also be exercised by 'shaping or determining' the entire political climate, so that individuals are not even aware they are being influenced. As the political climate of European integration develops, and the unassailable status of equalities grows, churches in the EU are increasingly forced to be much more proactive in order to protect their interests. In Denmark, for example, the Lutheran Church has set up an office in Brussels to lobby on behalf of 'liberal Protestants' in Europe, linking in with representatives from Swedish, Finnish and German churches. The Conference of European Churches already maintains an EU office in Brussels to liaise with the decision makers.

Indeed, France provides a helpful comparative example of the secular culture of the EU challenging religious values. The French Catholic Church was a powerful institution at the start of the twentieth century but in 1905 a law was passed in order to curtail its political influence. French society remains relatively homogeneous, with only 8 per cent of its current population made up of ethnic minorities (Bale 2005: 25; Barrett *et al.* 2001), and the de facto influence of the Catholic Church has remained across France, in terms of its values and culture, in a similar way to the national churches of Scotland and England. France's revolutionary tradition, however, provides an interesting contrast with the tradition that has evolved in some 'Protestant' nations of empowering the Church's involvement in politics by linking it to the State. In 2004 the comprehensive separation of Church and State in France was brought up to date as the Chirac government resolved to apply the secular principle to the case of 'conspicuous' ('ostensible') religious symbols in the classroom.

The French parliament subsequently banned pupils from wearing Muslim headscarves (the most high-profile and contentious aspect of the new law), Sikh turbans, Jewish skullcaps or 'prominent' Christian crosses in state schools, arguing that these practices contradicted the principle of *laïcité* embodied in the 1905 law that formally separated Church and State. The impact of European integration can be perceived here. The twenty-first-century French application of Church–State separation is in keeping with the harmonised neutral values of a secular EU – but somewhat alien to the British context. Parallels can also be drawn with the British Airways controversy, in that both have international and supranational implications, rather than simply being restricted to domestic politics. The question of how modern, multicultural political systems define the boundary between religion and politics is not only a British or French debate but a European issue – but that in itself has a major impact on domestic politics.

Strong parties, weak churches II: the repeal of 'Section 28'

So far, we have painted a picture of the Christian Church in Britain (Anglican, Presbyterian and Roman Catholic) floundering somewhat among a wash of supra-national and domestic equalities legislation. No better case of this can be identified than the repeal of 'Clause 28, Section 2A of the Local Government Act 1988' – known as 'Section 28' – which banned the 'promotion' of homosexuality in schools. This section will examine this in detail as it offers us the best example of the increasingly desperate lengths some branches of the Christian Church will go to, to try to halt what they regard as the sweeping tide of secularism that has overwhelmed Britain.

The Act had been passed by the then Conservative Government. While the then Prime Minister, Mrs Thatcher, was an economic libertarian, she was morally conservative, and this piece of legislation epitomised that traditionalist approach towards the family and the maintenance of the key structures of British society. It was also a convenient instrument to utilise in her battle with Labour-run local authorities, whose entire social policy agenda stood contrary to her core political philosophy. However, in one fell swoop, the Conservatives effectively lost an entire generation of gay voters who, while economically right-wing, could not bring themselves to vote Conservative.

Over ten years later, the issue would once again come to the fore of British party politics. One of the first acts of the new Labour–Liberal Democrat-run Scottish Executive, post-devolution, was to repeal 'Section 28'. The Act was viewed by the newly devolved Scottish Executive as a piece of 1980s Conservative legislation that an autonomous Scottish Parliament should abolish, but in the process underestimated the views of 'conservative' Scotland. In a national private referendum funded by the multimillionaire owner of Stagecoach and evangelical Christian, Brian Souter, and vigorously supported by the Scottish Catholic Church, 1,094,440 people voted against repealing the Act. While the Scottish Executive pressed ahead with repeal (albeit in a watered-down version), the episode remains one of the most divisive in devolved Scottish politics. Relations between Souter and Scottish Catholic leaders and the Labour Party were irrevocably damaged by it. The more competitive party system offered by devolution has presented opportunities for the former to punish the latter.

By the early summer of 2007, the issue had reappeared for a third time – this was an eventful period for those interested in the politics of regional United

Kingdom governance. On 3 May, the Scottish National party (SNP) narrowly won the Scottish Parliament election,[2] while on 27 June, Gordon Brown, a Labour MP for a Scottish constituency, became British prime minister. Together, these events raised the question of whether the cohesion of the United Kingdom was loosening, exactly 300 years after the Act of Union. Brown gained control of Downing Street just as his party had lost power in Scotland – highlighting the constitutional anomalies linked to Scottish MPs legislating on English matters, but the reverse not being possible due to asymmetric devolution. Questions of self-determination and national identity have become the concern of the whole of the United Kingdom, not just its geographic peripheries, with proposed reforms ranging from the introduction of regional assemblies in England to the exclusion of Scottish MPs from voting on matters that do not directly concern them.

The 2007 Scottish Parliament election campaign was punctuated by highly significant interventions from two of the country's most prominent 'conservative' Christians, offering their support to the aims and objectives of the Scottish National party. First, a substantial donation of £500,000 was made to SNP funds by Mr Souter – this monetary gift constituted the largest sum ever received by the SNP and helped the party run a very effective election campaign. Second, the most senior figure in the Catholic Church in Scotland, Cardinal Keith O'Brien, Archbishop of St Andrews and Edinburgh, publicly endorsed the SNP's 'Independence in Europe' objectives (BBC News, 15 October 2006). His intervention demonstrated a radical departure from the established link between the Labour party and Catholic voters in Scotland.

This institutional relationship between faith-based interests and the SNP requires closer analysis. The 2007 SNP manifesto makes no mention of specific social policies relating to moral issues or religious faith, yet significant public Christian figures viewed the party as being their most attractive voting option. The closest the manifesto comes to even mentioning religion is where it states that 'the SNP will not promote or support legislation or policies which discriminate on the grounds of race, disability, age, gender, faith or religion, social background or sexual orientation' (Scottish National Party 2007a: 66). Indeed, looked at within an even wider context, the SNP is a self-professed 'civic' nationalist movement, placing the emphasis on the socio-economic benefits of independence from the UK, and explicitly distancing itself from issues relating to personal identity or values. In a speech to the Council on Foreign Relations in New York City in October 2007, SNP leader Alex Salmond stated:

> the re-emergence of Scotland is based on a peaceful, inclusive, civic nationalism – one born of tolerance and respect for all faiths, colours and creeds and one which will continue to inspire constitutional evolution based on a positive vision of what our nation can be. Our nationalism is not one fuelled by negativity but rather is one inspired by hope.
>
> (Salmond 2007)

Furthermore, evidence from the 2000 Scottish Social Attitudes Survey suggests that SNP identifiers constitute the least religious group of any of the party supporters – 49 per cent claim not to belong to any religion while only 13 per cent of those do attend church on a regular basis (Curtice *et al.* 2002: 99–100).

This chapter offers two explanations for this apparent anomaly, both of which are linked to the improved political opportunity structures created by devolution: (1) the immediate consequences of introducing a proportional representation electoral system has allowed faith-based interests to 'punish' Labour and the Liberal Democrats for repealing 'Section 28'; (2) those same interests are attracted by the even greater autonomy over social policy formulation that would be delivered by an independent Scotland. The term 'political opportunity structure' has its origins in the American literature on the activity of social movements but has been applied in a range of different contexts. Indeed, there has been much dispute over the specific meaning of the concept although Doug McAdam clarifies its four key dimensions thus: 'the relative openness or closure of the institutionalized political system'; 'the stability or instability of that broad set of elite arguments that typically undergird a polity'; 'the presence or absence of allies'; and 'the state's capacity and propensity for repression' (McAdam 1996: 27). The first three dimensions are particularly pertinent to the discussion that follows. In terms of the consequences of improved opportunities, McAdam argues that as well as frequently mentioned dependent variables such as 'the timing of collective action' and 'the outcomes of movement activity', scholars should also be concerned with 'movement form' or tactics (McAdam 1996: 29), and it is this last variable that this chapter will focus on predominantly.

The SNP's 2007 election campaign was helped substantially by both Cardinal O'Brien's endorsement and by Brian Souter's donation. The latter was the largest ever gift received by the party – it was singled out for special mention in a press release praising Souter as 'one of the outstanding entre-preneurs of his generation, totally self-made and hugely successful' (Scottish National Party 2007b). Some political commentators at the time argued that Souter's donation would allow the SNP to 'outspend' Labour (Barnes 2007) and by December 2007 this was proven to be the case when the Electoral Commission released its official figures showing that the former had spent £1,383,462 compared with the latter's £1,102,866 (Electoral Commission 2007).

The SNP's campaign involved a significant amount of advertising activity, with pictures of Alex Salmond and Nicola Sturgeon, the party's deputy leader, appearing on large billboards in Scottish towns and cities, and also in national newspapers. Election literature was posted directly to Scottish households, while recorded voice messages from Salmond were left on thousands of voters' telephones. Salmond himself used a helicopter to tour every part of the country – the only party leader able to afford to do so. There was even the introduction of 'SNP tv' – an online television series broadcast nightly on the party website in an attempt to appeal to younger voters. It is impossible to prove that Souter's donation helped the SNP win the election but there is no doubt that it made a significant and positive contribution to the party's campaign. However, as a consequence of Souter's very prominent set of conservative Christian values – he is an active member and financial backer of the evangelical Church of the Nazarene in Perth – there existed an element of controversy about his substantial donation to the SNP.

Meanwhile, the Cardinal's intervention becomes even more significant when it is placed against the backdrop of the important role played by self-identifying Catholic voters in the sustained electoral success of the Scottish Labour party. In terms of parliamentary representation at Westminster, Labour has been the largest political party in Scotland since 1959, and has also consistently maintained its percentage share of the vote, rarely dipping below 40 per cent. In 1989, James Kellas wrote that the 'Catholic voter contributes in no small measure to the continuity of Labour support in Scotland and to the weakness of the SNP' (Kellas 1989: 110), while looking at evidence from the first Scottish Parliament Election Survey results in 1999, Lindsay Paterson *et al.* argue that 'across all models, religion plays an important part in distinguishing between Labour and SNP support, Roman Catholics being less likely to vote for the SNP'; they conclude that this long-established pattern has not yet been disrupted by the 'new politics' of devolution (Paterson *et al.* 2001: 63). According to evidence from the British and Scottish Election Study series, 68 per cent of Catholics voted Labour at the 1959 general election while in 1997, 81 per cent did so. In contrast, Catholic support for the SNP had not risen above 20 per cent in the same period (Seawright 1999: 97). In their analysis of the 2001 Scottish Social Attitudes Survey, Steve Bruce and Tony Glendinning (2003: 99) also conclude that Catholics remain less likely to vote SNP than Protestants,[3] while Paterson's analysis of the 2003 Survey also confirms this (Paterson 2006: 52). For Cardinal O'Brien to recommend that people should vote SNP was as significant a moment in Scottish politics as Brian Souter helping the party outspend Labour for the first time at a Scottish election – and ultimately win.

Since the first devolved elections in 1999, the SNP has gradually become a credible party of government, aided by the proportional, mixed member (MMP) electoral system. The system involves two votes – one to elect constituency MSPs (a total of seventy-three) and one to elect the regional list MSPs (a total of fifty-six). This system has helped to break the decades-long Labour domination of Scottish politics and allowed interest groups to use the more competitive nature of devolved elections to their advantage – for example, if a majoritarian system had been used, Labour would still have won thirty-seven out of seventy-three constituencies in 2007, compared with the SNP's twenty-one. A general election campaign does not offer the same sort of opportunities for Scottish interest groups – voting patterns remain stable with Labour winning forty out of fifty-nine Scottish constituencies in 2005. However, a devolved election is quite different – in 2003, seven parties and three independents gained representation at Holyrood, and in 2007 the SNP offered the best opportunity to inflict longer-term electoral harm on Labour, having formed the Official Opposition since 1999.

While conceding that the pattern across advanced industrial democracies is not always uniform, Russell Dalton and Mark Gray argue that

> enlargement of the electoral marketplace should mean increased access and influence on politics for the public, and thus represents an expansion of the democratic process. The creation of new venues for citizen input . . . provide new avenues for interests that might not be well represented in other electoral forums.
>
> (Dalton and Gray 2003: 35)

A more competitive party system offers improved opportunities for interest groups of all types – not just faith-based organisations. Also, while not the focus of this chapter, the fact that small parties such as the Scottish Christian party and the Scottish Christian Peoples Alliance have put forward an increasing number of candidates at devolved elections illustrates this point further – for example, another senior Scottish Catholic clergyman, Bishop Joseph Devine, chose to endorse publicly the Scottish Christian Peoples Alliance in the run-up to the 2007 election, publicly citing the Labour government's introduction of civil partnerships as one of his reasons (BBC News, 11 March 2007). At a UK level, such an endorsement would be futile, but at a devolved level it has much more impact.

Such behaviour on the part of interest groups is essentially tactical (see McAdam, 1996: 29–31) – it is possible that, at some point in the future, Labour will also benefit from greater party competition in Scotland if the SNP government takes policy decisions with which faith-based interests disagree, causing them to turn to the next largest party for an alternative electoral option. In other words, the change to a proportional electoral system may have long-term consequences but the specific impact upon group activity is relatively fluid in the short term. However, as the next section will discuss, there is also evidence that, in any case, these interests are adopting a fundamentally more long-term strategy.

Even prior to legislative devolution, Scotland enjoyed a great deal of autonomy owing to administrative devolution – a consequence of the incremental recognition that it had social needs distinct from other parts of the UK, especially in the post-war era. The gradual growth in power of the Scottish Office, after its founding in 1885, reflected an acknowledgement that central government in London was a blunt tool and insensitive to the 'special needs' of education, health and social care professionals on the ground in Scotland (see Mitchell 2003). Indeed, many of these can actually be traced back centuries to the distinctive traditions of the Scottish legal, educational and religious institutions that continued to operate after the Act of Union with England in 1707. Today, the Scottish government has devolved responsibility for social policy areas linked to marriage, adoption and divorce, as well as matters as diverse as the role of religious education in schools and initiatives aimed at tackling the high levels of alcohol and drug consumption in Scotland. Together, these provide a range of targeted focal points for faith-based groups interested in exerting influence.

Indeed, the Scottish Parliament was founded on the four key principles of power sharing, accountability, accessibility and equal opportunities (Consultative Steering Group 1999: 5) so the prospects of political influence are actually explicitly made more realistic. A natural corollary of this is that an independent Scottish Parliament, as advocated by the SNP, would have even more power over these policy areas – and with fewer competing interests. In other words, while devolution is not the same as independence, it does establish the premise that Scotland should have greater autonomy over these areas of social policy, and as Christopher Ansell and Jane Gingrich argue, '[a]ccess is easiest when government is within practical reach of the citizenry' (Ansell and Gingrich 2003: 140). So, unlike the previous example where we see the interests playing a short-term party-political game, here we see them actually attempt to improve the long-term political opportunity structures themselves.

For example, in his account of the campaign for devolution in the 1990s, BBC Scotland political editor, Brian Taylor, highlights the deliberate way the Scottish Catholic hierarchy campaigned to have the issue of abortion devolved to Edinburgh, in the hope that it could have more political influence in that area of legislation (Taylor 1999: 140). Ultimately, this was destined to be a futile campaign but a greater scope for influence over the areas of social policy already mentioned was secured. For the 2007 election, the Church actually composed an official questionnaire for Catholic parishioners to put before Scottish Parliament candidates, and it also provides an indication of the sort of devolved policy concerns of its leaders: first, and perhaps most prevalent, are 'family values', for example, the dislike of civil partnerships, 'gay adoption' and so-called 'quickie divorces'; second, the protection of denominational Catholic state schools; and third, the protection of the 'sanctity of life' in relation to abortion and stem-cell research (BBC News, 15 April 2007).

In October 2006, six months before the Holyrood elections, Cardinal O'Brien announced in a newspaper interview that he would be 'happy' if Scotland became an independent nation state:

> There is currently some frustration among the Scots about the say they have over what happens here, and that is part of what is pushing the independence movement. I can see this coming, perhaps not in the next few years, but before too long.
>
> (BBC News, 15 October 2006)

It is interesting to note the emphasis the Cardinal places on having 'a say over what happens here' – he is implying that independence would secure an even greater devolution of power, and therefore increased influence over social policy areas of interest. Alex Salmond commented: 'Scotland's Cardinal is a man of vision and stature. Obviously he avoids party politics but I am delighted that he has issued positive signals about independence and self-determination for the nation' (BBC News, 15 October 2006).

Meanwhile, at the time of his donation being made public, Brian Souter stated:

> As long as I can remember, the case for the union has been hugely financed by cash from London, while the case for independence has lacked resources. I hope my donation will help redress this imbalance . . . The time has come for Alex Salmond to deliver a dynamic government in Scotland which will respect our past, respond to our present problems and reflect the future aspirations of the Scottish people.
>
> (Hutcheon 2007)

These comments can be compared with those made by Cardinal O'Brien, and suggest similar motivations. The point about a future government 'respect[ing] our past' could be a reference to the fact that Scotland's 'moral climate' is traditionally more conservative than the rest of the UK's.[4] While referring to the Scottish Executive's 'Section 28' repeal plans in one appearance on the BBC's Question Time programme, Souter even went so far as to argue that 'Islington morality' should not be 'forced' upon 'Scottish children' (Gray and Milmo 2000). This can be likened to the greater levels of religiosity that exist in the United States, compared with Western Europe (see Norris and Inglehart 2004: 72–3), and their respective distinctive political cultures.

In 2007, Souter's motivations were interpreted by some as being one-dimensional; that is, he supports Scottish independence for reasons connected to his 'Section 28' campaign – and for the same sort of structuralist reasons as the Scottish Green party and the Scottish Socialist party – as an expedient means to a specific political end. The Green MSP, Patrick Harvie, urged all parties to condemn homophobia after Souter's donation was publicised:

> I call on all parties standing in the Scottish election to disassociate themselves from homophobic prejudice such as Mr Souter's former political enterprise. It is essential that serious politicians avoid any taint of pandering to bigotry, whether that be racial, religious, homophobic or any other kind.
>
> (BBC News, 17 March 2007)

Indeed, so controversial was Souter's electoral involvement that the SNP's deputy leader even felt the need publicly to deny that the donation was anything to do with a 'moral agenda' (Hutcheon, 2007). The outcome of the

'Section 28' debate might have been viewed as a failure by Souter and the Catholic Church but it nevertheless demonstrated that some sort of direct influence could be exerted more easily than was the case prior to devolution. As Catherine Bromley *et al.* (2006: 6) argue, the 'incident left many a minister rather bruised, and it perhaps inclined them thereafter to exercise caution in their pronouncements on social and moral issues'. Furthermore, the episode reinforced the basic premise upon which devolution was founded – that Scotland should have direct autonomy over areas of public policy where values distinctive from the rest of the UK have existed. Indeed, while 'Section 28' was ostensibly a gay rights issue, it was also very much an issue related to education – one of the three fundamental pillars of the Scottish political system, along with law and religion, and an area where practitioners are particularly sensitive about what constitutes Scottish good practice. One of the criticisms made of the Conservative government in the 1980s was that it did not respect Scottish educational traditions (see Paterson 1994) and this may have played a part in the thinking of the newly devolved administration when it decided to tackle the issue in the first place. Regardless, if a political consensus exists that Scottish problems are best tackled with Scottish solutions, it is easy to see how some interest groups feel there exists an even better way of having their 'solutions' implemented – via independence.

This part of the book has not chosen to focus on the Scottish dimension to the 'Section 28' episode solely because it was more prominent there – it also highlights a very important point. Conservative Christians are willing to take any measures they can – even support the break-up of the UK – if it would help them achieve their objectives. It also neatly shows how, regardless of the context – European or sub-national – the influence is the same. Indeed, we see a similar pattern in the US where pro-life campaigners argue that the States should have more power, not for some idealistic notion of constitutional purism but for highly rational and expedient reasons – they hope that many states, if they had the autonomy over outlawing abortion, would do so, and the Supreme Court in Washington would have no jurisdiction. Scottish independence offers some evangelical Protestants and Conservative Catholics their best hope of exerting their own influence. Despite the heated public debate over the repeal of Section 28 in 2000, Peter Kearney argues the Catholic Church regards the outcome of the debate as a failure. The legislation was watered down slightly, and the combined campaigning of Winning, Brian Souter and the *Daily Record* contributed to that change, but the 'Clause' was still repealed, and the Church did not achieve its objectives, according to Kearney (Interview with author, 25 March 2002).

Furthermore, Winning's numerous strongly worded public statements also suggest he was not as politically astute as many believed. Some of his pronouncements were ill-advised, for example his comparing the gay lobby in Britain with Nazis during the Section 28 controversy. As Bruce and Glendinning argue (2003), 'when pronouncements on personal sexual behaviour are least popular with churchgoers and very unpopular with the rest of the population, frequent press attention to the Church's teachings in these areas may have done nothing to improve its popularity'. Parry also hints at this paradox, alluding to Winning's 'attention-grabbing comments on the issues of the day and his fearlessness in mixing it with politicians, virtually none of whom could align themselves completely with his mix of theological conservatism and social radicalism' (2002: 145).

Once again, we see rational choice in relation to public opinion at play in British party politics.

Conclusions

While the European Union institutions have not always been directly involved in all these cases, they are responsible for helping to create a secular political climate that is questioning the role of religion across European societies, including the UK (see the 'multiple modernities' thesis, page 10). They have wider implications for Church–State relations, employment rights and interest-group politics. Churches can no longer expect automatically to enjoy a pre-eminent position in their domestic societies, and the traditionally close formal relationship between politics and religion in most European nation states has been fundamentally altered. Brussels is increasingly providing a focus for churches to lobby decision makers for their own ends, becoming one interest group among many, albeit one with potentially substantial influence.

Meanwhile, it can be cautiously argued that the 2007 Scottish Parliament election marked another stage of development in the role of religious interest groups in British politics, following the trend away from the established Western European model of official Church–State relations (see Madeley and Enyedi 2003), and towards a more pluralist American-style system where a variety of different types of religious lobbies – but often conservative, evangelical or fundamentalist – are highly prominent, if not highly influential, voices. That is not to argue that there has also been an increase in the political influence of religious groups or individuals in Western Europe – for one thing, such an argument is impossible to substantiate. However, it is true to say that the sort of structuralist changes involved in devolution or secession discussed here clearly have direct behavioural consequences. In the same way that Robert Putnam has shown that the presently transitional nature of the role of religion in American society has had political consequences (Putnam, 2000: 161), we can see similar trends developing in Western Europe – the traditional nation state is being hollowed out both from above (by the EU) and from below (via devolution and federalism) and the official model of one 'national' Church comprehensively reflecting national values is also concurrently being challenged.

Chapter 6 concluded that it was little wonder British politicians did not 'do God' – this chapter shows that, while the British churches 'do politics', the balance of political power between the different players in the game is quite different.

8 Conclusions

The British model of politics and religion

British politics is in something of a state of flux. The New Labour project that promised to reshape and renew the UK is now over, and an era of coalition government has begun. The constitutional reforms that, in many ways, were the hallmark of Tony Blair's time as Prime Minister, look set to continue with electoral reform, the power of recall and fixed term parliaments just some of the many proposals being considered. The expenses scandal of 2009, coupled with the international economic downturn, plunged the previously serene world of Westminster politics into crisis, with the number of MPs retiring in 2010 the largest single total (150 out of 646) since the war. It remains to be seen how deeply the crisis will affect the way that party politics are conducted in the UK but the problem that lay at the heart of it was about much more than simply parliamentary privileges being abused: the very real anger British voters felt in the summer of 2009 was the result of a dismay at the way their elected representatives had lost sight of their core role – to serve the public – and instead focused on serving themselves. The entire concept of career (not necessarily professional) politicians who climb their way up the party ladder into heady positions of power without really experiencing real life or holding down a real job is being rethought as politicians of all parties try desperately to reconnect with British voters, and convince them that they are 'just like them'.

It is not within the scope of this book to analyse any of this in too much depth – however, this book is as much about British politics as it is about religion and politics, and the way the institutional framework shifts and develops is very relevant indeed. The main argument of this book has not been that religion 'still matters' to British electoral and party politics – it has been to argue that it now matters in a different way, and one that requires to be taken seriously by scholars. The rise of ethical and human rights-based issues, the role of churches acting as modern interest groups, mixed with a greater fluidity in electoral behaviour as a consequence of partisan dealignment, have combined to create an environment where the power of Christianity as a values-based movement has been refreshed and reset.

When assessing the role of religion in a modern advanced industrial democracy such as the UK, there is a need to do more than simply track downward trends in normal Sunday church attendance, or point to the absence of a confessional party, or even, the lack of religious-based conflict. While the last aspect was relevant to the political context in Northern Ireland for many decades, the peace process has also taken away attention from that dimension of British politics, which, in any case, was not a focus of the study. A more rational approach is more insightful – it reveals a picture of a powerful Christian lobby in certain areas of social policy, as well as wider correlations between voting behaviour and Christian values. The shifting sands of Westminster politics may take time before settling down again, and the role of religious-based actors is critical.

Meanwhile, for international scholars of politics and religion, Britain provides an interesting case – the lack of a written constitution makes the way British party politicians deal with crucial life and conscience-based issues very important. There are signs that this aspect is starting to increasingly attract the attention of political scientists (for example, see Kettell 2009b), both in terms of the parameters of the debate, but also the way the actors seek to deal with the issues – for example, the role of the Church bishops in the House of Lords. The present author would argue that there is still a need for comparative political behaviour specialists to more methodically separate out the difference between the politics of immigration, and the security-related issues of the post 9/11 world, and voting behaviour at elections/party behaviour. In the same way that party scholars have ignored immigration as a factor too much in the past, they have also started to move away from religion, despite the different dimensions that have been discussed. 'The Christian Church is very difficult to take on – it has over 2000 years of experience . . .' (Sophie in't Veld, MEP, Interview with author, 9 April 2010). There is something about Sophie in't Veld's comment that fits in with this view. First, it encapsulates very effectively the argument that, just because people do not agree with Christianity or believe in God, does not mean that they can simply ignore it as a political or social actor; second, it also successfully articulates the idea that, just because church attendances have been falling in recent decades in Western Europe, it does not mean that either they will continue to fall indefinitely or that such a fall need necessarily be linked to a commensurate decline in political influence – as the British case proves, churches are well organised and often politically astute institutions that continue to hold a great deal of power and influence.

This book was divided into three main sections – political behaviour, Church–State relations and religious issues. Rather than simply repeat or recap solely what has been covered in those three sections, this concluding chapter will, instead, be divided into two main parts in order to set out the main, overarching arguments of the monograph: 1) the rise in issue-based voting connected to a range of social policy areas; and 2) the way the British parties respond rationally to this. It will then finish with a short section discussing the overarching field of the study, namely the relationship between religion and political participation in a Western European context, and where the British case fits in to that interface.

That key dimension is linked to the question of whether or not there is such a thing as a British 'model' or 'case' of religion and politics; more precisely, whether there is an exclusively British relationship between Christianity and representative democracy – that was effectively the research question for the book as a whole, and the one that this chapter will seek to address in its final thoughts. It centres on the overarching theme of the way a two-thousand-year-old ideology such as Christianity relates to an essentially modern and constantly developing concept such as representative democracy. Put slightly more directly, we are obliged to ask: is Christianity good for quality of democracy and social capital issues in Britain? If it is, then it can probably be much more convincingly argued that a 'British model' does not simply fit neatly into the established party structure of Western Europe, but rather offers a distinctive typological alternative, given what has already been said about the secularist European traditions. It also compounds the foolishness of ignoring religion in the British context, on the false premise that society is at such a high level of secularisation that it does not merit the effort.

Falling political participation in general is one of the great challenges facing advanced industrial democracies in Western Europe and North America – the British expenses scandal mentioned at the start of the chapter is merely replicating in different ways corrupt Congressmen in Washington along with some of the less savoury sides of the Brussels lobbying industry. Disillusion with democratic politics at a time of unprecedented predominance of democracies around the world is not an oxymoron – in fact, it represents the very high standards that voters in countries such as the UK expect from their elected representatives. Tying in such themes to the role of religion in democratic politics is both timely and sensible – this book has tried to do more than simply chart in a descriptive way how Christianity and politics mix in Britain; instead, it has applied a rational choice theoretical framework in order to explain why Christianity and politics mix in Britain, arguing that while a more institutionalist approach is not without its merits, it fails to reveal the true extent of the political influence of Christianity in British politics and government, as well as the reasons for that.

There is a great deal of evidence that British politicians respect the political role of the various mainstream denominations of the Christian Church, partly because it is expedient to do so from a public opinion perspective (with positive cost benefits), but also partly because the British Christian Church has shown itself to be capable of acting in a way that is compatible with the basic principles of democracy. In many other Western member states in the EU, an *institutional* explanation is much more satisfactory when looking at the link between religion and politics – the persistence of organisations such as the Christian Democrats means that that relationship is much more about structuralism than rationalism. Christian Democracy is itself an ideology that can trace its origins back to a wide-scale distrust of the influence of Christianity in politics which necessitated a partisan response. The absence of this from British politics is not a reason for scholars to ignore religion but, on the contrary, a very good reason to study it in more depth, applying a different methodological framework.

Linked to this, while the 'religious economy' has its roots as a concept in the American literature, it should be stressed once more that this book has not attempted to get involved in issues of whether or not political structures – including state churches – have an impact upon societal religiosity (which is firmly within the rational choice domain and the economics of religion). Rather, it is arguing the reverse – that the existence of state churches such as the Church of England and the Church of Scotland, along with other factors such as distinctive party organisational structures, has an impact upon political behaviour and subsequently public policymaking. The American model has provided the inspiration but not an exact template for this study of the British case, although that in itself is interesting given the deeper links that exist between the UK and the US, and the sometimes fraught relationship the former has with the EU.

Valence voting and issue politics: the rational base

Ultimately, by applying a public choice framework, *Christianity and Party Politics* makes the argument that a distinctively 'British model' is the consequence of the continuing importance of religious-based voting behaviour – including both the denominational *cleavage* but also the relationship between religiosity and factors such as party choice and overall turn-out – to British electoral politics. Chapter 2 argued that the religious cleavage therefore remains strong in British party politics. This is especially significant when we consider the growing influence of single issue, postmodern politics, where British politicians and parties have to deal with challenges such as how to legislate stem cell research or define equal rights within an employment and education context where definitions are often less than two-dimensional. Chapters 6 and 7 discussed the rise of more *conscience-based* issues related to equalities and ethics – Christian values clearly still matter to British politics because it is *rational* for them to still matter. The religious economy can be seen – within the British context, at least – to be both multidimensional, and flowing in more than one direction. The issue marketplace gives churches a voice as interest groups which significantly neutralises any commensurate decline in their influence that may come with a decline in their attendance figures (and that is not even taking into account the fact that many British voters do still attend/identify with a church – see Chapter 2).

As Chapter 2 argued, while it would be wrong to suggest that somehow elections in Britain are won or lost on the basis of religious beliefs – as some scholars have argued is the case in US Congressional ballots – the religious vote remains substantial enough that the parties rationally respond by respecting it, and listening carefully to it. The way that vote manifests itself is twofold: first, there continues to be a split in the Christian vote between

Protestants voting Conservative and Catholics voting Labour. On the face of it, such a split could be interpreted as being either irrelevant, given the numbers involved in some cases (for example, non-conformists voting Liberal), or even counterproductive to the overall aggregate influence of the Christian message/lobby. However, what is clear is that these divisions continue to have resonance primarily because they have practical party political ramifications.

The Labour Party – rationally – continues to be conscious of the Catholic vote, knowing that it is still a secure base for electoral support. That is not to say that this relationship does not encounter strain sometimes – like all relationships – especially when the Labour Government is advancing its equalities agenda, or being forced to legislate to facilitate scientific progress, but the overall picture is one of respect and an awareness of sensitivities. At a time of declining membership as well as a declining share of the vote (it has been falling sharply since 1997), the metropolitan, think tank-obsessed Labour leadership is simply unable – electorally – to be dismissive of ordinary, working-class Catholics who regard the party as their own. Similarly, the Conservatives continue to align themselves to the values of the Church of England, the Monarchy and the Union, believing that these traditional institutions and structures provide security and stability. A new green logo and a photogenic leader have not altered the fundamental beliefs of the party. The image of the Tory Party as the party of the establishment while Labour looks after the working class, including immigrants from other ethnic minority groups, is a powerful one, and loaded with political capital. The Christian dimension to that interface is both central and ongoing.

Indeed, the fact that Britain diverges from the rest of Europe and sees its Catholic vote go to socialists rather than conservatives is itself worthy of comment. Ultimately, it is the result of class – Catholics, concentrated in large British urban centres such as Liverpool and Glasgow after nineteenth-century immigration from Ireland, voted Labour to protect their socio-economic interests, which were more of a priority at the time, rather than their religious beliefs. However, such a pattern does not remove religion from British party politics – rather it, first of all, still disperses the Christian vote across parties, and second, means that the Catholic Church can still exert pressure from within, often via Catholic MPs in the House of Commons, as well as Catholic Lords, to try to influence social policy debates. Whether or not they are successful is debatable but they unquestionably help to shape public debates in the area of life and human genetics.

However, in addition to all of this, in many ways, it is the second dimension to the voting patterns that provides even more evidence that British parties *need* Christians. This book has outlined in detail the very real correlation between religious faith and political participation, in relation to electoral turn-out, and also partisan identification. In short, Christians are an extremely reliable source of democratic engagement – and linked to that, wider social capital. In the same way as parties have learned to court the 'grey vote' – older people are much more likely to vote than younger people – they have also realised that there are votes to be gained with religious Britons. Note the way that all three main parties employ teams of membership development staff to concentrate entirely on their Christian members – not for them the broad-brush belief that 'nobody goes to church any more, do they?'. In the midst of tough times for parties, with falling membership and identification levels, Christians are a welcome source of civic trust to all of their membership and activist registers.

Clearly, the British political system looks as secularised as its society has become but the reality of the picture is actually one of 'multiple modernities' – different value systems coexisting alongside one another, and often having equal worth and equal influence. Furthermore, there is no scientific evidence that British politics is somehow on some sort of trajectory towards a day when no one believes in God, no one supports state churches, and no one has to consider the ethical dimensions to issues related to scientific advances or modern sexual relationships. As Chapters 6 and 7 explained, somewhat conversely, as active religious observance has declined, the ethical and moral challenges faced by society have concurrently multiplied. The advances made by scientists are matched by the challenges of how society legislates those advances, and for that reason, the place of religious and moral interests in relation to the policymaking process, and political parties, is assured.

In some ways, this is particularly the case given the way the unwritten constitution of Britain functions – its organic and flexible capacity places the onus even more on parties and party politicians to have thought-out social policies in areas that, in other states, can be left to supreme courts, or single issue interest groups. This is not to argue that parties have to have fully thought-out positions on issues such as abortion or euthanasia but it does mean they have to work out which issues they grant both parliamentary time and free votes to, and which they do not, while, as Chapter 7 explained, equalities issues are highly partisan and do indeed require the politicians to reflect where their respective values of conservatism, liberalism and social democracy fit in with the wider British lifestyles picture.

Linked to this, it is also clear Christian Britons are – up to a point – voting on economic and social issues with their faith in mind – and that this tends to favour the Conservatives. While the data is less convincing here, and we need to be very careful not to overstate this, especially given the strength of the denominational vote also in existence – there is evidence of a link between atheists and the parties of the left/progressive/liberal centre, and other scholars have referred to this, as well. As Chapter 3 argued, this allows the Conservatives to continue to present themselves as the party of Britain, the party of British national pride, and of British Christian values. Admittedly this is quite fortuitous – after all, there is really no hard evidence whatsoever that the Tory Party's policy on, say, marriage and families is anything other than expedient and linked to a deeper attempt to 'do what works', as Iain Duncan Smith puts it (Interview with author, 4 March 2010); it is patently not simply a one-dimensional attempt to attract Christian voters. However, it is still a neat overlap that the Conservatives are able to take advantage of, and use to their advantage, and again it fits in with image points made earlier. It can also be argued that the existence of an albeit small and weak Christian Right in the UK makes a parallel with the US rather than continental Europe even more accurate in this specific context, at least.

Chapter 3 also noted that the liberal Christian vote is not really coherent (some vote Labour, some vote Liberal Democrat – indeed, some may even vote Conservative). In response, while we must reiterate the point about the fortuitous nature of the Conservative Party receiving the active Christian vote, almost by default, we should also acknowledge the growing presence of evangelical Christians in the party – notably absent from either of the other two. Evangelicals are a growing group of Christians in the UK, which again contradicts the argument that religion is in decline. The attempts by the Conservatives to capture that vote via David Burrowes, Tim Montgomerie and the Conservative Christian Fellowship is subtle but determined, and a dimension that David Cameron is clearly happy to encourage from a suitable distance.

The Church in Parliament and Christian party networks: the rational response

The state churches of Scotland and England continue to exist in their political guise primarily because of the above rational base – in short, it would be electorally unpopular for British party politicians to try to change this. The Christian vote – while dispersed and fragmented in many ways – is also substantial enough to collectively offer a political voice and interest. An excellent example was mentioned in Chapter 6 – on the issue of euthanasia, or assisted dying, the churches literally speak with one voice, and the bishops in the Lords have no qualms about exercising their right to vote in such contexts, voicing the fears of millions of British Christians: Protestant, Catholic and other.

As Chapter 4 argued, Anglican bishops sitting and voting in the British Parliament are not simply interesting because they are there, and they say important things – it is also very strong evidence of the sort of arguments put forward in Chapters 2 and 3, that is religion still matters to British politics owing to voting behaviour and parties. As Baroness Whitaker put it, it is a brave politician that 'takes on' the churches – not necessarily because, as her secular or humanist lobby argue, they have hidden resources or some sort of inexplicable hold over the media and leading politicians – but because, quite simply politicians realise that there are a lot of votes out there to be won and lost. Politicians pick the battles that they can win – with limited parliamentary time, and an agenda of fulfilling election manifesto promises to be delivered, getting involved in untangling the centuries-old mysteries of the British constitution when it could potentially be mishandled is not something that any politician of any party can afford to risk. The most appropriate comparison is with the monarchy – while the average British subject (citizen) is not overly concerned whether or not there is a royal family, if politicians were to try to get rid of it, many people would undoubtedly react negatively.

Linked to this, there is also real evidence of an even more direct impact upon the parties – the fact that they use their resources to staff desks and offices with the sole purpose of recruiting Christian members. Admittedly, this is given a perfectly reasonable façade – that of strengthening networks between Christians already in the party, educating non-Christians in the party, and all in the name of bringing more Christians into public life and party politics. For example, the umbrella group, 'Christians in Politics', claims to put religious faith above petty partisan interests and encourages more Christians to go into public life, regardless of which party route they go down. While noble – indeed, exactly the sort of consensual approach that there is clear evidence British voters want to see more of – that sort of aspiration is not the reason why we can find Christian officers with laptops and telephones at Millbank Tower, Victoria Street or Cowley Street. They are there because the parties know there is a market for Christian votes, and are happy to provide funding and facilities to pursue that vote. The level of influence and money that each group commands is a very real sign that the parties appreciate that there is something in it for them too – after all, none of them are without financial difficulties and have to be realistic about where to focus their efforts. While the evidence presented in Chapter 2 suggests a correlation between the Conservatives and church-goers, that is only one dimension of a wider picture, and might not necessarily always be the case. There are Christians in all parties, and while it is perhaps understandable that there are fewer atheist Conservatives, that does not mean the party has a stranglehold over that particular religious demographic.

The extent to whether or not all of this is as powerful a factor as the more high-profile existence of openly Christian parties across much of Northern Europe – relatively – is also debatable. There is much literature on just how Christian the Christian Democrats actually are in countries such as Germany, Belgium and the Netherlands. While their historical origins are not in any doubt, the actual meaning of the term 'Christian Democrat' has lost much of its power and meaning. In Scandinavia, its parties are certainly interested in socially conservative issues – much more so than on the continent – but they lack influence and seats in government, while not directly as a consequence, cer-tainly as a related factor. On the other hand, fully funded Christian factions within secular parties are – potentially – a more vivid symbol of religious power in Western Europe in 2010.

This is especially the case when we bear in mind the rise of the moral issue discussed in Chapters 6 and 7, and in the last section. The first point made was that British Prime Ministers never like to lose a vote at Westminster, regardless of whether or not it is overtly partisan in its detail, with the 2008 HFE Bill held up as an excellent example. Linked to this, with no supreme court prior to 2009 or written constitution, and no British tradition of human rights, in fact – the parties also really do risk public opinion if they are perceived to be getting something wrong. It is a brave MP who gets up in the Commons and argues that stem cell research should not be funded, it was argued in Chapter 6. Such emotive and personalised issues are extremely difficult for the parties to handle – the clever and sophisticated strategies deployed by spin doctors in modern party machines cannot do much if their politicians are perceived to be against scientific advances or anti-Christian, or something equally emotive. Linked to this, the pressure that can, in fact, be applied by churches can have a partisan angle due to the sort of voting patterns discussed in Chapter 2. Indeed, we have already noted that the Conservative Party is not averse to putting a partisan angle on all of this, albeit in a fairly innocuous and subtle way, while the entire equalities agenda is extremely divisive politically.

British Christianity and representative democracy: a marriage made in heaven?

So is religion good for the quality of British democracy? Superficially, state churches provide a tolerant voice, all parties contain Christians, and the challenges of moral issues are dealt with relatively fluidly by parties rather than constitutionally or legally. To be clear, this book cannot claim that Christianity is good for social capital or – more specifically – representative democracy in Britain. This would be a normative statement and not within the remit of this book.[1] However, what this book can argue is that Christianity appears to be perceived to be good for British representative democracy. Christian state churches are allowed to have a voice in Parliament and special legal privileges. Parties employ campaigners to try to capture the 'Christian vote' with no one party monopoly on religious believers or church attendees. Religious and moral issues are debated openly in public forums, without any significant social division.

However, while this book is not putting forward the argument that all countries should have bishops in the upper house – it is acknowledging that there is a case for some sort of representation that is not solely party political in parliamentary settings and that is apparently acceptable to British voters. The tradition of having a democratic check on elected officials is a sound one, and the idea that the system has representatives from different walks of life in the House of Lords should not be discounted on the basis that it is out of date. Bishops were there at the start of Parliament, and have been instrumental in its development since then – the fact that they are still there is testimony to their effectiveness, trust and respect, rather than simply because the politicians have not noticed them, or bothered to get rid of them. Their ability to operate as professional politicians (if not career politicians) as well as professional prelates, is impressive and has a moderating effect on both parliamentary politics and the social pronouncements of the Church. Indeed, anyone who has spent time researching the way the Palace of Westminster and

Portcullis House work will know that very little happens there for no reason. The prominence of Lord Bishops wandering around the corridors of power in their purple stocks is something a government could have tackled many years ago, especially a reforming, left-of-centre government such as Tony Blair's New Labour administration – but chose not to.

Also, while this book is not arguing that Christian Democracy is an ineffective partisan ideology, the question of whether or not CD parties are actually religious in any meaningful way in 2010 is perhaps open to question. The way Angela Merkel actually incorporates her Christian values into running the third largest economy in the world is uncertain. This book is not arguing that an evangelical interest group is always bad for democracy – although there is no question it causes great division and upset inside the United States. The development of the Christian lobby away from being aligned exclusively with the Republicans is surely good for American democracy, with the likes of Rick Warren becoming more prominent as figures from the 1980s fade. Above all, however, this book is merely concluding that the British way of Christianity continuing to have a role in a more subtle, non-divisive way, is one that is worthy of scholarly attention.

Clearly, the UK does not fit entirely neatly into the traditional Habermasian notion of religion being kept 'private' – this point has nothing to do with CD parties, the power of the Vatican or even constitutional Church–State relations but is rather linked to the idea that a modern advanced European political system should be wary of churches having too much 'public' power, and restrict it. In this regard, the distinctiveness of Britain as a European nation where the values of individualism outweigh a more communitarian or collectivist approach, is still very much to the fore. If we were forced to (rather crudely, it must be said) place the UK on a scale with the US at one end and EU member states at the other, it would probably be somewhere in between, but perhaps edging more towards its Atlantic cousin. There is no anti-clerical tradition in the UK, and no history of significant religious conservatism as there is in France, the Netherlands, Belgium, Italy or Spain. Germany is unique due to its history. Even the Nordic countries, while certainly the most similar to the UK (along with their continued support for monarchy), have clearly embraced the leftist/equalities agenda much more obviously, and do have a (albeit small) Christian Democratic tradition.

Linked to this, what really makes the UK unlike other European nations in 2010 is that British voters and parties do not necessarily seem to rationally support (for whatever reason) the marginalisation of religion in modern society because religion is not in any substantial way associated with social or political division. The United States of America's *raison d'être* is religious freedom, and despite the various negative deviations from that model – the extremes of the religious right since the 1980s being perhaps the most obvious – that basis continues to have tremendous resonance across all levels of American society and all sectors of American politics. Britain is not America and America is not Britain, and the present author is not trying to claim that the similarities between the two countries are entirely consistent or comprehensive – not least, the way that American politicians openly talk about God is clearly not matched by British politicians. Nevertheless, in 2010, the UK does not fit neatly into the continental European model and, for that reason, we need to make this intellectual distinction, and make it clearly and confidently.

Indeed, the origins of the American separation of Church and State are actually remarkably similar to the motivations for keeping Church and State linked in the UK. The separation in America was the consequence of a desire to protect people's religious freedoms from the State – in other words, by keeping the State away from churches, religion would be protected within the political system. As Chapter 7 discussed, this model is the exact opposite of the French/European-style *laïcité*, which was motivated by a philosophy to protect the State from the Church, and create a secular society. America may have a legal, constitutional separation of Church and State, but it does not have secularism. The specifics of the reason for America being founded – non-conformist puritans wanting to practise their faith, away from the state interference of British Anglicanism – have now become essentially irrelevant, and the fact that both countries valued the (Protestant) Christian religion so importantly that they politicised it, has instead become the key point to note. Now, the difference between that approach and the European one of wanting to depoliticise religion altogether, is the most visible dimension/axis.

As a consequence, mainstream public opinion is not divided into parties on the basis of secular versus religious values – there are no confessional parties in either the UK or the US, and no sizeable anti-clerical movement either. Indeed, even the relationship between the Christian Right and the Republican Party in America is recent, electorally expedient, and ultimately positive. That is, it is not about forming a political alliance as a reaction towards secularism but a proactive decision to protect and promote shared Christian values. Neither party in America can claim to totally own the Christian vote, and the same is the case for the three parties in the UK. Linked to this, the ideological division between left and right in Europe is not matched in the Anglo-American context – there exists no rigid correlation between Christianity and Conservatism as there is across the EU via the Christian Democrats. In the UK, there is the Christian Socialist movement, while the Catholic vote for the Democrats used to be a consistent feature of American elections.

Clearly, this is not a perfect match. For a start, the way that religious issues become hugely influential in the US, with interest groups campaigning hard on abortion or life issues, is not replicated in Britain, where the parliamentary system prevents voters from only being interested in the personality and values of candidates. Also, the very large number of Christians in America make the religious vote a much more valuable resource for parties than in the markedly less religiously observant UK. Furthermore, the way the American Supreme Court guards the moral agenda of the country is quite distinct from the way the British Parliament is forced to debate the issues, and often in a partisan way. Nevertheless, it is possible to talk of an 'Anglo-American' sphere where the values of Christianity are not necessarily viewed with suspicion by the State, parties or politicians.

For economists of religion, it has been argued that the UK can provide evidence that such a methodological approach can (broadly applied through a public choice framework) have its merits outside the US. Perhaps Britons do not change their religious denominations quite as much as Americans,[2] but that does not mean that the 'Adam Smith model' does not continue to have resonance in the land where it originated. The establishment of the state churches in the UK is an ostensibly limiting factor but the market sees the churches act rationally, and minimises this themselves by appearing inclusive and progressive. It has already been acknowledged that this is the religious market working in reverse, but still working.

Smith, of course, was also interested in social capital – including the moral market – and the idea that it is rational/self-interested to be interested in the welfare of the greater good. This book is not necessarily presenting any clear evidence that the UK has a better level of social capital because of this religious market, but it is seeking to link the two issues, in terms of their overall relevance. The editors of *The Economist* actually go down the Weberian route of supporting the argument that there is a link between Protestantism and economic growth. This book is not interested in making such grand statements, and it is also not within its remit, but it does acknowledge the existence of models that link modern Christianity and representative democracy. In particular, the relationship between churches acting as *interest groups* and *political parties* in the British context has been the central focus – that institutional link is close, alive and worthy of scholarly analysis. Both sets of institutions face membership crises, both sets have overlapping personalities and both sets are ultimately engaged in similar aims – to make society better. Both are ideological, both are political and both are interested in holding power. Both lie at the heart of British society, and, in short, both need one another equally.

For too long, scholars have mistaken religion not being a significant source of political or social *conflict/division* in the UK with it *not mattering at all*. British voters may well not get overly exercised by religious issues and British parties may well not fight with one another over the place of religion in British society – but that does not mean that religious issues are not an ever-present and important feature of the British political landscape. Christianity continues to be a key social cleavage in Britain, and it is a cleavage that impacts upon electoral and party politics as a consequence. British political science scholars have ignored religion, and particularly Christianity, for too long – the present author is not unsympathetic to the reasons for this, as it is perhaps not as immediately obvious an area upon which to focus as the impact of the media, multilevel governance or foreign policy. Looked at from a different perspective, the way the UK has not always been included in social scientific studies of Christianity is also perhaps not surprising, given its apparently high levels of secularisation.

Nevertheless, it is surely the duty of scholars to see things that journalists and policymakers themselves cannot see, and analyse their importance, and power. When bills are being either progressed or blocked in the British Parliament by the votes of Church of England bishops, that is worthy of attention. When voters are deciding how to vote in elections on the basis of their Christian values, that is worthy of attention. When moral or life issues become political issues, primarily because of the way the political system is constituted, that is worthy of attention. Indeed, there is no sign that any of these dimensions are diminishing in their importance – in fact, quite the reverse. The modernisation of British society and politics may be unstoppable but ethical questions will always persist, with moral and religious actors exerting political influence on the British public policymaking process. This book is the first attempt to comprehensively chart and explain how and why that happens.

Notes

1 Introduction: the neglected dimension of British politics

1 The focus of this book does not include the politics of Northern Ireland, owing to the specific nature of the relationship between religion and politics in the province.

2 Mr Brown was brought up in a Scottish Presbyterian household with values such as hard work and prudence placed to the fore by his father, a Church of Scotland minister.

3 Britain is unique among European and North American nation states in having no single codified document containing a Bill of Rights or detailed summary of how the different parts of the political system relate to one another.

4 A dominant Church is not a state Church but kept separate from the State precisely because it is so large and/or powerful – for example, the Catholic Church in France.

5 Since the late 1970s, religious interests, particularly on the political right, have been prominent in national American politics, with the two most important religious right organisations of that period both founded in 1978 – the 'Christian Voice' and the 'Moral Majority'.

6 Indeed, two prominent British scholars argue that voters are looking for – among other things – public figures they can trust, who are in politics for public service not financial gain, and to do more than simply 'administer' (Stoker 2006; Hay 2007).

7 In formal terms, the constitutional separation of Church and State.

8 The three terms won by Tony Blair from 1997 to 2010, and by the Conservatives under Margaret Thatcher are modern exceptions to this rule. The Conservative–Liberal Democrat coalition formed in May 2010 is the first since the national unity government of the Second World War.

9 The Conservatives narrowly missed winning an overall majority on their own, taking 306 seats, just ten short of what they required. The Liberal Democrats won only 57, and are the junior partners in the coalition.

10 This book will interchange the terms 'religion' and 'Christianity' given that the focus of this book is the UK and the mainstream Christian churches.

11 Chapter Four will go into more detail in relation to the interest group literature on churches.

12 Indeed, such questions have been asked by social scientists in relation to religion for a long time – Max Weber, for example, wrote extensively about the relationship between Protestantism and capitalism (*The Protestant Ethic and the Spirit of Capitalism*, 1905). However, it should be added that this book is not going to go into much detail over the more theoretical literature that discusses the nuances of the Protestant versus Catholic traditions of Northern and Southern Europe respectively. While the comparative context is important, ultimately this is a single case study of a country with a long Christian tradition.

2   Religion and voting behaviour in Britain: from denominational 'cleavage' to the 'alpha vote'

1   It was Grace Davie who first made the distinction between people nominally belonging to a specific denomination or church, and them actively *believing* in God (1994).
2   This distinctiveness spans both the fact that Catholic voters in Britain prefer the left-wing, rather than right-wing, party, as well as the lack of any confessional party.
3   For an analysis of the place of religion in European politics, see the January 2003 special edition of *West European Politics*, vol. 26, no.1, co-edited by Enyedi and Madeley. See also Madeley's edited volume (2002) *Religion and Politics* (Dartmouth: Ashgate). For a more detailed analysis of the relationship between religion and voting behaviour, see Broughton and ten Napel's edited volume (2000) *Religion and Mass Electoral Behaviour in Europe* (London: Routledge).
4   Mrs Thatcher introduced a law that made references to human sexuality in secondary schools illegal, while John Major launched the (ultimately unsuccessful) 'Back to Basics' campaign.
5   The author would like to thank John Micklethwait for his helpful discussion in relation to this area.

3   More Methodism than Marxism?: Christianity and the British party system

1   It should also be noted that contemporary political scientists continue to ignore the issue. If one looks at the most recent studies of the three parties (Bale 2010; Russell and Fieldhouse 2005; Shaw 1994), only Russell and Fieldhouse mention religion or Christianity, and even then, barely at all. Even Eric Shaw's more recent religiously themed *Losing Labour's Soul: New Labour and the Blair Government 1997–2007* (2007) neglects to cover the topic.
2   One methodological point requires to be clarified before we proceed. It was briefly mentioned in Chapter 1 that the author considered sending a survey questionnaire to all British Members of Parliament, asking them about their religious views and beliefs. This was ultimately rejected as a productive strand to the project due to its bluntness as an instrument – while space can be left on the forms for comments that can be analysed more qualitatively, the more quantitative data is not especially informative (see Steven 2003). While finding, for example, that the religious beliefs of British MPs are different from wider British society, would be very interesting, trying then to quantify that into a meaningful conclusion about political influence is more complicated. In any case, many of the potential target MPs are no longer in Parliament, owing to the 2010 British General Election. However, the author is in charge of the British data set for the more extensive European research project: 'The religious preferences of Members of the European Parliament' (RelEP), involving members of RECON (Reconstituting Democracy in Europe), a European network funded by the European Commission, and the findings of this project will be released in 2011.
3   See also Angelo Panebianco's more recent 'electoral–professional' party (1988).
4   Again, it is not necessarily within the scope of this book to discuss at length how clear the link is between more issue-based voting behaviour and 'catch-all' party organisations but, clearly, the two are related in different ways.
5   The present author does not support this theory – the GOP ('Grand Old Party') existed long before the rise of the Moral Majority, Jerry Falwell and Pat Robertson (see Sullivan 2008).

 6 While the Christian Democratic parties are not exclusively Catholic, e.g. the Scandinavian ones are essentially Protestant and the CDU in Germany is a mixture, it is in Catholic countries that they are most firmly rooted.
 7 Robertson set up the evangelical, anti-abortion Christian Coalition after his unsuccessful Presidential bid.
 8 Although there have been moves made recently to tighten up the organisational framework, and to create a more uniform structure. In Scotland, where its parliamentary representation has been extremely low since 1997, the party's official membership figures continue to rival that of the SNP and Labour.
 9 This is despite the fact that it was the Conservative Party that took Britain into the European Community in 1973 and signed the Maastricht Treaty in 1992, both without holding referendums.
10 Indeed, CSM sent the largest number of delegates to the 2009 annual conference of any of the party's affiliated groups or organisations.
11 For example, the French Socialists are by far the most vociferous in their opposition to Muslim headscarves and burkas: 'The burka is a prison for women and has no place in the French Republic' (BBC News, 6 January 2010).
12 This is the case for the staff of the CCF and LDCF also – see concluding comments.
13 For example, see Winnett (2009).
14 Blair's father, Leo, had even planned to stand as a Conservative Party candidate in the constituency of Durham.
15 It should perhaps also be pointed out that there are other dimensions here that are worthy of more analysis in their own right – for example, the relationship between the development of the welfare state and reformed Protestant Christianity (see Van Kersbergen and Manow 2009).
16 Although it might be added that Mrs Thatcher – while often accused of not being terribly 'conservative' – was nevertheless religious, and continues to serve as a member of the All-Party Group on Methodism.

4 Still the 'Conservative Party at prayer'? The role of Church of England bishops in Parliament

 1 In reference to the Church's radical report on urban renewal, *Faith in the City* (1985).
 2 The two Archbishops of England (Canterbury and York) have a permanent seat, as do the two bishops representing the two oldest dioceses (Durham and Winchester). The other twenty-two gain their seat on personal seniority, i.e. how long they have been a bishop.

5 A Presbyterian conscience: the Church of Scotland, the Labour Party and the politics of social justice

 1 ACTS (Action of Churches Together in Scotland), the ecumenical organisation that includes all the main Scottish denominations, appointed Dr Blount, then a Church of Scotland minister in Falkirk, in 1998 to the position of Parliamentary Officer, to act as a link between faith-based organisations and the new Parliament. There is also a Catholic officer, and an Evangelical Alliance officer.
 2 SIFC is funded by a Scottish Executive grant, and meets annually with the First Minister.

6 Little wonder 'We don't do God': ethics, life issues and the power of the Christian lobby

1 The British parliamentary system has a strong tradition of forcing Members to vote in the way that their party wants.

2 The correct term for someone who lives in Britain is a 'subject' of Her Majesty The Queen. The term 'citizen' has only been introduced since the Maastricht Treaty of 1992.

3 See Chapter 2.

7 Still fighting a losing battle? Equalities and the weakness of the Christian lobby

1 This is not to argue that churches are always against the equalities agenda but, as we will see in the chapter, they do tend to adopt a more traditionalist approach. This is also not to argue that a lack of influence equates to a lack of relevance – this chapter will explain how Christian values continue to be prominent in this context, if not necessarily effective.

2 Seat total = 129: SNP – 47 seats, Labour – 46 seats, Conservatives – 17 seats, Liberal Democrats – 16 seats, Greens – 2 seats, Independent – 1 seat.

3 The national Church of Scotland's silence during the 2007 election campaign reflects the broad nature of its theology. Like the Church of England, the Church of Scotland does not have a Catechism, and so its viewpoints are contained only in the deliverances of its General Assembly, which are subject to change.

4 Kellas (1989: 179) describes the various pieces of legislation linked to abortion, divorce, Sunday observance, human sexuality and alcohol licensing that were passed at a UK level but delayed or modified in Scotland in the 1960s and 1970s.

8 Conclusions: the British model of politics and religion

1 That having been said, both Campbell and Putnam (2010) and Micklethwait and Wooldridge (2009) all argue that Christianity has been good for democracy in America – and that there, Christianity is viewed to be inherent to democracy (rather than the European model of secularism).

2 It should be noted that Americans, while much greater consumers of religion than Europeans, only actually switch between Christian denominations.

References

Adam Smith Institute (2010) 'About the Adam Smith Institute' www.adamsmith.org/about-the-adam-smith-institute/ (accessed 6 June 2010).

Allardyce, J. (2009) 'Salmond: "Faith is my driving force"' www.timesonline.co.uk/tol/news/uk/scotland/article6727842.ece (25 July 2010).

Almond, G. and Verba, S. (1963) *The Civic Culture* (Princeton, NJ: Princeton University Press).

Alpha Course (2010) 'Ever wondered what it's all about?' http://uk.alpha.org/home (accessed 6 June 2010).

Andersen, A., Tilley, J. and Heath, A. F. (2005) 'Political knowledge and enlightened preferences: party choice through the electoral cycle', *British Journal of Political Science*, 35: 285–302.

Ansell, C. and Gingrich, J. (2003) 'Reforming the administrative state' in B. Cain, R. Dalton and S. Scarrow (eds), *Democracy Transformed?* (Oxford: Oxford University Press), 140–63.

Bachrach, P. and Baratz, M. (1962) 'Two faces of power', *American Political Science Review*, 56 (4): 947–52.

Bachrach, P. and Baratz, M. (1970) *Power and Poverty: Theory and Practice* (New York: Oxford University Press).

Baggott, R. (1995) *Pressure Groups Today* (Manchester: Manchester University Press).

Bakvis, H. (1981) *Catholic Power in the Netherlands* (Kingston: McGill-Queen's University Press).

Baldwin, T. (2009) 'Religious right encroaches on Tory party despite Cameron's stance', www.timesonline.co.uk/tol/comment/faith/article6926191.ece (accessed 21 November).

Bale, T. (2005) *European Politics: A Comparative Introduction* (Basingstoke, Palgrave Macmillan).

Bale, T. (2010) *The Conservative Party from Thatcher to Cameron* (Cambridge: Polity).

Barley, L. (2006) *Churchgoing Today* (London: Church of England).

Barnes, E. (2007) 'Tycoon gives SNP £1/2m to beat Labour', *Scotland on Sunday*, http://scotlandonsunday.scotsman.com/latestnews/Tycoon-gives-SNP-12m-to.3355450.jp (accessed 18 March 2007).

Barrett, D. B., Kurian, G. T. and Johnson, T. M. (2001) *World Christian Encyclopedia* (Oxford: Oxford University Press).

Baumgartner, F. R. and Leech, B. L. (1998) *Basic Instincts* (Princeton, NJ: Princeton University Press).

BBC News (2000) 'UK to extend embryo research' http://news.bbc.co.uk/1/hi/sci/tech/1078672.stm (accessed 19 December).

BBC News (2002) 'Kirk warns of care home threat' http://news.bbc.co.uk/1/hi/scotland/1758543.stm (accessed 13 January).

BBC News (2002) 'Prison watchdog "will have bite"' http://news.bbc.co.uk/1/hi/scotland/2144204.stm (accessed 22 July).

BBC News (2002) 'Argos Sunday working climbdown' http://news.bbc.co.uk/1/hi/scotland/2407891.stm (accessed 6 November).

BBC News (2004) 'Churchman who wants to end poverty' http://news.bbc.co.uk/1/hi/uk/3645119.stm (accessed 21 April).

BBC News (2005) 'Howard backs abortion law change' http://news.bbc.co.uk/1/hi/uk/4344851.stm (accessed 14 March).

BBC News (2006) BBC News (2006) 'Cardinal happy to see UK break-up' http://news.bbc.co.uk/1/hi/scotland/6052552.stm (accessed 15 October).

BBC News (2006) 'Archbishop attacks BA cross rules' http://news.bbc.co.uk/1/hi/england/north_yorkshire/6166746.stm (accessed 21 November).

BBC News (2007) 'Bishop declares anti-Labour vote' http://news.bbc.co.uk/1/hi/scotland/6439723.stm (accessed 11 March).

BBC News (2007) 'Stagecoach tycoon donates to SNP' http://news.bbc.co.uk/1/hi/scotland/6462119.stm (accessed 17 March).

BBC News (2007) 'Candidates face quiz by Catholics' http://news.bbc.co.uk/1/hi/scotland/6557477.stm (accessed 15 April).

BBC News (2007) 'Blair feared faith "nutter" label' http://news.bbc.co.uk/1/hi/7111620.stm (accessed 25 November).

BBC News (2009) 'Brown pledges MP code of conduct' http://news.bbc.co.uk/1/hi/uk_politics/8075723.stm (accessed 31 May).

BBC News (2010) 'France Socialist party opposes burka ban' http://news.bbc.co.uk/1/hi/world/europe/8443989.stm (accessed 6 January).

BBC News (2010) 'Archbishops urge "hopeful" voting at election' http://news.bbc.co.uk/1/hi/uk_politics/election_2010/england/8655312.stm (accessed 30 April).

BBC News (2010) 'Nick Clegg pledges biggest political reforms since 1832' http://news.bbc.co.uk/1/hi/uk_politics/8690882.stm (accessed 19 May).

Becker, G. (1996) *Accounting for Tastes* (Cambridge, MA: Harvard University Press).

Bennie, L., Brand, J. and Mitchell, J. (1997) *How Scotland Votes* (Manchester: Manchester University Press).

Berger, P. (1967) *The Sacred Canopy: Elements of a Sociological Theory of Religion* (New York: Anchor).

Berger, P., Davie, G. and Fokas, E. (2008) *Religious America, Secular Europe?* (Aldershot: Ashgate).

Biggar, N. and Hogan, L. (eds) (2009) *Religious Voices in Public Places* (Oxford: Oxford University Press).

Blais, A. (2007) 'Turn-out in elections' in R. Dalton and H-D. Klingemann (eds), *Oxford Handbook of Political Behavior* (Oxford: Oxford University Press).

Blewitt, T., Hyde-Price, A. and Rees, W. (eds) (2008) *British Foreign Policy and the Anglican Church* (Aldershot: Ashgate).

Bochel, J. and Denver, D. (1970) 'Religion and voting: a critical review and a new analysis', *Political Studies*, 18 (2): 205–19.

Boyle, R. and Lynch, P. (1998) *Out of the Ghetto: The Catholic Community in Modern Scotland* (Edinburgh: John Donald).

Bromley, C., Curtice, J., Hinds, K. and Park, A. (2003) *Devolution: Scottish Answers to Scottish Questions* (Edinburgh: Edinburgh University Press).

Bromley, C., Curtice, J., McCrone, D. and Park, A. (eds) (2006) *Has Devolution Delivered?* (Edinburgh: Edinburgh University Press).

Broughton, D. and ten Napel, H-M. (eds) (2000) *Religion and Mass Electoral Behaviour in Europe* (London: Routledge).

Brown, A., McCrone, D. and Paterson, L. (1998) *Politics and Society in Scotland* (Basingstoke: Macmillan).

Brown, C. (1992) 'Religion and secularisation' in A. Dickson and J. H. Treble (eds) *People and Society in Scotland 1914–1990* (Edinburgh: John Donald), 48–80.

Brown, C. (2001) 'The myth of the established Church of Scotland' in J. Kirk (ed.) *The Scottish Churches and the Union Parliament 1707–1999* (Edinburgh: Scottish Churches Historical Society), 48–74.

Brown, C. (2003) 'Campbell interrupted Blair as he spoke of his faith: "We don't do God"' www.telegraph.co.uk/news/uknews/1429109/Campbell-interrupted-Blair-as-he-spoke-of-his-faith-We-dont-do-God.html (accessed 4 May).

Brown, F. (1994) 'Influencing the House of Lords: the role of the Lords Spiritual, 1979–1987', *Political Studies*, 42 (1): 105–19.

Brown, G. (2010) 'Tomorrow we fight on' www2.labour.org.uk/tomorrow-we-fight-on---text-of-speech-by-gordon-brown-at-labour- (accessed 11 May 2010).

Bruce, S. (2002) *God is Dead: Secularization in the West* (Oxford: Blackwell).

Bruce, S. and Glendinning, T. (2003) 'Religion in modern Scotland' in C. Bromley, J. Curtice, K. Hinds and A. Park (eds) *Devolution: Scottish Answers to Scottish Questions* (Edinburgh: Edinburgh University Press) 86–115.

Butt, S. and Curtice, J. (2010) 'Duty in decline? Trends in attitudes to voting' in A. Park, J. Curtice, K. Thomson, M. Phillips, E. Clery *et al.* (eds) *British Social Attitudes: The 26th Report* (London: Sage), 1–18.

Campbell, A., Converse, P., Miller, W. And Stokes, D. (1960) *The American Voter* (New York: John Wiley).

Campbell, D. and Putnam, R. (2010) *American Grace: How Religion Divides and Unites Us* (New York: Simon and Schuster).

Campbell, D. and Quin Monson, J. (2008) 'The religion card: gay marriage and the 2004 Presidential Election', *Public Opinion Quarterly*, 72 (3): 399–419.

Carnie, J. (1986) 'Parliament and Scottish moral legislation' in *The Scottish Government Yearbook 1986* (Edinburgh: Unit for Study of Government in Scotland), 49–69.

Casanova, J. (1994) *Public Religions in the Modern World* (Chicago, IL: University of Chicago).

Charlemagne (2004) 'Real politics, at last?', *The Economist*, 30 October, 52.

Christian Socialist Movement (2010) 'What we stand for' www.thecsm.org.uk/Groups/87274/Christian_Socialist_Movement/About_CSM/What_we_stand/What_we_stand.aspx (accessed 7 June 2010).

Christian Today (2008) 'MP: faith is compatible with Liberal politics' available at: www.christiantoday.com/article/mp.faith.is.compatible.with.liberal.politics/21844.htm (9 November).

Church of England (1985) *Faith in the City: A Call for Action by Church and Nation* (London: Church House).

Church of Scotland (1988) *Reports to the General Assembly* (Edinburgh: St Andrew).

Church of Scotland (1989) *Reports to the General Assembly* (Edinburgh: St Andrew).

Church of Scotland (1999) *Reports to the General Assembly* (Edinburgh: St Andrew).

Church of Scotland (2001) *Reports to the General Assembly* (Edinburgh: St Andrew).

Church of Scotland (2002) *Reports to the General Assembly* (Edinburgh: St Andrew).

Clarke, H., Sanders, D., Stewart, M., Whiteley, P. (2004) *Political Choice in Britain* (Cambridge: Cambridge University Press).

Clarke, H., Sanders, D., Stewart, M., Whiteley, P. (2010) *Performance Politics and the British Voter* (Cambridge: Cambridge University Press).

Clements, A. (2008) 'Stem-cell research – public opinion' http://business.timesonline. co.uk/tol/business/specials/stemcell_research/article3903552.ece (accessed 10 May).

Conservative Christian Fellowship (2010) 'About us' www.ccfwebsite.com/new-about-us.shtml (accessed 7 June 2010).

Conservative Party (2010) 'Recognising marriage in the tax system' www. conservatives.com/News/News_stories/2010/04/Recognising_marriage_in_the_tax_ system.aspx (accessed 10 April).

Consultative Steering Group (1999) *Shaping Scotland's Parliament* (Edinburgh: Scottish Office).

Cowley, P. and Stuart, M. (2006) 'Party splits remain on abortion' available at www. revolts.co.uk/cat_briefing_papers.html (University of Nottingham).

Coxall, B. (2001) *Pressure Groups in British Politics* (Harlow: Longman).

Curtice, J., McCrone, D., Park, A. and Paterson, L. (2002) *New Scotland; New Society: Are Social and Political Ties Fragmenting?* (Edinburgh: Edinburgh University Press).

Dahl, R. (1961) *Who Governs? Democracy and Power in an American City* (New Haven, CT: Yale University Press).

Dalton, R. (1999) 'Political support in advanced industrial democracies' in P. Norris (ed.), *Critical Citizens: Global Support for Democratic Governance* (Oxford: Oxford University Press), 57–77.

Dalton, R. (2002) *Citizen Politics in Western Democracies* (New York: Chatham House).

Dalton, R. and Gray, M. (2003) 'Expanding the electoral marketplace' in B. Cain, R. Dalton and S. Scarrow (eds), *Democracy Transformed?* (Oxford: Oxford University Press), 23–43.

Dalton, R. and Wattenberg, M. (2000) *Parties without Partisans: Political Change in Advanced Industrial Democracies* (Oxford: Oxford University Press).

Dalton, R. and Weldon, S. (2005) 'Public images of political parties: a necessary evil?', *West European Politics*, 28 (5), 931–51.

Davie, G. (1994) *Religion in Britain since 1945* (Oxford: Blackwell).

Davie, G. (2005) 'Research 2005 Recent media coverage' www.cofe.anglican.org/ info/statistics/ (accessed 10 May 2010).

Denholm, A. (2007) 'End church veto over jobs, say teachers', *The Herald*, 16 May, 1.

Denver, D. (2003) *Elections and Voters in Britain* (Basingstoke: Palgrave Macmillan).

Denver, D. (2007) *Elections and Voters in Britain* (Basingstoke: Palgrave Macmillan).

Devine, T. M. (ed.) (2000) *Scotland's Shame?* (Edinburgh: Mainstream).

Der Spiegel (2010) 'Germany's Conservatives head for the political center' www. spiegel.de/international/germany/0,1518,671478-2,00.html (accessed 13 January).

Dinan, D. (2005) *Ever Closer Union: An Introduction to European Integration* (Basingstoke: Palgrave Macmillan).

Downs, A. (1957) *An Economic Theory of Democracy* (New York: Harper and Row).

Duncan, F. (2006) 'A decade of Christian Democratic decline: the dilemmas of the CDU, ÖVP and CDA in the 1990s', *Government and Opposition*, 41 (4): 469–90.

Duverger, M. (1954) *Political Parties* (London: Wiley).

Dyson, A. (1985) '"Little else but the name" – reflections on four church and state reports' in G. Moyser (ed.) *Church and Politics Today* (Edinburgh: T and T Clark), 282–313.

Edge, P. (2006) *Religion and Law: An Introduction* (Aldershot: Ashgate).

Eisenstadt, S. (2000) 'Multiple modernities', *Daedalus*, 129 (1), Winter, 1–29.

Electoral Commission (2007) 'Campaign spending by political parties at the 2007 Scottish Parliament elections' www.electoralcommission.org.uk/your-area/scot campaignexpend.cfm (accessed 7 June 2010).

Elliott, F. and Hurst, G. (2007) 'Cardinal Cormac Murphy-O'Connor wades in to embryo research debate with Catholic meeting' www.timesonline.co.uk/tol/comment/ faith/article2943595.ece (accessed 26 November).

European Commission (2010) 'European Commission campaigns to reduce gender pay gap' http://ec.europa.eu/unitedkingdom/press/press_releases/2010/pr1017_en. htm (accessed June 2010).

European Parliament (2008) 'All party working group on the separation of religion and politics' http://politicsreligion.com/group.html (accessed 7 June 2010).

European Union (2000) 'Council directive . . . establishing a general framework for equal treatment in employment and occupation' http://europa.eu/scadplus/leg/en/ cha/c10823.htm (accessed 7 June 2010).

Evangelical Alliance (2003) 'Introduction to Evangelical Alliance' http://billofrights. nihrc.org/submissions/submission_105.pdf (accessed 7 June 2010).

Evans, G. and Norris, P. (eds) (1999) *Critical Elections: British Parties and Voters in Long-Term Perspective* (London: Sage).

Fielding, S. (2002) *The Labour Party: Continuity and Change in the making of 'New' Labour* (Basingstoke: Palgrave Macmillan).

Flanigan, W. and Zingale, N. (2006) *Political Behavior of the American Electorate* (Washington, DC: CQ Press).

Forrester, D. (1993) 'The Church of Scotland and public policy', *Scottish Affairs*, 4: 67–81.

Frum, D. (2003) *The Right Man: The Surprise Presidency of George W Bush* (New York: Random House).

Gerber, A., Gruber, J. and Hungerman, D. (2008) 'Does church attendance cause people to vote? Using Blue Laws' repeal to estimate the effect of religiosity on voter turn-out', National Bureau of Economic Research working paper (Cambridge, MA), September.

Giddens, A. (1988) *The Third Way: The Renewal of Social Democracy* (Cambridge: Polity).

Gledhill, R. (2008) 'Churchgoing on its knees as Christianity falls out of favour' www.timesonline.co.uk/tol/comment/faith/article3890080.ece (accessed 8 May).

Gledhill, R. and Charter, D. (2005) 'Cardinal tells Catholics to reject Labour over abortion' www.timesonline.co.uk/tol/news/uk/article427996.ece (accessed 15 March).

Goldstein, K. (1999) *Interest Groups, Lobbying and Participation in America* (Cambridge: Cambridge University Press).

Grant, W. (2000) *Pressure Groups and British Politics* (Basingstoke: Macmillan).

Gray, C. and Milmo, C. (2000) 'Boy George ridicules tycoon over Section 28 repeal' www.independent.co.uk/news/uk/crime/boy-george-ridicules-tycoon-over-section-28-repeal-706641.html (accessed 12 May).

Guardian online (2010) 'Leaked House of Lords Reform Paper' www.guardian.co.uk/politics/2010/apr/20/leaked-house-of-lords-reform-paper (accessed 20 April).

Guth, J., Kellstedt, L., Green, J. and Smidt, C. (2002) 'A distant thunder? Religious mobilization in the 2000 elections', in A. J. Cigler and B. A. Loomis (eds), *Interest Group Politics* (Washington, DC: CQ Press), 161–84.

Guth, J., Kellstedt, L., Green, J. and Smidt, C. (2007) 'Getting the spirit? Religious and partisan mobilization in the 2004 Elections' in A. Cigler and B. Loomis (eds) *Interest Group Politics* (Washington, DC: CQ Press), 157–81.

Habermas, J. and Derrida, J. (2003) 'Nach dem Krieg: Die Wiedergeburt Europas', *Frankfurter Allgemeine Zeutung*, www.faz.net/s/Rub117C535CDF414415BB243B 181B8B60AE/Doc~ECBE3F8FCE2D049AE808A3C8DBD3B2763~ATpl~Ecommon ~Scontent.html (accessed 31 May).

Hall, P. (2002) 'Great Britain: the role of government and the distribution of social capital' in R. Putnam (ed.) *Democracies in Flux: The Evolution of Social Capital in Contemporary Societies* (Oxford: Oxford University Press), 21–59.

Harrop, M. and Miller, W. (1987) *Elections and Voters* (Basingstoke: Macmillan).

Hay, C. (2007) *Why We Hate Politics* (Cambridge: Polity).

Haynes, J. (1998) *Religion in Global Politics* (Harlow: Longman).

Heath, A., Jowell, R. and Curtice, J. (1991) *How Britain Votes* (Oxford: Pergamon).

Heath, A., Jowell, R. and Curtice, J. (eds) (1994) *Labour's Last Chance* (Aldershot: Dartmouth).

Heath, A., Jowell, R. and Curtice, J. (2001) *The Rise of New Labour* (Oxford: Oxford University Press).

Heclo, H. (1978) 'Issue networks and the executive establishment' in A. King (ed.) *The New American Political System* (Washington, DC: American Enterprise Institute), 87–124.

Hickson, K. (ed.) *The Political Thought of the Conservative Party since 1945* (Basingstoke: Macmillan).

Holmes, M. (2001) *The Eurosceptical Reader 2* (Basingstoke: Palgrave Macmillan).

Hundal, S. (2010) 'The right hand of God', *New Statesman* (accessed 26 April).

Hunter, F. (1953) *Community Power Structure* (Chapel Hill, NC: University of North Carolina).

Hurst, G. and Henderson, M. (2008) 'David Cameron: Catholics should not misrepresent embryo Bill' www.timesonline.co.uk/tol/news/politics/article3611458.ece (accessed 25 March).

Hutcheon, P. (2007) 'Souter jumps back on SNP bandwagon with £1/2m donation', *Sunday Herald*, http://findarticles.com/p/articles/mi_qn4156/is_20070318/ai_n18737959?tag=rel.res2 (accessed 18 March).

Jordan, G. and Richardson, J. (1987) *Governments and Pressure Groups in Britain* (Oxford: Clarendon).

Katz, R. and Mair, P. (1995) 'Changing models of party organization: the emergence of the cartel party', *Party Politics*, 1 (1): 5–28.

Keating, M. (ed.) (2007) *Scottish Social Democracy: Progressive Ideas for Public Policy* (Oxford: Peter Lang).

Kellas, J. (1989) *The Scottish Political System* (Cambridge: Cambridge University Press).

Kettell, S. (2009a) 'Did secularism win out? The debate over the Human Fertilisation and Embryology Bill', *The Political Quarterly*, 80 (1): 67–75.

Kettell, S. (2009b) 'On the public discourse of religion: an analysis of Christianity in the United Kingdom', *Politics and Religion*, 2: 420–43.

Kidd, C. (2009) 'The irresistible itch', *London Review of Books*, 31 (23): 9–10.

Kirchheimer, O. (1966) 'The transformation of the Western European party systems' in J. LaPalombara and M. Weiner (eds) *Political Parties and Political Development* (Princeton, NJ: Princeton University Press), 177–200.

Kirkup, J. (2008) 'Catholic leader defends Gordon Brown from Anglican bishops' criticism' www.telegraph.co.uk/news/newstopics/politics/labour/4029423/Catholic-leader-defends-Gordon-Brown-from-Anglican-bishops-criticism.html (accessed 30 December).

Knapp, A. and Wright, V. (2001) *The Government and Politics of France* (London: Routledge).

Kotler-Berkowitz, L. (2001) 'Religion and voting behaviour in Great Britain: a reassessment', *British Journal of Political Science*, 31: 52–4.

Künkler, M. and Meyer-Resende, M. (2007) *A Missing Link: Why Europe Should Talk about Religion when Promoting Democracy Abroad* (Berlin: Democracy Reporting International).

LeDuc, L., Niemi, R. and Norris, P. (eds) *Comparing Democracies 2: New Challenges in the Study of Elections and Voting* (London: Sage).

Leustean, L. and Madeley, J. (eds) (2009) *Religion, Politics and Law in the European Union* (London: Routledge).

Liberal Democrats Christian Forum (2010) 'About LDCF' www.ldcf.net/index.php?option=com_content&view=article&id=47&Itemid=62 (accessed 7 June 2010).

Lindblom, C. (1977) *Politics and Markets: The Worlds' Political-Economic Systems* (New York: Basic).

Linklater, M. and Denniston, R. (eds) (1992) *Anatomy of Scotland* (Edinburgh: Chambers).

Lipset, S. M. and Rokkan, S. (eds) (1967) *Party Systems and Voter Alignments: Cross-National Perspectives* (New York: Free Press).

Lowery, D. and Gray, V. (2000) *A Neo-pluralist Perspective on Research on Organized Interests*, presented at the annual meeting of the Midwest Political Studies Association, Chicago.

Lucardie, P. and ten Napel, H-M. (1994) 'Between confessionalism and liberal conservatism: the Christian Democratic parties of Belgium and the Netherlands' in D. Hanley (ed.) *Christian Democracy in Europe: A Comparative Perspective* (London: Pinter), 51–70.

Lukes, S. (1974) *Power: A Radical View* (Basingstoke: Macmillan).

McAdam, D. (1996) 'Conceptual origins, current problems, future directions' in D. McAdam, J. McCarthy and M. Zald (eds), *Comparative Perspectives on Social Movements* (New York: Cambridge University Press), 23–40.

McAndrew, S. (2010) 'Religious faith and contemporary attitudes', in A. Park, J. Curtice, K. Thomson, M. Phillips, E. Clery *et al.* (eds) *British Social Attitudes: The 26th Report* (London: Sage), 87–113.

McLean, I. (2001) *Rational Choice and British Politics* (Oxford: Oxford University Press).

McLean, I. (2009) *What's Wrong with the British Constitution?* (Oxford: Oxford University Press).

Madeley, J. (ed.) (2002) *Religion and Politics* (Aldershot: Ashgate).

Madeley, J. and Enyedi, Z. (eds) (2003) *Church and State in Contemporary Europe: The Chimera of Neutrality* (London, Frank Cass). Also available as special issue of *West European Politics*, 26 (1).

March, J. and Olsen, J. (1984) *Rediscovering Institutions: The Organisational Basis of Politics* (New York: Free Press).

Marr, A. (1992) *The Battle for Scotland* (London: Penguin).

Martin, D. (1978) *A General Theory of Secularization* (Oxford: Blackwell).

Meny, Y. and Knapp, A. (1998) *Government and Politics in Western Europe* (Oxford: Oxford University Press).

Micklethwait, J. and Wooldridge, A. (2009) *God Is Back: How the Global Rise of Faith is Changing the World* (London: Allen Lane).

Midwinter, A., Keating, M. and Mitchell, J. (1991) *Politics and Public Policy in Scotland* (Basingstoke: Macmillan).

Mill, J. S. (1861) *Considerations on Representative Democracy*.

Miller, W. and Niemi, R. (2002) 'Voting, choice, conditioning and constraint', in L. LeDuc, R. Niemi and P. Norris (eds) *Comparing Democracies 2: New Challenges in the Study of Elections and Voting* (London: Sage), 169–88.

Mitchell, J. (2003) *Governing Scotland* (Basingstoke: Palgrave Macmillan).

Moyser, G. (ed.) (1985) *Church and Politics Today* (Edinburgh: T and T Clark).

National Health Service (2009) 'Abortions' www.isdscotland.org/isd/5940.html (accessed 26 May).

Newton, K. and Van Deth, J. (2005) *Foundations of Comparative Politics* (Cambridge: Cambridge University Press).

Norris, P. and Inglehart, R. (2004) *Sacred and Secular: Religion and Politics Worldwide* (Cambridge: Cambridge University Press).

Norton, P. (2010) 'The status of Bishops' http://lordsoftheblog.net/2010/03/17/the-status-of-bishops/ (accessed 17 March).

Office of the Chief Statistician (2005) *Analysis of Religion in the 2001 Census: Summary Report* (Edinburgh: HMSO).

Office for National Statistics (2004) 'Religious populations' Census www.statistics. gov.uk/cci/nugget.asp?id=954 (11 October).

Office for National Statistics (2010) 'Divorces' www.statistics.gov.uk/cci/nugget. asp?id=170 (accessed 5 February).

Olson, M. (1965) *The Logic of Collective Action: Public Goods and the Theory of Groups* (Cambridge, MA: Harvard University Press).

Panebianco, A. (1988) *Political Parties: Organisation and Power* (Cambridge: Cambridge University Press).

Park, A., Curtice, J., Thomson, K., Phillips, M., Clery, E. *et al.* (eds) (2010) *British Social Attitudes: The 26th Report* (London: Sage).

Parry, R. (2002) 'Leadership and the Scottish governing classes' in G. Hassan and C. Warhurst (eds) *Tomorrow's Scotland* (London: Lawrence and Wishart), 141–53.

Paterson, L. (1994) *The Autonomy of Modern Scotland* (Edinburgh: Edinburgh University Press).

Paterson, L. (2002) 'Scottish social democracy and Blairism: difference, diversity and community' in G. Hassan and C. Warhurst (eds) *Tomorrow's Scotland* (London: Lawrence and Wishart).

Paterson, L. (2006) 'Sources of support for the SNP' in C. Bromley, J. Curtice, D. McCrone and A. Park (eds) *Has Devolution Delivered? The New Scotland Four Years On* (Edinburgh: Edinburgh University Press), 46–68.

Paterson, L., Brown, A., Curtice, J. Hinds, K. McCrone, D. *et al.* (2001) *New Scotland, New Politics?* (Edinburgh: Polygon).

Pattie, C., Seyd, P. and Whiteley, P. (2004) *Citizenship in Britain: Values, Participation and Democracy* (Cambridge: Cambridge University Press).

Pew Forum on Religion and Public Life (2008) *Faith in Flux Changes in Religious Affiliation in the U.S.* http://pewforum.org/Faith-in-Flux.aspx.

Pierce, A. (2005) 'Horror as Cameron brandishes the B word' www.timesonline. co.uk/tol/news/politics/article574814.ece (accessed 5 October).

Polsby, N. (1980) *Community Power and Political Theory* (New Haven, CT: Yale University Press).

Pulzer, P. (1967) *Political Representation and Elections in Britain* (London: Allen and Unwin).

Putnam, Robert (2000) *Bowling Alone: The Collapse and Revival of American Community* (New York: Simon and Schuster).

Rhodes, R. (1988) *Beyond Westminster and Whitehall: The Sub-Central Government of Britain* (London: Unwin).

Roman Catholic Church, 'The Catechism' www.vatican.va/archive/catechism/ p3s2c2a6.htm#IV (accessed 7 June 2010).

Russell, A. and Fieldhouse, E. (2005) *Neither Left nor right? The Liberal Democrats and the Electorate* (Manchester: Manchester University Press).

Salmond, A. (2007) 'Speech to the Council on Foreign Relations' www.cfr.org/ publication/14497/speech_by_alex_salmond_first_minister_of_scotland.html (accessed 12 October).

Salmond, A. (2009) 'First Minister addresses General Assembly' www.snp.org/ node/15326 (accessed 25 May).

Scottish Churches Housing Action (2010), 'Housing issues' www.churches-housing. org/housing_issues2.php?id=5 (accessed 7 June 2010).

Scottish National Party (2007a), *It's Time: The 2007 Manifesto*, Edinburgh: Scottish National Party.

Scottish National Party (2007b), 'SNP Welcome Brian Souter's Public Support and Donation' www.snp.org/press-releases/2006/snp-welcome-brian-souter2019s-public-support-and-donation (accessed 10 March 2008).

Seawright, D. (1999) *An Important Matter of Principle: The Decline of the Scottish Conservative Party* (Aldershot: Ashgate).

Seawright, D. (2000) 'A confessional cleavage resurrected? The denominational vote in Britain', in D. Broughton and H-M. ten Napel (eds) *Religion and Mass Electoral Behaviour in Europe* (London: Routledge), 44–60.

Shaw, E. (1994) *The Labour Party Since 1979: Crisis and Transformation* (London: Routledge).

Shaw, E. (2007) *Losing Labour's Soul: New Labour and the Blair Government 1997–2007* (London: Routledge).

Singh, R. (2003) *Contemporary American Politics and Society* (London: Sage).

Sky News (2010) 'PM: I never unleashed hell on my Chancellor' http://news.sky. com/skynews/Home/Politics/Alistair-Darling-Number-10-Unleashed-The-Forces-Of-Hell-On-Me/Article/201002415558080?f=rss (accessed 24 February).

Smidt, C., Kellstedt, L. and Guth, J. (2009) *The Oxford Handbook of Religion and American Politics* (New York: Oxford University Press).

Smith, A. (1977 [1776]) *An Inquiry into the Nature and Causes of the Wealth of Nations* (Chicago, IL: University of Chicago Press).

Smith, M. (1995) 'Pluralism' in D. Marsh and G. Stoker (eds) *Theories and Methods in Political Science* (Basingstoke: Macmillan), 209–27.

Spohn, W. (2001) 'Eisenstadt on civilizations and multiple modernity', *European Journal of Social Theory*, 4 (4): 499–508.

Stark, R. and Iannaconne, L. (1994) 'A supply-side re-interpretation of the "secularization" of Europe', *Journal for the Scientific Study of Religion*, 33 (3): 389–97.

Steven, M. (2003) *The Political Influence of the Church of Scotland, Post-Devolution: Public Policy-Making and Religion in Scottish Politics*, unpublished Ph.D. thesis.

Stewart, J. (1958) *British Pressure Groups* (Oxford: Clarendon).

Stoker, G. (2006) *Why Politics Matters* (Basingstoke: Palgrave Macmillan).

Sullivan, A. (2008) *The Party Faithful: How and Why the Democrats are Closing the God Gap* (New York: Scribner).

Taylor, B. (1999) *The Scottish Parliament* (Edinburgh: Polygon).

Tearfund (2007) *Churchgoing in the UK* www.tearfund.org/webdocs/Website/News/Final%20churchgoing%20report.pdf.

Thatcher, M. (1987) 'No such thing as society' www.margaretthatcher.org/speeches/displaydocument.asp?docid=106689 (accessed 23 September).

Theos (2008) 'Would you vote for an atheist?' http://ukpollingreport.co.uk/blog/archives/1564 (accessed 28 October).

They Work for You (2009) 'Peers' www.theyworkforyou.com/peers (accessed 7 June 2010).

Tocqueville, A. de (2004 [1835; 1840]) *Democracy in America* (trans. A. Goldhammer (New York: Library of America).

Traynor, I. (2007) 'As the EU turns 50, pope says it's on path to oblivion' www.guardian.co.uk/world/2007/mar/26/eu.catholicism (accessed 26 March).

Truman, D. (1951) *The Governmental Process* (New York: Knopf).

Truman, T. (1959) *Catholic Action and Politics* (Melbourne: Georgian House).

Van Hecke, S. and Gerard, E. (eds) (2004) *Christian Democratic Parties in Europe Since the End of the Cold War* (Leuven: Leuven University Press).

Van Kersbergen, K. (1994) 'The distinctiveness of Christian Democracy', in D. Hanley (ed.) *Christian Democracy in Europe: A Comparative Perspective* (London: Pinter), 31–47.

Van Kersbergen, K. and Manow, P. (2009) *Religion, Class Coalitions and Welfare States* (Cambridge: Cambridge University Press).

Voas, D. and Crockett, A. (2005) 'Religion in Britain: neither believing nor belonging', *Sociology*, 39 (1): 11–28.

Voas, D. and Ling, R. (2010) 'Religion in Britain and the United States', in A. Park, J. Curtice, K. Thomson, M. Phillips, E. Clery *et al.* (eds) *British Social Attitudes: The 26th Report* (London: Sage), 65–86.

Walker, G. and Gallagher, T. (eds) (1999) *Sermons and Battle Hymns: Protestant Popular Culture in Modern Scotland* (Edinburgh: Edinburgh University Press).

Warner, C. (2000) *Confessions of an Interest Group: The Catholic Church and Political Parties in Europe* (Princeton, NJ: Princeton University Press).

Webb, P. (2000) *The Modern British Party System* (London: Sage).

Webb, P., Farrell, D. and Holliday, I. (2002) *Political Parties in Advanced Industrial Democracies* (Oxford: Oxford University Press).

Weber, M. (1905) *The Protestant Ethic and the Spirit of Capitalism*.

Weber, M. (1978) *Economy and Society* (trans. P. Breiner) (Berkeley, CA: University of California Press).

Whiteley, P. and Winyard, S. (1987) *Pressure for the Poor: The Poverty Lobby and Policy-Making* (London: Methuen).

Wilcox, C. (1992) *God's Warriors: The Christian Right in the Twentieth Century* (Baltimore, MD: Johns Hopkins University Press).

Wilcox, C. and Larson, C. (2006) *Onward Christian Soldiers: The Religious Right in American Politics* (New York: Westview).

Wilson, P. (2003) 'Faith-based organizations, charitable choice, and government', *Administration and Society*, 35 (1): 29–51.

Winnett, R. (2009) 'Gordon Brown draws on religion to warn "markets need morals"' www.telegraph.co.uk/news/newstopics/religion/5084464/Gordon-Brown-draws-on-religion-to-warn-markets-need-morals.html (accessed 31 March).

Worcester, R. (2005) 'The Catholic vote in Britain helped carry Blair to victory' www.ipsos-mori.com/newsevents/ca/ca.aspx?oItemId=247 (accessed 23 May).

Index